GW00640828

HARDEN'S

bars
pubs

London

Publisher's announcements

Other Harden's titles

London Restaurants 2003
UK Restaurants 2003
Good Cheap Eats in London 2003
London Food Shops 2002/03
Hotel Guide 2003/04
London for Free

The ideal corporate gift

Harden's London Restaurants, *Harden's UK Restaurants* and
Harden's London Bars & Pubs are available in a range of
specially customised corporate gift formats.

For further information on any of the above, please call
(020) 7839 4763 or visit www.hardens.com.

© Harden's Limited 2003

ISBN 1-873721-47-1 (paperback)

British Library Cataloguing-in-Publication data:
a catalogue record for this book is available from
the British Library.

Printed and bound in Finland by
WS Bookwell Ltd

Research Manager: Antonia Russell
Production Manager: Elizabeth Warman
Research assistants: Frances Gill, Megan Lesperance

Harden's Limited
14 Buckingham Street
London WC2N 6DF

CONTENTS

KEY

 Traditional pub
(and/or beer a speciality)

 Wine bar
(and/or wine a speciality)

 Lounge bar
(and/or interesting range of cocktails or spirits)

 Good Food

 Gay
(includes Lesbian bars)

 DJ

 Live music

 Dance floor
(dancing is also possible at many places just labelled 'DJ')

 Outside tables
(excludes places with a few pavement tables)

 Happy hours

 Open late
(beyond midnight)

Telephone number – all numbers should be prefixed with '020' if dialling from outside the London area.

Map reference – shown immediately after the telephone number.

Website – the first entry in the small print.

Opening hours – unless otherwise stated, drinks are served seven days a week from 11am through to the normal statutory closing times (11pm, Mon-Sat; 10.30pm Sun).

Credit and debit cards – unless otherwise stated, Mastercard, Visa, Amex and Switch are accepted.

Dress – where appropriate, the management's preferences concerning patrons' dress are given.

Smoking – cigarette smoking restrictions are noted.

FROM THE EDITORS

This second edition of our guide to drinking in London –
the first was published in 1995 – reflects a scene utterly
transformed. In those prehistoric days, such concepts as
lounge bars, DJs (in bars) and gastropubs were either
unknown or so rare they seemed like one-offs. Even the
cocktail bar – hardly a revolutionary concept – was a
beast rarely sighted in practice. London's great legacy of
Victorian (and earlier) boozers had only just begun
(thanks to the 1989 Beer Orders) to shake off the 'dead
hand' of big brewery ownership.

And as we go to press, new changes to the law may
inspire yet further improvements to the bar and pub
scene. With the government finally making good on its
promise to tackle licensing laws, the arcane practice of
Last Orders at 11pm looks set finally to bite the dust.
With the advent of easier late-night drinking, London
should finally be able to make a serious claim to being a
24-hour city.

Our aim with this book has been a simple one:
to produce a truly portable drinking companion, with
maps, to help you find new and interesting joints of any
particular type you're looking for.

As with our restaurant guides, we've been anxious to do
justice to the whole range of possibilities, from the most
traditional inns and pubs, via wine and cocktail bars, to
the slickest new style and lounge bars.

If you like what you read – but especially if you don't –
we want to hear from you. Please just send an email to
mail@hardens.com headed "Bars and Pubs" with any
feedback on existing reviews or suggestions for new
ones.

We will be pleased to send complimentary copies of the
next edition of this guide to all those whom we judge to
have made a real contribution to it.

Cheers!

Richard Harden   **Peter Harden**

Directory

a.k.a. WC1

18 West Central St 7836 0110 4–1C

Attached to The End nightclub, this is a decent, spacious bar in which to kick off a Big Night Out, and its post-industrial (former sorting office) setting attracts a younger crowd. During the week, its 'Midtown' location ensures a decent mix of City and West End types (but, as it's rather off the beaten track, tourists from nearby Covent Garden rarely infiltrate).

/ **Website:** www.akalondon.com **Details:** Mon-Thu 6pm-3am, Fri 6pm-4am, Sat 7pm-5am. **Food:** D only. **DJ:** Tue-Sat. **Happy hour:** Tue-Fri 6pm-7.30pm (beer, wine, spirit & mixer £2).

Abbaye EC1

55 Charterhouse St 7253 1612 9–2A

Belgian beers are what these large – in fact, surprisingly large at the Smithfield original – mussels halls are all about. (You can eat at any time the place is open, but it's as much a bar as a restaurant.) Over two dozen bottled brands are available, with Hoegaarden and Leffe (brown and blond) on tap.

/ **Details:** closed Sat & Sun; no-smoking area. **Food:** till 10.30pm.

The Abingdon W8

54 Abingdon Rd 7937 3339 5–2A

A stylish but comfortable design has made this former boozer – which, in 1995, was given a thorough make-over by the same designer as Beach Blanket Babylon – into a venue that's well worth knowing about in this leafy part of Kensington. The cosy bar is a popular destination in its own right – if you want to eat, it's best to pre-book one of the cosy booths at the back.

/ **Details:** Mon-Fri noon-2.30pm & 6.30pm-11pm, weekends noon-3pm & 6.30pm-11pm. **Food:** till 11pm.

Admiral Codrington SW3

17 Mossop St 7581 0005 5–2C

Rarely does a pub come with such a weight of social history as at this Chelsea boozer which, in the '80s, became infamous as 'Sloane Central'. A few years ago, however, it was elegantly revamped by Society decorator Nina Campbell, and today attracts a crowd which owes as much to Prada as it does to Barbour. The restaurant at the rear is an attraction in its own right. / **Website:** www.longshot.co.uk **Details:** Mon-Sun noon-3pm & 7pm-11pm. **Food:** L&D (L bar snacks only), till 10.30pm.

Akbar W1

77 Dean St   7437 2525   3–1D

Added during the expensive renovation of Soho's venerable Red Fort Indian restaurant, this basement bar (with its own entrance) creates a suitably opulent impression. It's a large space with three main seating areas divided into low tunnels decked out with sofas, cushions, low tables and velvet drapes. Choose from one of many exotic cocktails, plus interesting subcontinental snacks. / **Details:** *Mon-Fri noon-1am, Sat 6pm-1am; no credit cards.* **Food:** *till 11.15pm.* **DJ:** *Thu-Sat.*

Al's EC1

11-13 Exmouth Mkt   7837 4821   9–1A

Something for everyone, and at pretty much all hours – this Clerkenwell canteen is a diner by day and a bar by night, serving some good European beers (including Hoegaarden and Leffe). On Fri & Sat, the basement becomes a cocktail bar, with DJs until 2am. Find your way back in the morning for the hang-over special all-day breakfast. / **Details:** *Mon-Fri 8am-2am, Sat 10am-2am, Sun 10am-10.30pm.* **Food:** *till 9.30pm.* **DJ:** *Fri-Sat in Winter.* **Happy hour:** *Mon-Thu 8pm-10pm.*

Albert NW1

11 Princess Rd   7722 1886   8–3B

A mere stone's throw from the Primrose Hill's two über-pubs (the Engineer and the Lansdowne), this agreeable boozer makes a more traditional and relaxed destination than its trendy neighbours. Rather like The Engineer, it boasts a very pleasant garden and decent food – the main difference is that, on a sunny day here, you might actually get a seat! / **Details:** *no Amex; no-smoking area.* **Food:** *L till 2.30pm, D till 10pm, all day weekends.*

The Albert SW1

52 Victoria St   7222 5577   2–3C

For Victorian grandeur, few places better this Westminster pub, which – on its island site near New Scotland Yard – conveys the impression of a becalmed battleship of the Empire. (It's the only building nearby not to have been bombed to bits by the Luftwaffe). Downstairs, admire the original hand etched glass windows (1852) – upstairs there's a traditional carvery of sufficient popularity with MPs to have a division bell. (If the place has a drawback, it's that all this heritage appeal makes it a stop on the tour bus circuit.) / **Food:** *L till 3pm, D till 9.30pm, bar snacks all day till 10pm.*

Albertine W12

1 Wood Ln   8743 9593   7–1B

There's something very welcoming about this small and simply-furnished Shepherd's Bush wine bar, where the selection of wines (most by the glass) is written up on the blackboards at the rear. There's some simple food available, too, much of it enjoyed by production types from Beeb Central (just down the road). / **Details:** *Sat 6.30-11pm, closed Sun; no Amex.* **Food:** *D till 10.30pm.*

Alexandra SW4

14 Clapham Common Southside   7627 5102   10–2C

Despite its somewhat uninviting exterior, this sprawling, three-floor Victorian boozer by Clapham Common tube is actually rather good. Noisy it may be, but it's a useful rallying point, with efficient service and a friendly crowd (and upstairs, where it's less hectic, you might even get a seat). There are 22 varieties of lager on offer and six of bitter, while entertainments include comedy nights every Sun. (History anoraks note: sessions of parliament were held here in WWII). / **Details:** *no credit cards.* **Food:** *Sun L only.*

All Bar One

289 Regent St, W1   7467 9901
3-4 Hanover St, W1   7518 9931
36-38 Dean St, W1   7479 7921
5-6 Picton Pl, W1   7487 0161
7-9 Paddington St, W1   7487 0071
108 New Oxford St, WC1   7307 7980
19 Henrietta St, WC2   7557 7941
48 Leicester Sq, WC2   7747 9921
58 Kingsway, WC2   7269 5171
84 Cambridge Circus, WC2   7379 8311
587-591 Fulham Rd, SW6   7471 0611
152 Gloucester Rd, SW7   7244 5861
126 Notting Hill Gate, W11   7313 9362
197 Chiswick High Rd, W4   8987 8211
64-66 The Mall, Ealing Broadway, W5   8280 9611
1 Liverpool Rd, N1   7843 0021
131 Upper St, N1   73549535

All Bar One (continued)
1 Hampstead Ln, N6   8342 7861
2-4 The Broadway, Crouch End, N8   8342 7871
79-81 Heath St, NW3   7433 0491
60 St John's Wood High St, NW8   7483 9931
1 Chicheley St, SE1   7921 9471
28-30 London Bridge St, SE1   7940 9981
34 Shad Thames, SE1   7940 9771
32-38 Northcote Rd, SW11   7801 9951
7-9 Battersea Sq, SW11   7326 9831
527-529 Old York Rd, SW18   8875 7941
37-39 Wimbledon Hill Rd, SW19   8971 9871
9-11 Hill St, TW9   8332 7141
42 Mackenzie Walk, E14   7513 0911
93a Charterhouse St, EC1   7553 9391
127 Finsbury Pavement, EC2   7448 9921
18 Appold St, EC2   7247 6841
34 Threadneedle St, EC2   7614 9931
107 Houndsditch, EC3   7283 0047
16 Byward St, EC3   7533 0301
103 Cannon St, EC4   7220 9031
44-46 Ludgate Hill, EC4   7248 1356
Even though – or maybe because – there's now one on almost
every corner, these large, airy bars, still seem to be pulling in
the punters. Whatever the reason, they remain a cut above
their copycat rivals. Crowds of office juniors on the pull are an
ever-present evening hazard (or attraction?), but many
branches make mellow weekend destinations. Given they
produce so much of it, the food could be very much worse.
/ **Website:** www.sixcontinents.com **Details:** *City branches closed all or part of*
weekend; no-smoking areas available. **Food:** *L&D & bar snacks.*

Alma SW18

499 Old York Rd   8870 2537   10–2A
It's as a rugger-buggers' boozer that this popular Wandsworth
institution is best known, but if you avoid match days you'll see
that it's actually quite a fine Victorian pub. It's owned by Young
& Co., and serves a good selection of their bitters (and their
lager). There is a separate dining annexe on the ground floor,
with food service quite a large part of the operation.
/ **Website:** www.thealma.co.uk **Food:** *till 10pm.*

Alphabet W1

61-63 Beak St   7439 2190   3–2D
*It was once an achingly hip hang-out, but this Soho 'oldie'
(all things are relative) has weathered well, and still hums at
weekends, when there are DJs in the bar downstairs. The sofas
in the window are a prime spot for watching the local media
crowds go by. / **Website:** www.alphabetbar.com **Details:** Sat 4pm-11pm.
Food: till 10.30pm, no L Sat-Sun. **DJ:** Thu-Sat.*

Amber W1

6 Poland St   7734 3094   3–2D
*The smooth two-floor operation, south of Oxford Street, is the
creation of the team who created Alphabet (a couple of
minutes walk away). There's tables upstairs, booths and a
dance floor in the basement, and the warm, neutral décor
throughout is stylish and expensive-looking. Cocktails and wine
list come with a Latin American twist. / **Website:** www.amberbar.com
Details: Mon-Sat 5pm-1am, closed Sun. **Food:** till midnight. **DJ:** Thu-Sat.
Live music: percussionist, Wed.*

The Anchor SE1

34 Park St   7407 1577   9–3B
*With its extensive terrace and a walled garden for barbecues,
this large Borough tavern is one of the best central riverside
pubs in which to while away a summer's day (or indeed a
winter evening in front of a roaring fire). The mainly 18th-
century building has recently been renovated, but the smaller
rooms (often used for private events) retain considerable
panelled period charm. / **Website:** www.theanchorbankside.co.uk
Details: no-smoking area. **Food:** till 9pm.*

Anchor Tap SE1

20A, Horselydown Ln   7403 4637   9–3D
*Hidden in the warren of streets behind Tower Bridge Road,
this attractive wooden-fronted pub (the 'tap' pub of the former
Courage brewery) is a great antidote to the modern bars that
have sprung up around Shad Thames. Old-fashioned décor,
Sam Smith's beers and a games room off the main bar seem to
attract a fairly mature local crowd, and there's a large beer
terrace for warm days. / **Details:** no Amex; no-smoking area. **Food:** L till
3pm, D till 9pm (closed Sun D), bar snacks till 9pm.*

Angel SE16

101 Bermondsey Wall East   7237 3608   11–2A
With fine views over the Pool of London, with Tower Bridge in the distance, this nautically-themed Rotherhithe tavern (now owned by Samuel Smith's) is worth bearing in mind when you feel like a trip down to the river. The building is 19th-century (and looking a bit tired nowadays), but the site is an historic one – almost 700 years old, and mentioned by Pepys. / **Details:** no Amex. **Food:** till 8pm (weekends till 6pm).

The Angelic NW1

57 Liverpool Rd   7278 8433   8–2D
It's easy to overdo the use of the word 'palatial' when it comes to grand Victorian pubs, but it seems particularly appropriate when applied to this tastefully updated Islington institution, which has been made over into a very impressive modern boozer. Food is quite a large part of the operation and drinks wise the emphasis is on wine and lager (with a selection including Gulpener – a wheat beer). Don't miss the grandiose upstairs room. / **Website:** www.theangelic.co.uk **Details:** Sat from 10am; no Amex. **Food:** L&D.

Anglesea Arms SW7

15 Selwood Ter   7373 7960   5–2B
This early 19th-century free house must be one of the most successful pubs in inner south west London – it certainly has one of the most pukka positions (in the middle of a row of white stucco houses in the heart of a South Kensington residential street). Especially in warm weather, it's regularly heaving with well-bred, young locals, who – having filled up the small paved garden – spill out on to the pavement. / **Details:** no Amex. **Food:** L till 3pm, D till 10pm, all day weekends.

The Anglesea Arms W6

35 Wingate Rd   8749 1291   7–1A
One of the capital's first places to be described as a gastropub, this phenomenally popular destination, a short stroll from Ravenscourt's Park, is many Londoners' favourite watering hole. Lots come for Dan Evans's fabulous cooking, but drinkers aren't regarded as second-class citizens, and the bare, but characterful bar attracts a crowd of all ages. / **Details:** no Amex. **Food:** till 10.45pm.

The Antelope SW1
22 Eaton Ter   7824 8512   5–2D
Characterfully located on a side-street between Sloane and Eaton Squares, this late 18th-century pub benefits from a strong and very genuine atmosphere (and it can get very crowded and smoky). Despite the place's obvious 'heritage' charms, the crowd – a mixture of locally-barracked guardsmen and heavily-pinstriped City types – is largely tourist-free. The most popular choice of drink is a pint of one of the bitters (which include Old Speckled Hen, Adnams, and London Pride). / **Details:** *closed Sun.* **Food:** *till 2pm.*

L'Apogee WC2
Leicester Sq   7437 4556   4–3B
A pleasant spot for a glass of wine or cocktail, just off Leicester Square (next to the Prince Charles cinema) – not necessarily an exciting place but a useful rendezvous in a busy part of town. Bar snacks and full meals are available, and there are tables outside. / **Details:** *8pm-1am; no Amex.* **Food:** *8pm-11pm.* **DJ & Live music:** *Fri-Sat.*

The Approach Tavern E2
47 Approach Rd   8980 2321   1–1D
This friendly-looking pub, in a leafy side street, is one of the hidden delights of Bethnal Green. Bombed during WWII, it has been partly 'trendified' in recent times (there's an art gallery upstairs, Czech beers on draught, and the patio is heated), but it retains some great features, including a jukebox filled with 'oldies'. The punters are a happy mix of locals, students and staff from the nearby London Chest Hospital; and as well as lager, there's a good array of bitters, including IPA, Prospect, Old Bob and London Pride. / **Details:** *no Amex.* **Food:** *L till 2.30pm (weekends 3.30pm), D till 9.30pm.*

Aqua Cafe Bar
Ocean Music Venue E8

270 Mare St   8533 0111   1–1D
*Situated in the former library opposite the Town Hall,
this impressive neo-classical building now houses Hackney's first
purpose-built music venue (Ocean Music Venue), which plays
anything from R&B to Disco. Its pleasant, modern bar/café
fronts onto the street and is fitted out with a retro look.
It serves the usual range of lagers, cocktails and wine,
and some reasonably-priced spirits. / **Website:** www.ocean.org.uk*
Details: *Mon-Thu 10am-11pm, Fri & Sat 10am-2am, Sun 6pm-10pm;
no Amex.* **Food:** *L till 3, D till 10 (Mon-Fri only).* **DJ:** *Wed-Sun.*

Aragon House SW6

247 New King's Rd   7736 1856   10–1A
*Opened shortly before we went to press, this new venue
overlooking Parson's Green is part of the same imposing
building as the British Legion. The ground floor bar/restaurant
has been decorated in a vaguely baronial style – apparently to
be mirrored in a basement room opening soon. The plan is
eventually for it to become a members' club, but it's early days.
/ **Details:** Mon-Sun 9am-11pm.* **Food:** *till 10pm.*

Archduke Wine Bar SE1

Arch 153, Concert Hall Appr.   7928 9370   2–2D
*Nightly jazz is a feature of this spacious establishment in
railway arches by the South Bank Centre – long known as the
best place hereabouts for a drink before or after a concert
(and now also for a steadying glass after a turn in the 'Eye').
The quality of the wines far exceeds that of the bar snacks –
there is also a restaurant. / **Details:** closed Sun; no-smoking area.*
Food: *till 10pm.*

Argyll Arms W1

18 Argyll St   7734 6117   3–1C
*The décor and scale of this grand pub, near the Palladium,
make it, at least architecturally speaking, one of the great
Victorian boozers (and its interior preserves many wonderful
original fittings). By day, it's the haunt of shoppers and local
office-workers, but on Friday and Saturday nights a younger
crowd takes over. Much of their consumption is of lagers like
Grolsch and Carlsberg – the range of bitters includes Adnams,
London Pride and IPA. / **Details:** no-smoking area.* **Food:** *L till 3pm,
bar snacks till 9pm.*

The Art Bar SW3

87-89 Walton St 7589 8558 5–2C
Quite a hit since it opened early in 2002, this quite stylish Knightsbridge watering-hole has become popular with younger City folk and Euros, on their way home to Chelsea, Fulham or beyond. A wide range of drinks is available, from cocktails to beer. / **Details:** *Mon-Sat 5pm-midnight, Sun 5pm-10.30pm.* **Food:** *till 11.30pm.*

The Artesian Well SW8

693 Wandsworth Rd 7627 3353 10–1B
With its wacky, vaguely nautical mish-mash of a design (from the people behind the seminal Beach Blanket Babylon) – not to mention a late licence at weekends – this converted Battersea boozer has made itself a popular south-of-the-river destination. They make quite an effort on the food front, and also with entertainment (there's dance classes during the week, and also jazz some days). / **Website:** *www.artesianwell.co.uk* **Details:** *Tue & Wed noon-midnight, Thu noon-2pm, Fri & Sat noon-3am, Sun noon-10pm (closed Mon).* **Food:** *L till 3pm, D till 10pm.* **DJ:** *Fri & Sat.*

The Assembly EC3

14-15 Seething Ln 7626 3360 9–3D
This trendy-looking new bar/restaurant looks as though it should be in Clerkenwell or Hoxton, but has somehow ended up in the rather less fashionable area south of Fenchurch Street station. A funky wooden booth is its most eye-catching feature, and the overall impression is of a more-than-usually stylish modern bar. There's a kitchen on view, and food is a significant part of the operation. / **Details:** *closed weekends.* **Food:** *till 9pm.*

Atlantic Bar & Grill W1

20 Glasshouse St 7734 4888 3–3D
The former queues of eager wannabes tend to be more conspicuous by their absence nowadays, outside the entrance to Oliver Peyton's spacious Art Deco basement bar (under the Strand Palace Hotel), which in the mid-'90s was THE bar of the moment. It seems to be making some efforts to shake off the complacency which has afflicted it in recent years, though, and while there's still a (nominal) door policy and prices are still breathtaking, the cocktails are good, and the late licence remains a major attraction. / **Details:** *Mon-Fri noon-3pm & 6pm-12.30am, Sat 6pm-3am, closed Sun.* **Food:** *till midnight, bar snacks till 3am.* **DJ:** *weekends.*

The Atlas SW6

16 Seagrave Rd   7385 9129   5–3A
Opposite a storage depot in the backstreets of Fulham (near Earl's Court 2), this ordinary-looking boozer had been made over into an incredibly popular gastropub (with cooking in Mediterranean style). At meal times it fills up quickly, so if you're after a quiet pint or glass of wine get there early. / **Details:** *no Amex.* **Food:** *L till 3pm, D till 10.30pm.*

The Audley W1

41-43 Mount St   7499 1843   3–3A
When a former Duke of Westminster was building this corner of Mayfair, he was determined that the pub should – in accordance with his wealth and status – be the grandest in the capital. The result is this opulent Victorian boozer – all polished wood and gilded cornicing – which, to this day, remains one of the most impressive places in town to sink a pint. / **Food:** *till 9.30pm.*

Auld Shillelagh N16

105 Stoke Newington Church St   7249 5951   1–1C
This characterful Irish boozer is as 'traditional' an example of the type as you'll find in the Smoke. It's small but very friendly, serves a fine pint of Guinness and regularly plays host to live Irish bands. A loyal local fan club adds to the atmosphere. / **Website:** *www.theauldshillelagh.com* **Details:** *no-smoking area.*

Auntie Annie's NW5
180 Kentish Town Rd   7485 3237   8–2B
For once an Irish bar that announces its presence with a bright yellow exterior. Once you've got past the glare, this Kentish Town free house is just a nice ordinary pub, with a good selection of whiskeys and the occasional fiddle night. / **Food:** *L&D.*

The Australian SW3

29 Milner St   7589 6027   5–2D
This pretty, creeper-clad Victorian pub looks very superior from the outside, and the interior does not disappoint (unless you're looking for things Antipodean, which are notable by their absence). Although it's located not that far from Sloane Square, its off-the-beaten-track location makes it truly a destination for the locals (especially the younger ones). / **Food:** *L till 3pm, D till 9pm, weekends till 5pm.*

The Avenue SW1

7-9 St James's St   7321 2111   2–2B

*For an example of impressive '90s style, you won't do much better than this large St James bar/restaurant (which is often glibly, but wrongly, described as being 'like New York'). It's quite a 'cross-over' sort of place – not scaring off the local art-dealers and estate agents, but still attracting groovier types before a night in the West End. / **Website:** www.theavenue.co.uk **Food:** till 11pm.*

B@1

85 Battersea Rise, SW11   7978 6595   10–2B
7a, Petersham Rd, TW9   7978 6595   1–3A

*The tiny Battersea original of this lively bar duo is packed pretty all week with noisy Battersea blokes and Clapham chicks. Decently-priced jugs of killer cocktails (from a globe-trotting menu) and blaring disco tunes fuel the party atmosphere. There's also a branch in Richmond. / **Website:** www.beatone.co.uk **Details:** Mon-Sat 5pm-11pm, Sun 5pm-10.30pm. **Happy hour:** Mon-Thu 6pm-8pm, Fri & Sat 6pm-7pm (cocktails 2 for the price of 1).*

Babble
Landsdowne House W1

59 Berkeley Sq   7758 8255   3–3B

*Perhaps it's not the most upmarket venue in Mayfair, but this large bar has quite a capacity, and boasts such attractions as a generous happy hour (5pm-7pm) and bookable basement booths – ideal for a party of up to 15 people. There's dancing too, mainly to the sounds of the '70s and '80s. / **Website:** www.latenightlondon.co.uk **Details:** Mon-Wed noon-1pm, Thu noon-2pm, Fri noon-3pm , Sat 6pm-3am, closed Sun. **Food:** L&D (closed Sun). **Happy hour:** 5pm-7pm (all wine (except house), cocktails & spirits half-price, £10 off champagne).*

Babel SW11

3-7 Northcote Rd   7801 0043   10–2B

*A lounge bar – one of the longer-runners in this ever more popular 'strip' – that caters to a chilled set of Claphamites in modern chrome surroundings. It's open plan, so the noise of the crowd, lounging on sofas and pouffes, can get very loud indeed. The usual range of cocktails and beers are on offer at fairly reasonable prices. / **Website:** www.faucetinn.com **Details:** no-smoking area. **Food:** bar snacks 6pm-10pm Mon-Fri, Sat-Sun L. **DJ:** Thu-Sat.*

Babushka

648 King's Rd, SW6   7736 4501   10–1A
41 Tavistock Cres, W11   7727 9250   6–1B
125 Caledonian Rd, N1   7837 1924   8–3D
58-62 Heath St, NW3   7431 0399   8–1A
40 St Matthew's Rd, SW2   7274 3618   10–2C

*A Russian-inspired vodka chain with five branches – the latest,
Hampstead, opened in July 2002 – all of which have a
deserved following. Each offshoot has its own look and feel –
Brixton looks Stalinist from the outside, but the interior is filled
with leather sofas, candles, chilled people and music.
Its Notting Hill sibling has a certain claim to fame as it sits on
the site of the former Firkin pub which appeared in 'Withnail &
I'.* / **Website:** *www.styleinthecity.co.uk* **Details:** *Mon-Sat noon-11pm (W11 &
SW2 5pm-11pm only; N1 & SW2 Sat until midnight), Sun noon-10.30pm;
SW3, no Amex.* **Food:** *L&D.* **DJ:** *nightly.* **Happy hour:** *N1 5pm-7pm
(homemade vodka £1 a shot).*

Bacchanalia WC2

1a, Bedford St   7240 3945   4–3C

*It may perhaps not quite live up to its name, but this large
basement bar is a handy place for a quick drink just off the
Strand, and certainly much nicer than it looks from the outside.
The décor and the food are in the classic wine bar tradition,
but beer is available, too.* / **Details:** *closed Sun.* **Food:** *L till 3pm, D till
10.30pm.*

Backpacker N1

126 York Way   7278 8318   8–3C

*Sitting in the dentist`s chair takes on new meaning at this
infamous hang out, where you can pay to have shots poured
down your throat. You get the idea: this is partying Aussie style
with enough lager to drown a battleship. Weekend happy hour
is taken seriously – pay your entrance and then you can drink
as much as you like in the next two hours. Then on to the
dance-floor. If all this sounds like your idea of a great night out,
get yourself down to King's Cross immediately.* / **Details:** *closed
Mon-Thu, Fri & Sat 7pm-2am, Sun 3.30-midnight; no credit cards.* **DJ & Live
music:** *nightly.* **Happy hour:** *Fri-Sat 8pm-10pm (Men entry £7, Women £5,
then drink is free).*

The Balham Tup SW12
21 Chestnut Grove   8772 0546   10–2B
*There's nothing particularly remarkable about the Balham branch of this chain of airy boozers (although their game of indoor cricket sounds interesting). It's a friendly, if often quite raucous place to hang out at weekends, to watch the football or for Sunday lunch. / **Website:** www.massivepub.com **Details:** no Amex. **Food:** till 10pm. **DJ:** Sat. **Live music:** Live band or DJ Sat and special events.*

Balls Brothers
20 St James's St, SW1   7321 0882
50 Buckingham Palace Rd, SW1   7828 4111
34 Brook St, W1   7499 4567
Hays Galleria, Tooley St, SE1   7407 4301
11 Blomfield St, EC2   7588 4643
158 Bishopsgate, EC2   7426 0567
5-6 Carey Ln, EC2   7600 2720
6-8 Cheapside, EC2   7248 2708
Kings Arms Yd, EC2   7736 3049
52 Lime St, EC3   7283 0841
Mark Ln, EC3   7623 2923
Mincing Ln, EC3   7283 2838
St Mary at Hill, EC3   7626 0321
Bucklersbury Hs, Budge Row, Cannon St, EC4   7248 7557
*If there is such a thing as a 'plain vanilla' wine bar, this well-established chain – run by merchants in the business for a century and a half – is the epitome of the breed. Premises are comfortably furnished in traditional style, and offer an extensive, if conventional, list. Some of the branches do good sandwiches, and the restaurants (at six of the branches, mostly open for lunch only) are popular City stand-bys. (Balls Brothers also owns the Hop Cellars and the Bar Under the Clock, listed separately.) / **Website:** www.ballsbrothers.co.uk **Details:** closed weekends. **Food:** L&D.*

Baltic SE1

74 Blackfriars Rd   7928 1111   1–2C

This Polish bar/restaurant has at least three things in common with nearby Tate Modern – it's in Southwark, it's a dramatic conversion of an 'old' industrial space, and it has been hugely successful. On the booze front, vodka – over 30 types, with flavours from bison grass to caraway – killer cocktails and bottled beers are key. Those in search of more solid nourishment can sample blinis or snacks at the bar or a proper meal in the restaurant at the back.
/ **Website:** www.balticrestaurant.co.uk **Details:** Mon-Fri noon-midnight, Sat 6pm-midnight. **Food:** bar snacks all day, L till 3pm, D till 11.30pm.

Bank WC2

1 Kingsway   7379 9797   2–1D

This large, noisy – perhaps slightly impersonal – bar/restaurant has a very handy location on the fringe of Covent Garden, which makes it an ideal rendezvous between the City and the West End. The circular bar – with huge windows looking on to the street – has established itself as a popular spot for an after-work cocktail or trendy lager. / **Website:** www.bankrestaurants.com
Details: Mon-Fri 7.30am-10.30am, noon-3pm, Sat & Sun 11.30am-3.30pm, Mon-Sat 5.30pm-11.30pm, Sun 5.30pm-10pm. **Food:** L&D.

Bar And Dining House N1

2 Essex Rd   7704 8789   8–3D

Near Islington Green, this former Victorian boozer has been given a vaguely '60s/Boho make-over and offers the attraction (at weekends) of a late licence. The cellar Tiki bar features regular DJs and occasional live bands, when it reverberates to strains of hip hop, funk and reggae. Most punters are on bottled lager or vino, and there's also quite a big food operation.
/ **Details:** Mon-Wed 5pm-11pm, Thu 5pm-1am, Fri & Sat 5pm-2pm, Sun noon-10.30pm. **Food:** D 6pm-10pm, all day Sun. **DJ:** 3-4 nights/week.

Bar Baran E8

50-52 Broadway Market   7249 0666   1–1D

Part of this lounge-bar's attraction is its location in Broadway Market (a sort of Bohemian village in Hackney). It combines bistro-style food, funky music, art and drink in a dark interior with wooden décor and tables, and good cocktail and wine lists – given that all sounds great, we didn't find it quite as atmospheric as you might hope. / **Website:** www.barbaran.com **Details:** Mon-Sat from 5pm, Sun 11am-11pm; no Amex. **Food:** D only, Sun L&D. **DJ:** Fri & Sat (latin jazz, old skool, garage). **Happy hour:** Mon-Fri 6pm-8pm.

Bar Bourse EC4

67 Queen St   7248 2200   9–3C

This lively basement bar/restaurant near Cannon Street tube is a stylish and refreshing alternative to chain outlets or the more standard City pubs and wine bars. It's not a bargain or a beery place, though – champagne and cocktails are definitely the order of the day. / **Details:** closed weekends. **Food:** L till 3pm, bar snacks 5pm-9pm. **DJ:** every couple of weeks, Thu.

Bar Code W1

3-4 Archer St   7734 3342   3–2D

In a backstreet near Piccadilly Circus, this Soho bar (above a comedy club) manages the neat trick of being incredibly central, yet feeling something of a secret – just right for the gay singles scene which this dimly-lit cube of a room accommodates. Seats around the edge offer a comfortable spot for weighing up the talent before wading in to the action. / **Website:** www.barcodesoho.com **Details:** Mon-Sat 4pm-1am, Sun 4pm-11pm; no Amex. **DJ:** Fri-Sat. **Happy hour:** all day till 7pm (pints £2).

Bar des Amis du Vin WC2

11-14 Hanover Pl   7379 3444   4–2D

In a little alley by the Royal Opera House, this hidden-away basement wine bar – which was left mercifully untouched when they tarted up the restaurant above – remains one of the best meeting spots in Covent Garden. A good list of reasonably-priced wines is complemented by an excellent Gallic cheeseboard. Popularity is such that the place can feel like a Tokyo subway train, especially before curtain-up. / **Website:** www.cafedesamis.co.uk **Details:** closed Sun. **Food:** till 11pm.

Le Bar du Café Delancey NW1

4 Delancey St   7387 3544   8–3B

*A pretty little bar – with awning and café-style outside tables –
which is part of the large, well-known Camden Town brasserie,
with check table cloths to complete the illusion of La France
Profonde. As you'd expect, wines from across the Channel are
the house speciality, with cocktails (and snacks) also available.
/ Details: Mon-Sun 9am-11pm; no Amex. **Food:** till 10.30pm.*

Bar Du Musée SE10

17 Nelson Rd   8858 4710   1–2D

*This formerly tiny, narrow and dark wine bar (which also serves
beer and spirits) now boasts an impressive rear extension which
gives access to a surprisingly spacious garden – especially worth
knowing about in the touristy heart of Greenwich. There's also
a restaurant, serving modern European brasserie fare.
/ Details: Mon-Sat noon-midnight, Sun noon-10.30pm. **Food:** L till 3pm
(weekends 5pm), D till 10.30pm.*

Bar Estrela SW8

111-115 S Lambeth Rd   7793 1051   10–1C

*This bustling Portuguese café/bar is a relaxed and friendly place
in which to have a drink or eat some tapas and watch the TV
(if you speak the lingo). In the summer it can get very crowded
with the locals spilling out onto the pavement. / Details: Mon-Sun
8am-midnight. **Food:** till 11.30pm.*

Bar Gansa NW1

2 Inverness St   7267 8909   8–3B

*A late licence, Spanish beers, Mexican cocktails and a good
range of tasty tapas really have made this lively and colourful
bar somewhere which really can be described a linchpin of
Camden Town. The only drawback is that it's so well known
that you may be lucky to get a table, certainly later in the
evening. / Details: Mon-Tue 10am-midnight, Wed-Sun 10am-1am; no Amex.
Food: Sun-Wed till 11pm, Thu-Sat till 12.30am.*

Bar Kick E1

127 Shoreditch High St   7739 8700   9–1C

*A festive, brightly-lit hang-out (an offshoot of Exmouth Market's
Café Kick) which occupies a notably unlovely stretch of
Shoreditch High Street. It's regularly packed, however, with a
wholesome, freshly scrubbed crowd of twentysomethings, lured
by an evening of table footie at the large array of tables.
When exhaustion sets in, revivers come in the shape of beers
and cocktails; also Mediterranean fare that is served in the
café.* / **Website:** www.cafekick.co.uk **Details:** Thu-Sat till midnight,
Sun 11am-11pm; no Amex. **Food:** L till 3.30pm, D till 10.30pm, Sat all day till
midnight, Sun all day till 10pm. **DJ:** Thu-Sun. **Happy hour:** Mon-Sun
4pm-7pm (beers £1.50 beers, cocktails £3.50).

bar local SW4

4 Clapham Common Southside   7622 9406   10–2C

*A relaxed hang-out for over-25s, this long and narrow spot –
by Clapham Common tube, and formerly the restaurant Tuba –
opened as a bar in late-2001. It's not as hectic (or wannabe)
as some Clapham joints, but groovy enough when they have DJs
at the weekend. Basic bar fare is also on offer at reasonable
prices.* / **Website:** www.barlocal.co.uk **Details:** Mon-Fri 5pm-midnight,
Sat noon-midnight, Sun noon-11.30pm. **Food:** 5pm-10.30pm. **DJ:** Thu-Sun.

Bar Lorca N16

175 Stoke Newington High St   7275 8659   1–1C

*On the corner with Stoke Newington Church Street,
this sizeable and atmospheric bar/restaurant – with its yellow
walls, ceramic plates and mosaic bar – has a distinct Latino feel
to it. It's relaxed and friendly and doesn't try to be über-trendy,
attracting a local crowd who indulge in a little salsa dancing
every Friday (and there are live bands on other nights).*
/ **Website:** www.barlorca.com **Details:** Mon-Thu noon-1am, Fri & Sat
noon-2am, Sun noon-midnight; no Amex. **Food:** till 11.30pm. **DJ:** nightly.
Live music: salsa Fri, bands Sun and Thu. **Happy hour:** Mon-Sat 6pm-9pm
(£3.50 cocktails).

Bar Madrid W1

4 Winsley St 7436 4649 3–1D

"Welcoming hen nights and large parties" – is the proud claim on the website of this large venue, just north of Oxford Street. It's been around for ages and has long had the reputation as a fun, twentysomething pick-up joint. Monday is Brazilian club night, while most other nights Salsa classes provide numerous mingling opportunities. Different nights promote different drinks, with most of the fun fuelled by bottled lager and pitchers of cocktails. / **Website:** www.barmadrid.co.uk **Details:** Mon-Fri 4.30pm-3am, Sat 6.30pm-3am, closed Sun. **Food:** till 3am. **DJ:** nightly from 9.30pm. **Live music:** Mon Brazilian band, Tue-Sat salsa £3, free Thu-Sat. **Happy hour:** till 9pm (half-price shots, wine £8, jugs of mixed drinks £7.50, £1 off spirits, cocktails £2.50).

Bar Red W1

5-6 Kingly St 7434 3417 3–2C

Two floors of cool, unadorned space have helped make this Soho bar a popular destination for a crowd that's mature by local standards – some of them are even in their thirties! At the weekends, it's quite a pre-clubbing haunt; during the week they work hard on the food 'offer', with substantial oriental (and tapas) dishes on hand. / **Website:** www.bar-red.com **Details:** Mon-Fri 5pm-midnight, Sat 6pm-midnight, closed Sun. **Food:** 5pm-11.30pm. **DJ:** Wed-Sat.

Bar Risa NW1

11 East Yd, Camden Lock 7428 5929 8–3B

The main attraction of this place is its location – overlooking Camden Lock – where you can rest your weary limbs after tramping around the market. It has a good number of outside tables which are very popular during the summer months. Inside is a modern bar/café with exposed beams and brickwork. / **Website:** www.jongleurs.com **Food:** L till 4.30pm.

Bar Rocca N8

159A, Tottenham Ln 8340 0101 8–1D

A vibrant and friendly bar, in a former Victorian chapel, where there's usually something going on, from salsa (Tue) to karaoke (Sun) via DJs (especially on Fri & Sat, when the place is open till 1am). / **Details:** Mon-Thu 5pm-midnight, Fri & Sat 11am-1.30am, Sun 11am-midnight; no Amex. **Food:** L&D. **DJ:** Fri & Sat. **Happy hour:** Mon-Fri 5pm-8pm (£1 off spirits).

Bar Room Bar

32 Gerrard St, W1 7494 1482 4–3A
451 Fulham Rd, SW10 7352 8636 5–3B
269 Uxbridge Rd, W12 8749 1857 7–1A
383 King St, W6 8748 6076 7–2A
Station Rd, Wood Green, N22 8889 9436 8–1C
48 Rosslyn Hl, NW3 7431 8802 8–2A
111 Kennington Rd, SE11 7820 3682 10–1C
26 Camberwell Grove, SE5 7703 4553 1–2C
441 Battersea Park Rd, SW11 7223 7721 10–1B
162 Victoria Park Rd, E9 8985 5404 1–1D

London boasts ten of these lively modern pubs, of which many – unusually for a corporately-owned chain – have their own distinct character. Of course, there are similarities – every branch has sofas, a menu that majors in wood-fired pizzas, DJs, art displays, a big screen TV and computer games – but the each location has developed differently (often based on their former incarnations). The Kennington branch, for example makes a feature of its huge roof terrace overlooking the Imperial War Museum, while the funky Chinatown interloper has a big 'crush bar' area suited to West End drinking.
/ **Website:** www.thespiritgroup.com **Details:** Mon-Sat noon-11pm, Sun noon-10.30pm (SW10 & W6, Fri & Sat midnight – W12 Thu midnight, Fri & Sat 1am – SE11 Thu 1am, Fri & Sat 2am – W1 opens at 1pm); no Amex. **Food:** L&D. **DJ:** Fri & Sat. **Happy hour:** 5.30pm-7.30pm (house wine £6 a bottle, doubles for singles on house spirits).

Bar Rumba W1

36 Shaftesbury Ave 7287 2715 3–3D

Cheap cocktails and salsa classes (Tue) are among the attractions of this late-night basement bar near the Trocadero, which boasts live music most nights and a large dance floor. Good air-conditioning (it needed it) and a recent spruce-up have made it much more comfortable than of old.
/ **Website:** www.barrumba.co.uk **Details:** Mon 9pm-3am, Tue 6pm-3am, Wed 9pm-3am, Thu & Fri 6pm-3.30am, Sat 9pm-5am, Sun 8pm-2am; no Amex. **Food:** 6-11pm. **DJ:** nightly. **Happy hour:** Tue, Thu & Fri 6-9pm (2 for 1).

Bar Soho W1

23-25 Old Compton St   7439 9301   4–2A

With its big windows and its prime position on London's cruisiest street, this large'n'loud heart-of-Soho establishment – half bar/half restaurant, and complete with glitter ball – is something of an of out-of-towners' delight. It attracts quite a lot of locals too, and it's usually packed. / **Details:** *Mon-Thu 4pm-1am, Fri & Sat 4pm-3am, Sun 4pm-12.30am.* **Food:** *from 6pm.* **DJ:** *nightly.*

Bar Sol Ona W1

17 Old Compton St   7287 9932   4–2A

Late on Friday or Saturday night, this inconspicuous Soho basement tapas bar (by Café Bohème) heaves with life as people willingly shell out the entry charge to keep on drinking until the wee hours (there's a small charge – under a fiver – from about 8pm most nights). Not that it's a bad place, but its attractions other than as a late-night drinking den are fairly limited. / **Details:** *management declined to provide information.*

The Bar Under The Clock EC4

74 Queen Victoria St   7489 9895   9–2C

With its modernistic style, you'd hardly guess that this basement City wine bar – in the cute lanes behind St-Mary-le-Bow – is an outlet of the ultra-traditional Balls Bros chain. It's a pleasant place, though, that doesn't strive too hard to be fashionable, and offers a good range of bottles at reasonable prices as well as a selection of bottled lagers and spirits. / **Website:** *www.ballsbrothers.co.uk* **Details:** *closed weekends.* **Food:** *L till 3pm, D till 9.00pm, bar snacks all day.*

Bar Vinyl NW1

6 Inverness St   7681 7898   8–3B

Two doors down from Bar Gansa this cool-looking bar – which claims something of a celeb following – opened five years ago. Its main claim to fame is that is has a record shop downstairs where lovers of vinyl can browse to their hearts' content. The bar itself is modern and offers a fair array of lagers (Grolsch, Staropramen, Budvar) and cocktails, and also food. Unsurprisingly given the location, weekends are especially popular. / **Website:** *www.vinyl-addiction.co.uk* **Details:** *Fri & Sat noon-midnight; no Amex.* **Food:** *L till 4pm, D till 11.30pm.* **DJ:** *Wed-Sun.*

Bardo SW3
196 Fulham Rd   7351 1711   5–3B
The only full-on cocktail bar on the strip known by the Tatler-reading classes as the Chelsea 'Beach' – this is a civilised and notably comfortable spot. Picture windows looking on to the street allow you to check out the action outside, but on the inside it feels far from being a goldfish bowl. Sushi and snacks are available to sustain you till the 1am close. / **Details:** *Mon-Sat 5.30pm-1am, Sun 5.30pm-11pm.* **Food:** *till 1am.* **DJ & Live music:** *DJ and bongos - varies.*

Barley Mow E14
44 Narrow St   7265 8931   11–1B
At its best in summer, when the tables on the circular terrace are at a premium, this prominent riverside pub (converted in the late '80s from the Dockmaster's House at the lock entrance to Limehouse Basin) has far-reaching Thames views. Otherwise it's a pretty standard boozer, but as it's considerably larger than its near neighbours (House, Grapes and Booty's), it has become a useful Docklands dwellers' rendezvous. / **Food:** *L till 3pm, D till 9pm.*

The Barley Mow W1
8 Dorset St   7935 7318   3–1A
The oldest inn in Marylebone is a suitably traditional affair, with wood panelling and such original features as two pawnbrokers' booths attached to a section of the bar. It caters to a mainly local crowd who go to read the paper or to gas with their friends, while supping on a pint of lager or one of the fair range of bitters. / **Details:** *closed Sun.* **Food:** *L only.*

Bartok NW1
78-79 Chalk Farm Rd   7916 0595   8–2B
Describing itself as London's only classical music bar (though jazz is sometimes played), this Chalk Farm joint is decked out in velvet (both curtains and sofas), and boasts large chandeliers to help create a suitable atmosphere. (In case you're wondering about the DJ symbol, the music might be traditional, Indian, or contemporary classical with "beat undernotes".)
Hoegaarden, Fosters and Stella are on tap, but the list of wine and cocktails tends to be more the order of the day.
/ **Website:** *www.meanfiddler.com* **Details:** *Mon-Thu noon-midnight, Fri & Sat noon-1am, Sun noon-midnight; no Amex.* **Food:** *till midnight (weekends 1am).* **DJ:** *nightly.* **Live music:** *bands Wed (classical, jazz, world).* **Happy hour:** *till 8pm, all Thu pm.*

Beach Blanket Babylon W11

45 Ledbury Rd   7229 2907   6–1B

When this Gaudiesque Notting Hill bar was opened in 1991 it set a new standard for London bar interiors. The place has stood the test of time pretty well, and although the crowd is perhaps not now as drop-dead hip as it once was, the atmosphere remains special and inviting. In the warren-like basement, there is an expensive Mediterranean restaurant not known for its great value. / **Website:** www.beachblanket.aol.com **Details:** no Amex. **Food:** L till 3pm, D till 11pm.

The Bear EC1

St John's Sq   7608 2117   9–1A

In an area progressively dominated by extremes, this pleasing boozer just off Clerkenwell Road (overlooking historic St John's Gate) can seem refreshingly unpretentious. The décor is bright and modern, while the drinks and food are reassuringly familiar – especially to regulars of Primrose Hill's Queen's or Battersea's Duke of Cambridge, which are also run by the same company, Geronimo Inns. / **Details:** closed weekends. **Food:** L noon-3pm, D 6pm-9.30pm. **DJ:** Thu-Fri.

Bed

310 Portobello Rd, W10   8969 4500   6–1A
57-59 Charterhouse St, EC1   7336 6484   9–2A

The original Bed is a converted pub, right at the top of the Portobello Road, with two floors both done out in a darkly-lit, lavish style bordering on Gothic. At the second branch in Smithfield, the style is Moroccan – a three level venue, nicely decked out throughout, with perhaps the cosiest, soukiest bit being the Bedrock bar at the bottom. Lagers or cocktails are the most popular tipples. Both places get louder as the night goes on (with DJs nightly). / **Details:** W10 Mon-Wed 5pm-1am, Thu-Sat noon-11pm, Sun noon-10.30pm; EC1 Mon-Wed 11am-midnight, Thu 11am-2am, Fri & Sat 11am-3am, Sun noon-10.30pm; EC1 no Amex. **Food:** till 9pm.

The Bedford SW12

77 Bedford Hill   8673 1756   10–2B

Weekly discos, comedy nights, dance lessons and a giant TV screen have made this large Balham boozer a notable local venue. The function rooms (including a galleried theatre) play host to a myriad of events all week long, while the saloon bar is a relaxed and comfortable space for drinking. Sunday lunch (served all afternoon) is a big draw, complete with entertainment. / **Website:** *www.thebedford.co.uk* **Details:** *Fri & Sat till 2am.* **Food:** *L till 3pm (Sun L till 5pm), D till 10pm.* **DJ:** *Fri-Sat.* **Live music:** *bands nightly.*

Bedroom Bar EC2

62 Rivington St   7613 5637   9–1D

For once, 'New York style' really does describe this achingly cool bar – with its white-painted brick walls and iron pillars, it's a dead ringer for a downtown Manhattan loft. A rather beautiful crowd sips cocktails and bottled lager, and chats over the background of whatever the DJ is spinning – which could be lots of things. / **Details:** *Wed & Thu noon-1am, Fri & Sat 7pm-2am, closed Sun-Tue; no Amex.* **DJ:** *Thu-Sat.*

Bell EC4

29 Bush Ln   7626 7560   9–3C

"We believe it is the oldest small pub in the City of London", says a sign outside this boozer tucked away down the side of Cannon Street station. There was a time when the City was full of places like this, but it's quite a rare beast nowadays – its popularity is such that non-traditionalists may find it on the cramped and smoky side. Bitters include Spitfire and Smiths Smooth. / **Details:** *Mon-Fri till 10pm, closed weekends; no credit cards.* **Food:** *L&D.*

The Bell & Crown W4

11-13 Thames Rd   8994 4164   1–2A

This well-run Fullers pub is arguably the best of the three hostelries in Strand-on-the-Green – a particularly picturesque part of the Thames towpath near Kew Bridge. The décor is of the pub-carpet, rather than the stripped-wood-floors variety, but with its real fires, nice conservatory and terrace it offers a dependable classic pub experience. / **Details:** *no-smoking area.* **Food:** *L till 3pm (Sun till 5pm), D till 9pm.*

The Belle Vue SW4

Clapham Common Southside   7498 9473   10–2C
*Right by Clapham Common tube this Bohemian gastropub serves up decent-enough grub to a typical, er, Clapham crowd. You can just drink, of course (about as many people opt for wine as the range of lagers and bitters) but seating priority is given to diners. / **Details:** Mon-Fri from 4pm; no Amex. **Food:** till 6.30pm.*

Bentley's W1

11-15 Swallow St   7734 4756   3–3D
*Burlington Bertie would have felt very at home in this Mayfair bastion of a seafood bar (which has a fish restaurant of some repute above) – a wonderfully central spot for a traditional blow out with a bottle of Champagne and perhaps a few oysters. The décor – dating from 1916 – is in a style of which few examples survive. / **Details:** Mon-Sat from 5pm, closed Sun. **Food:** D till 11pm. **Happy hour:** Mon-Fri 5.30pm-7pm (30% discount on all drinks).*

(The Blue Bar)
Berkeley Hotel SW1

Wilton Pl   7235 6000   5–1D
*Cliché-mongers have had a field-day with the 'ultra-cool' surroundings of the new bar of this formerly rather stuffy Savoy-group Knightsbridge hotel. For once, though, they have got it right, and the bar – which is indeed very chic and, er, blue – has succeeded in attracting a fashionable (and surprisingly youthful) following. / **Website:** www.savoygroup.com **Details:** Mon-Sat 4pm-1am, closed Sun; no-smoking area. **Food:** till 12.45am.*

Berners Hotel Bar
Berners Hotel W1

Berners St   7666 2000   3–1D
*Part of the restaurant area, this small bar fronts on to the street of this impressive hotel (built in 1835 as five separate houses, and converted a century ago). And the magnificent original ceilings (Grade II listed) are still in evidence. Hurry along, though, if you want to appreciate its current shabby-chic charms – a major refurb is apparently afoot. / **Food:** till 10.30pm. **Happy hour:** 5pm-7pm (cocktails £4).*

The Betsey Trotwood EC1

56 Farringdon Rd   7253 4285   9–1A

*This triangular Shepherd Neame pub has an attractive, scrubbed-up appearance, with décor that's a blend of original features and modern touches. It's located right by the Guardian's offices, so there are usually a few hacks propping up the bar with a pint either of the brewery's lagers (Holstein, Oranjeboom, Hurlimann) or its bitters (Bishops Finger, Spitfire, and Masters Brew). / **Details:** no Amex. **Food:** L till 3pm (Mon-Fri).*

Bierodrome

680 Fulham Rd, SW6   7751 0789   10–1A
173-174 Upper St, N1   7226 5835   8–3D
44-48 Clapham High St, SW4   7720 1118   10–2C

*This smart, modernistic chain of beer halls (from the same stable as the Belgo restaurants) offers an impressive, all-Belgian range, from rare Trappist brews to fruit-flavoured varieties; and with up to 10 on tap at any time. Belgian-ish snacks and more substantial fare complete the experience. / **Details:** Mon-Sun noon-midnight (WC2 11pm, closed Sun), SW4 Thu 1am, Fri & Sat 2am. **Food:** L&D & bar snacks.*

Big Easy SW3

334 King's Rd   7352 4071   5–3C

*If you're looking for an All-American experience in deepest Chelsea, you won't do much better than this long-established bar and 'crabshack'. It offers a good range of US beers, but the prices might raise a few eyebrows in Boise, Idaho. / **Details:** Sun-Thu noon-11.30pm, Fri & Sat noon-12.30am; no-smoking area. **Food:** till 12.20am (closed Sun). **Happy hour:** Mon noon-11pm, Tue-Fri 4pm-7.30pm (2 for 1).*

The Bishop's Finger EC1

Smithfield   7248 2341   9–2A

*A place of pilgrimage for beer and banger lovers alike. This modernised Shepherd Neame pub (the company's original London venture) serves up a weekday feast of gourmet sausages from Smithfield Market across the road, plus a range of the famous beers – choose from cask (Bishop's Finger, predictably, plus seasonal brews), keg (Masterbrew, Spitfire) or lager (Oranjeboom Pilsener). / **Website:** www.shepherd-neame.co.uk **Details:** closed weekends. **Food:** till 9pm.*

Black Bull SW10

358 Fulham Rd   7376 7370   10–1A

*Relief in a rather depressing stretch of the Fulham Road –
just before you go over the bridge from Chelsea into Fulham –
is provided by this forbidding-looking converted pub.
Once inside, though, the interior is warm and relaxed,
in loungey style, and is warmed by a real fire and different
drinks specials nightly.* / **Details:** *no Amex.* **DJ:** *Wed-Sat.*
Happy hour: *nightly & Mon-Thu till 8pm (2 for 1 cocktails, house wine
£5.95, Sun Bloody Marys £2, tequila slammers £1.20, flavoured Absolut £1.20,
5 beers £10, schnapps £1.20/shot).*

The Black Cap NW1

171 Camden High St   7428 2721   8–3B

*This amiable Camden Town bar (with a disco and drag acts
downstairs) is a long-standing gay destination, and pretty
unremarkable of its type. For sunny days, though, it boasts an
unusually pleasant beer garden.* / **Details:** *Mon-Thu noon-2am, Fri &
Sat noon-3am, Sun noon-12.30am.* **Food:** *till 5pm.* **Happy hour:** *Mon (spirit
& mixer £2.99).*

The Black Lion W6

2 South Black Lion Ln   8748 2639   7–2A

*If you're in Hammersmith on a sunny day, and the nearby Old
Ship is full to bursting (not unusual), you might like to consider
strolling down the riverside path to this quieter traditional
boozer (under the same ownership). If it wasn't near the river
and didn't have a large outside terrace it might not make the
guide, but it is and it does.* / **Food:** *till 9pm (Sun 6pm).*

The Blackfriar EC4

174 Queen Victoria St   7236 5474   9–3A

*Their grammar may not be up to much, but the management's
claim that this Nicholson's boozer is "London's most unique
public house" is not that far off the mark. It's the small building
itself – constructed and elaborately decorated in (very rare,
for London) art nouveau style, in 1916 – which makes it so
special, but (despite the volume of nearby traffic) it's the large
outside area which is the special attraction for today's City
workers.* / **Details:** *closed weekends.* **Food:** *till 2.30pm.*

Blacksmith's Arms SE16

267 Rotherhithe St   7237 1349   11–1B

Of interest mainly because there's so little else in the immediate area, this darkly-panelled Fullers pub – by Nelson's Dock Hilton hotel – is a friendly-enough – if otherwise unremarkable – place. Attractions include a pool table, and a restaurant upstairs. / **Website:** www.fullers.co.uk **Details:** no Amex. **Food:** Tue-Sat 6.30pm-9.30pm, Sun roast 12.30pm-5pm.

Blakes NW1

31 Jamestown Rd   7482 2959   8–3B

On the corner of Jamestown and Arlington Roads, this medievally-inspired Camden Town pub boasts huge Gothic-style doors. The style continues inside in a similar vein, and the crowd is cool and friendly. Above the bar, there's a small restaurant, which can be quite good. / **Food:** till 10.30pm.

Blakes Bar
Blakes Hotel SW7

33 Roland Gdns   7370 6701   5–2B

The tiny, eclectically decorated, very '80s basement champagne and cocktail bar of this famously romantic South Kensington hotel has lost little of its seductive charm with the passing of the years. If you're on anything resembling a budget, give the place a wide berth – if you're not, you'll probably have fun. / **Website:** www.blakeshotels.com **Details:** Mon-Sun 5.30pm-11pm. **Food:** bar snacks all day, D 7pm-11pm.

Bleeding Heart EC1

Bleeding Heart Yd, Greville St   7242 8238   9–2A

Long-time customers may still think of this intriguing warren (hidden away north of Holborn), as just a romantic and cosy wine bar (with an excellent list and good food), with a grander dining room attached. It's expanded considerably over the years, though, and – for those with drinking in mind rather than eating – the most obvious destination these days is the relatively recently-created (and highly popular) tavern, where beer is also on offer. / **Details:** Mon-Fri noon-2.30pm & 6pm-10.30pm, closed weekends. **Food:** till 10.30pm. **Happy hour:** 5pm-7pm.

The Blind Beggar E1
337 Whitechapel Rd   7247 6195   1–1D
Notorious as the place where, in 1966, Ronnie Kray shot George Cornell, this otherwise rather standard boozer (opposite the Royal London Hospital) does boast one great non-historic attraction – a large, ivy-covered beer garden for summer. / **Food:** *L till 2.30pm (Sun till 3.30pm).*

The Blue Anchor W6
13 Lower Mall   8748 5774   7–2B
On Boat Race day, you can't move with the crush of spectators who pack the space outside the pubs just upstream from Hammersmith Bridge (approximately the half-way point). And on any warm day of the year, the large riverside pavement outside this Georgian hostelry makes a nice spot for a pint while watching the river go by. Inevitably given its prime location, the crowd can be a bit touristy, though it does attract some 'local types' also. / **Food:** *L till 3.30pm, D till 8.30pm.*

(Blue Bar)
Blue Elephant SW6
4-6 Fulham Broadway   7385 6595   10–1A
If you fancy feeling like an extra in 'The King & I', then the new bar attached to Fulham's vast and justly-famed Thai restaurant is the place. Sit amidst palm trees and golden barges, while you consume some (not inexpensive) cocktails and superior nibbles. / **Website:** www.blueelephant.com **Details:** *Mon-Sun noon-1am.* **Food:** *till midnight.* **Happy hour:** *Mon-Fri 4pm-6.30pm.*

Blue Posts W1
28 Rupert St   7437 1415   2–1C
Just your average, mild-mannered pub – or at least it would be if it wasn't slap bang in the middle of the West End. It really is quite incredible that this simply-decorated corner spot hasn't been Irish-themed or turned into yet another 'trendy bar'. Perhaps it's because it seems almost invisible among all the flashing neon signs of Chinatown that it's lasted this long. There's Leffe, Hoegaarden and Stella on tap, or – for bitter drinkers – TT Landlord, Adnams and London Pride. / **Food:** *till 9pm.*

Bluebird SW3

350 Kings Rd   7559 1000   5–3C

This large and swanky Conran outfit – comprising a Sainsbury's foodstore, restaurant, café and bar – enjoys 'landmark' status, down Chelsea way (unsurprisingly as it occupies a huge, grade II listed building on the main drag). The bar occupies quite a large part of the impressively airy room on the first floor, which it shares with a (rather overpriced) grill restaurant.
*/ **Website:** www.conran.com **Details:** Mon-Sat 9am-1am, closed Sun.*
***Food:** D only, L bar snacks. **DJ:** Fri-Sat. **Live music:** piano & singer Sat night in members club.*

Blues W1

42 Dean St   7494 1966   4–2A

By the standards of Soho, this clean-lined bar (at the front of a large brasserie) isn't the most cutting-edge hip kind of place. It's fun and friendly, though, and its handy central location makes it a useful standby for a wide-ranging crowd. The decent cocktails won't break the bank (and nor will the grub).
*/ **Website:** www.bluebistro.com **Details:** Mon-Thu noon-midnight, Fri & Sat 5pm-1am, Sun 5pm-midnight. **Food:** till 11.30pm.*

Bluu N1

1 Hoxton Sq   7613 2793   9–1D

*Next to the longer-established Hoxton Square Bar & Kitchen, this relative newcomer occupies a more rambling space (parts of which older trendies may remember from its days as the Blue Note). With its brick walls and dark finishes, it certainly ticks off most of the requirements for a cool-looking modern bar, and DJs at weekends pump up the volume. / **Food:** Mon-Fri till 8pm (weekends 6pm). **DJ:** Thu-Sat.*

Boardwalk W1

18 Greek St   7287 2051   4–2A

It's not what you'd call a cool destination, but this theme-y looking club/bar is something of a Soho stalwart. Its prime advantage these days is a late-night licence – there's a charge (usually under a fiver) after 11pm.
*/ **Website:** www.latenightlondon.co.uk, www.boardwalksoho.co.uk*
***Details:** Mon-Sat 5pm-3am, closed Sun. **Food:** till 3am.*
***Happy hour:** 5pm-7pm (wine £8, £10 off champagne, cocktails £3, spirits £1.50).*

Bohème Kitchen & Bar W1

19-21 Old Compton St   7734 5656   4–2A

This is one of the few genuinely mixed (gay/straight) places in the heart of Soho. It's quite a loungey bar/restaurant – from the same owners as the mega-successful Café Bohème next door – and the food isn't bad at all. On sunny days, the (few) outdoor seats offer an excellent perch from which to watch the crowds cruise by. / **Website:** www.bohemekitchen.co.uk **Details:** Mon-Sat 11am-1am, Sun noon-11pm. **Food:** till 11.45pm (Sun 10pm).

(Back Bar) Boisdale SW1

15 Eccleston St   7730 6922   2–3B

On the fringe of Belgravia, this grand Scottish restaurant and bar – run by a real, live laird – has made quite a name for its wide range of Scotches (over 250 of them) and cigars (over 100) and, in the restaurant, its game and steaks from north of the border. It has a comfortable, traditional clubby feel, and some cool jazz regularly adds to the atmosphere. Despite its other attractions its the wine list (over 400 bins majoring in clarets) which most often attracts drinkers' attentions. / **Website:** www.boisdale.co.uk **Details:** closed weekends. **Food:** till 10.45pm.

Boisdale of Bishopsgate EC2

202 Bishopsgate   7283 1763   9–2D

Down an alleyway next to Dirty Dick's, this characterful new bar is an offshoot of the successful Belgravia bastion of traditional Scottish values. Its clubby charms have been pretty successfully re-created here for City gents, so lovers of claret and malts are particularly well catered for. / **Website:** www.boisdale.uk.com **Details:** closed weekends. **Food:** till 9pm.

Boland's Wine Bar SE24

22 Half Moon La   7733 2570   1–3C

If you're looking for a congenial wine bar down Herne Hill way, it's worth seeking out this small and friendly establishment, where a fair range of wines is served, as well as a range of bottled beers (plus some simple Gallic dishes). There are also a few tables outside. / **Details:** Mon-Sat noon-midnight, Sun noon-11pm; no Amex. **Food:** L till 4pm, D till 10pm. **Happy hour:** Mon-Fri 5.30pm-6.30pm.

Bollo House W4

13-15 Bollo Ln   8994 6037   7–2A
*Converted a couple of years ago, this spacious and easygoing venture on the Acton/Chiswick borders is a nice mix of modern gastropub and old-style boozer. When it opened, the food was a major reason to visit and – though it may have come off a notch – it's still better than at many other such places. / **Website:** www.thebollohouse.com **Food:** L till 3pm (weekends 5pm), D till 10.30pm.*

Bond's EC2

5 Threadneedle St   7657 8088   9–2C
*Ten years ago, the idea of a boutique hotel in the City that was half as stylish as this new opening near Bank would have seemed preposterous. With its airy setting, though (a reclaimed banking hall) this new venue provides the kind of glamorous setting for which – even these days – workers in the surrounding money-factories more usually need to travel 'up West'. / **Website:** www.etontownhouse.com **Details:** closed weekends. **Food:** D till 10.30pm.*

Boom Bar SW11

165-167 St John's Hill   7924 3449   10–2B
*This relaxed, trendy and buzzy bar near Clapham Junction is a cut above the rest in the area. The interior is well-designed and tasteful, with the bar taking up the back wall. Lighting is well-done and seating mixes booths and tables and chairs. Beers are available, but this is really more a cocktails and spirits sort of place. / **Details:** Mon-Thu from 5pm, Fri 5pm-midnight, Sat noon-midnight; no Amex. **Food:** D till 10.15pm (weekends till 4pm). **DJ:** Tue & Thu-Sun. **Live music:** live music Sun. **Happy hour:** Thu-Sun (£2 off normal price).*

Booty's E14

92a Narrow St   7987 8343   11–1B
*Until 1979, these low-ceilinged riverside premises were part of a 16th-century boat yard. Nowadays, they provide the setting for what looks like a plainly decorated wine bar, ornamented with black and white pictures recording the development of the Docklands. A small but smart place, it boasts an impressive view of the Thames. It's actually a free house and also has a wide range of lagers, bitters and other drinks. / **Food:** till 9.30pm, Sat till 7.30pm.*

Borough Bar SE1

10-18 London Bridge St   7407 6962   9–3C

A new opening from the Hartford group (Dakota, Canyon and so on), this airy bar has a slightly corporate, All Bar One-esque, feel about it. There's still not that much choice in these parts, though – certainly if you're looking for somewhere with a bit of scale – so it's worth checking out. / **Details:** *closed Sun; non smoking areas.* **Food:** *till 9pm.*

(Le Bar des Magis) Bouchon Bordelais SW11

5-9 Battersea Rise   7738 0307   10–2B

It's quite grand by Battersea standards, and the attractive Continental-style bar attached to this lively, long-established Gallic bistro has long been a popular destination in its own right. As you'd expect most customers opt for Les Vins, but there is also a good selection of Les Bières, Les Cocktails and so on. / **Website:** *www.lebouchon.co.uk* **Details:** *Mon-Sun 10am-11pm.* **Food:** *till 11pm.*

Boulevard WC2

40 Wellington St   7240 2992   4–3D

Given its tacky touristy Covent Garden location, this large, modern bar/brasserie ought to be awful. But it isn't – it's a friendly, well-run outfit that makes a very handy central meeting place. It's largely given over to eating, but you can just drink and there's a bar on the ground floor (and also in the basement, which is often hired out for events and parties). / **Website:** *www.boulevardbrasserie.com* **Details:** *Mon-Sun noon-midnight; no-smoking area.* **Food:** *L&D.*

The Bow Wine Vaults EC4

10 Bow Churchyard   7248 1121   9–2C

A particularly charming 'old City' location – in a pretty lane, under the impressive bulk of St Mary-le-Bow – contributes to the ambience of this traditional-style wine bar (which has a brasserie attached). It offers a good range of wines, reasonably priced. / **Website:** *www.motcombs.co.uk* **Details:** *closed weekends.* **Food:** *D only.*

The Box WC2

32-34 Monmouth St   7240 5828   4–2B
*Just by Theatreland's Seven Dials, this simple bar-café was one
of the advance party of hip, gay (well, predominantly gay) bars
to hit the centre of town. It remains pretty happening,
and serves a wide range of bottled beers and cocktails.*
/ **Details:** *no Amex.* **Food:** *till 5pm (Sun till 6pm).*

Bradley's Spanish Bar W1

42-44 Hanway St   7636 0359   4–1A
*This real curiosity – in a back alley near Tottenham Court Road
tube – boasts a tiny bar at street level, but (through a separate
entrance) there's also a slightly larger bar below. The dark
setting, with lots of little alcoves, is essentially (but not
exclusively) Spanish, and the clientèle – downing lagers and
beers from a good selection with no particular geographical
theme – is chilled and Bohemian.* / **Details:** *Sun from 3pm; no Amex.*
Food: *L&D.*

Bread & Roses SW4

68 Clapham Manor St   7498 1779   10–1C
*It's nice to come across a boozer with personality, and this
Trades Union owned Clapham gastropub certainly scores on
that front. (As you'll almost certainly know, it's named after a
famous incident in the early 20th-century American labour
movement.) The drinks selection includes a special house ale,
but there are a number of lagers on tap and many drinkers go
for wine. The decked garden out back comes into its own on for
ethnic Sunday lunch ('Family Day') – very New Labour.*
/ **Website:** *www.breadandrosespub.com* **Details:** *no Amex; no-smoking area.*
Food: *L till 3pm (weekends 4pm), D till 9.30pm.*

Bricklayers Arms W1

31 Gresse St   7636 5593   4–1A
*This mock-Tudor inn (actually built in the 18th century) looks a
bit out of place in a quiet cut-through near Charlotte Street and
is made more distinctive by the small lane that runs through the
side of the building. It has a traditional and woody interior,
making it an ideal antidote for those for whom the area (which
trendies describe as NoHo) is just a bit too hip nowadays.*
/ **Details:** *no Amex.* **Food:** *L till 3pm, D till 9pm (Fri-Sun L only).*

The Bricklayers Arms EC2

63 Charlotte Rd   7739 5245   9–1D

Permanently packed with a relaxed crowd of twentysomethings, buoyed up by sounds from the charts, this nicely faded free house just south of Old Street is proof that there's more to life than blond wood and halogen downlighters. / **Details:** Mon-Sat 11am-midnight, Sun noon-11.30pm; no Amex. **Food:** L till 2.45pm, D till 10.30pm. **DJ:** Wed-Sun.

The Bridge SW13

204 Castelnau   8563 9811   1–2A

This converted boozer, just south of Hammersmith bridge received a very stylish makeover at the end of 2002 (and already seems to be attracting the well-heeled residents of nearby chichi Harrods Village). It feels less like a pub and more like a loungey bar and restaurant the further you go in; out back there's a very nice-looking decked garden. The food's not bad, but not notable either. / **Food:** till midnight (closed weekends).

Bridge & Tunnel E2

4 Calvert Ave   7720 7739   9–1D

Imagine a chic air raid shelter and you'll get close to the 'look' of this dark venue off Shoreditch High Street. In the main bar, large velvet drapes help soften the grungy effect of the bare walls. There's also a lounging area, while the basement is just full-on clubby. Ownership by the nuphonic record label accounts for the huge, slightly threatening looking speakers on the walls (and the high-quality sound). Cocktails are the preferred tipple. / **Website:** www.bridgeandtunnel.co.uk **Details:** Mon-Sat 12.30pm-midnight (Fri & Sat later in club), Sun 4pm-midnight. **Food:** D till 11.30pm. **DJ:** nightly & Sun during the day. **Live music:** bands sometimes.

Bridge House SE1

218 Tower Bridge Rd   7407 5818   9–3D

Adnams' range of beers is always quite a draw, so this pub by Tower Bridge, run by the Southwold-based brewery, has a head start with fans of real ale. From the outside it looks like an old pub, but inside it's bright and airy, with colourful walls and pale wood flooring. All the company's beers (including the seasonal brews) and their (impressive) wine list are available, and there's a dining room upstairs. / **Food:** L till 3pm (Sun 4pm), D till 10pm (closed Mon, Sat L & Sun D).

Brinkley's SW10

47 Hollywood Rd   7351 1683   5–3B

If there is a younger 'Chelsea set' nowadays, this side-street bar/restaurant has a reasonable claim to being its rallying point, and the place is frantically busy from early-evening onwards. It looks rather like a cocktail bar, but ownership by merchant John Brinkley means that the selection of wine is actually its star attraction. At the rear, there's a restaurant where the charm of the setting rather eclipses that of the menu.
/ **Website:** www.brinkleys.com **Details:** Mon-Sun 6pm-11.30pm. **Food:** D till 11pm. **Happy hour:** till 9pm (beer £3).

The Britannia W8

1 Allen St   7937 6905   5–1A

There isn't a vast amount to say about this Victorian Young's pub, prettily located in a side street off High Street Ken'. It's a useful, honest-to-goodness traditional boozer serving a good range of lagers and bitters (and – as is customary for Young's pubs – a fair range of wine), and which has the benefit of an attractive rear conservatory. / **Website:** www.youngs.co.uk **Food:** L till 3pm, D till 9.45pm.

Brixtonian
Havana Club SW9

11 Beehive Pl   7924 9262   10–1C

Don't let the slightly unnerving side street location of this small cocktail bar put you off (where you go up an outside staircase to gain access). It specialises in rum-based cocktails (based on 200 or so different types) and Latino dancing – and, yes, it's usually as much fun as that description suggests. Top marks for cocktail naming goes to the catchily christened 'Brixton Riot'.
/ **Website:** www.brixtonian.co.uk **Details:** Mon-Wed noon-1am, Thu-Sat noon-2am, Sun noon-midnight. **Food:** D 5pm-10.30pm (L weekends only). **Happy hour:** 5pm-7pm ("martini hour").

Brown's Hotel W1

30 Albemarle St   7493 6020   3–3C

Despite the modernising influences of its latest owners (the Raffles group) clubbiness and tradition are still the forte of this creaky old hotel, in the heart of Mayfair. The principal feature of the somewhat wince-makingly named St George's Bar is a back-lit Victorian stained glass window and single malts are a house speciality. / **Website:** www.raffles-brownshotel.com **Details:** no-smoking area. **Food:** L till 5pm, D till 10pm.

Buchan's SW11
62-64 Battersea Bridge Rd   7228 0888   10–1B
Just south of Battersea Bridge, this long-established Scottish-themed wine bar has long been a key haunt of the local young professionals. There's a full-blown restaurant, or (good but quite pricey) bar snacks are also available. That the bar is named for John Buchan (author of The 39 Steps*) explains the number of wines and different varieties of Scotch on offer.*
/ **Website:** www.buchansrestaurant.com **Details:** Mon-Fri noon-2.45pm & 5.30pm-11pm, Sat 12.30pm-3.30pm & 5.30pm-11pm, Sun 12.30pm-4pm & 7pm-10pm. **Food:** L till 2.45pm, D till 10.45pm. **Happy hour:** Mon-Fri 5.30pm-7pm (1/3 off most drinks).

The Bucks Head NW1
202 Camden High St   7284 1513   8–3B
If you're up Camden Town way, this newish bar is to be found by the clothes section of the market and makes a useful standby in the area. Decked out simply with wooden tables, snacks and meals are available and there are regular DJs. At the time of writing, a music and dance licence has been applied for so it may be that developments are afoot.
/ **Website:** www.scottish-newcastle.com **Food:** till 9pm, Fri & Sat till 7pm. **DJ:** Thu-Sat.

Bug SW2
The Crypt, St Matthew's   7738 3184   10–2C
St Matthew's Church dominates Brixton's main traffic junction and its crypt provides an impressive setting for this basement bar, which has long had a reputation as a music venue. There are DJs pretty much nightly, playing funk, R&B and all that jazz and the whole place gets very loud and crowded. (Note: there's an adjoining restaurant of the same name – but eating there doesn't mean you can gain access to the bar).
/ **Website:** www.bugbrixton.co.uk **Details:** Wed 7pm-2am, Thu 8pm-2.30am, Fri & Sat 8pm-3am, Sun 8pm-2am (closed Mon & Tue); no Amex. **Food:** D only. **DJ:** Thu-Sun.

The Builder's Arms SW3
13 Britten St   7349 9040   5–2C
A convenient location for King's Road strollers – tucked away in a cute little street behind Waitrose – has helped make this excellent Chelsea gastropub a hugely popular destination. The food's a prime attraction, but it makes a relaxed and comfortable destination whether you're eating or not.
/ **Details:** no Amex. **Food:** L till 2.30pm, D till 9.30pm (Sun 9pm).

The Bull N1

100 Upper St   7226 3467   8–3D

*Rather loungier than the norm on north London's booziest major strip, this made-over Islington pub – haven't they all been? – covers up its guilty secret surprisingly well. You'd never guess that this former Firkin was under the same ownership as All Bar One. For an intimate drink, head up the spiral stairs to the one of the sofas on the mezzanine level. / **Food:** till 9.50pm.*

The Bull EC1

292 St John St   7278 8405   9–1A

*A Clerkenwell-style pub-conversion that's geographically closer to Islington is, perhaps, the best way of describing this large, modernised corner boozer. It avoids the gastropub tag by only offering lunchtime bar snacks, and serves a fair range of ales and lagers. Table football and a big TV screen in one corner, and board games and newspapers in another contribute to its wide-ranging appeal. / **Details:** Mon-Fri till 11.30pm, closed weekends; no Amex. **Food:** L only.*

The Bull & Gate NW5

389 Kentish Town Rd   7485 5358   8–2B

*It has quite an interesting interior, but it's as a music venue that this large, rather shabby Victorian boozer near Kentish Town tube is of most interest to today's drinkers – the place is a well-known showcase for new bands. / **Details:** no credit cards. **Food:** L (closed weekends). **Happy hour:** 11am-5pm (beer £2).*

Bull's Head SW13

373 Lonsdale Rd   8876 5241   1–3A

*Nightly blues and jazz – it's one of the top venues in town – is the top draw to this large Victorian Young's pub, near Barnes Bridge, whose rear music room is much grander than normal for this kind of venue. Supporting attractions come in the shape of a pleasant location near the Thames (though you don't see much of the river), a characterful bar (which received an attractive revamp a few years ago), and a cute bistro (The Stable) in the yard out back. / **Website:** www.youngs.co.uk, www.thebullshead.com **Details:** no-smoking area. **Food:** till 10.30pm.*

The Bull's Head W4

15 Strand on the Grn   8994 1204   1–2A

*This ancient and intriguingly rambling (grade I listed) Chef &
Brewer pub is on the towpath by the Thames, on the very
pretty stretch of water downstream from Kew Bridge.
The outside tables therefore have obvious attractions. Inside its
received a slightly suburban, but attractive and comfortable refit
which makes it feel more like a restaurant in parts. In keeping
with its slightly 'posh' style, wine is a popular choice of tipple,
though there are five bitters on tap. (History anoraks note: this
was Cromwell's HQ during the civil war.)* / **Details:** *no-smoking area.*
Food: *till 10pm.*

The Bunch of Grapes SW3

207 Brompton Rd   7589 4944   5–1C

*In some ways this prominently-located, late-Victorian pub is a
typical high-street boozer. Given that the high street in question
is Knightsbridge (this is the first pub you come to if you exit
Harrods by the front door, and turn left), it's a little bit nicer
than that initial description might suggest. Some impressive
etched glass adds to the ambience and all-in-all it's worth
remembering as a useful meeting place in a pricey area.*
/ **Details:** *no-smoking area in restaurant.* **Food:** *L till 3pm, D till 9.45pm.*

Bush Bar & Grill W14

45a Goldhawk Rd   8746 2111   7–1B

*When the crew who helped put restaurant 192 on the map
opened this chic bar/restaurant – hidden away in a yard off the
unlovely Goldhawk Road – it started to provide some substance
to the hype that Shepherd's Bush might just become the new
Notting Hill. The Grill here is a larger part of the operation
than the Bar, but the cosy seating and dramatic design mean
that drinkers – the cool crowd of da Bush – don't feel short
changed.* / **Website:** *www.bushbar.co.uk* **Details:** *no Amex.* **Food:** *till 11pm
(Sun 10.30pm).* **Happy hour:** *Mon-Sun 5pm-7pm (cocktails £3).*

The Bushranger W12

55 Goldhawk Rd   8743 3016   7–1B

It's a good number of years now since this revamped pub, next to Goldhawk Road tube station, was known as the Railway Tavern. It was one of the first wave of boozers to be converted into more modern hang-outs. It's still more traditional than most (with sawdust on the floor, for example), but that doesn't seem to put off a mellow following of twenty- and thirtysomethings. On sunny days, you can catch the rays on the upstairs balcony.
/ **Details:** *Mon-Fri 10am-midnight, Sat 9am-midnight, Sun 9am-11.30pm.*
Food: *B from 10am, L&D till 10.30pm.*

Cactus Blue SW3

86 Fulham Rd   7823 7858   5–2C

A cavernous but impressive hi-tech interior greets those who venture in to this Chelsea bar/restaurant whose menu is inspired by the southern states of the US of A. The Tex/Mex grub is not the world's best, but it's a fun place to go and down a few frozen margaritas. / **Details:** *Mon-Fri from 5.30pm, weekends noon-11.45pm.* **Food:** *D till 11pm.* **Happy hour:** *5.30pm-7.30pm.*

Café Bohème W1

13 Old Compton St   7734 0623   4–2A

A phenomenal success story – this prominent, corner-site cafe-bar-restaurant is a buzzing linchpin of Soho life. Its quite continental in style and you can get anything from a coffee or (from 11 pm) a beer to a full-blown meal at pretty much any time of day. It really comes into its own late night, when it's one of the best places to head post-clubbing. (Note, though, that – as we go to press – it's no longer open 24 hours).
/ **Details:** *Mon-Sat 8am-3am, Sun 8am-11pm.* **Food:** *B 8am-noon (till 5pm Sun), L&D noon-midnight, bar snacks also available.* **DJ:** *early pm Tue, Thu, Sun.* **Live music:** *live jazz.*

Café Kick EC1

43 Exmouth Mkt   7837 8077   9–1A

Football is what this tiny, shack-like café-bar is all about. There are a number of fusball tables, and the décor (like the TV) is wholly devoted to the Beautiful Game. However, with outside tables and a Boho Exmouth Market location, the atmosphere is surprisingly continental, and certainly without a hint of the lager lout. The owners have recently opened a slightly smarter sibling, Bar Kick (see also), in Shoreditch. / **Website:** *www.cafekick.co.uk*
Food: *L only.* **Happy hour:** *4pm-7pm (beer of the day £1.50, cocktails £3.50).*

Cafe Sol SW4

56 Clapham High St   7498 8558   10–2C

If you're young (say, under 25) and out on the pull, this raucous Mexican bar/café in Clapham may well be the place for you. Much of its appeal comes down to late-opening – it was one of the first places on the Clapham strip where you could hang out after hours. / **Details:** *Mon-Sat 12.30pm-2am, Sun 12.30pm-1am.* **Food:** *Sun-Thu till 11.45pm, Fri-Sun till 12.45pm.* **DJ:** *Fri-Sat (disco).*

The Calthorpe Arms WC1

252 Grays Inn Rd   7278 4732   9–1A

The last nice boozer before King's Cross? – before you enter the seedy zone around the station itself, this welcoming traditional pub makes a worthwhile stopping-off point. As well as the usual Young's brews it regularly features guest beers, and recent CAMRA awards are testament to the care taken in looking after them. / **Website:** *www.youngs.co.uk* **Details:** *no Amex.* **Food:** *L only.*

Camden Brewing Co NW1

1 Randolph St   7267 9829   8–3C

As you'd hope for a lounge/bar/café on the northern fringes of Camden Town, near a railway line, this is quite a cool place, with a funky chrome bar, and white leather sofas one end and 'Christine Keeler'-style chairs at the other. There's a fair selection of lagers on tap (Hoegaarden, Stella, Carlsberg Export) and some perfectly reasonable food too. / **Food:** *L till 3pm, D till 9pm.* **DJ:** *Fri-Sat.*

The Camden Head N1

2 Camden Walk   7359 0851   8–3D

Confusingly named, this smoky and warm High Victorian pub – with its impressive glass and its roaring (coal-effect) fires, is in fact in the heart of Islington's quiet backstreets – near the antiques market. Attractions include a comedy club on some nights, and a pleasant outside area for sunny days. / **Food:** *till 9.30pm.*

Cane NW6

283-285 West End Ln   7794 7817   8–1A
*Funky West Hampstead DJ bar, whose two most obvious
features are retro, rather '60s styling and a jukebox. There are
also seats out the front, which have the benefit of heaters.
Its punters get through a fair amount of spirits, but there's also
a fair trade in bottled lagers.* / **Details:** *no Amex.* **Food:** *L&D.*
DJ: *Thu-Fri & Sun.*

Canonbury Tavern N1

21 Canonbury Pl   7288 9881   8–2D
*This large, simply-furnished and quite civilised boozer enjoys a
lovely, off-the-beaten-track location near Canonbury Square.
It numbers table footie, a pool table, a fireplace, and a back
garden with tables among its attractions (but note that kids are
not allowed).* / **Details:** *no Amex; no-smoking area.* **Food:** *L till 2.45pm, D
till 8.45pm, Sat L till 4pm, D till 9pm, Sun till 6pm.*

Cantaloupe EC2

35-42 Charlotte Rd   7613 4411   9–1D
*The bar which helped to make Shoreditch hip is a large,
industrial-chic venue (with a slightly subdued restaurant at the
back). Some nights see a concentration of suits which has
robbed the place of its cutting-edge reputation, but it remains a
very popular destination with trendies too. They don't do
cocktails, but almost every sort of alcohol is available and there
are good tapas-style snacks.* / **Website:** *www.cantaloupe.co.uk*
Details: *Mon-Sat till midnight, Sun till 11.30pm.* **Food:** *L&D.* **DJ:** *Wed,
Fri-Sun.*

Canvas W11

177 Portobello Rd   7727 2700   6–1B
*Pale leather sofas set off the dark wood setting of this small,
'designery' Notting Hill cocktail basement (entered down steps
from the corner with Elgin Crescent). There are DJs nightly
towards the weekend, offering a wide variety of sounds.*
/ **Website:** *www.canvasbar.com* **Details:** *Mon-Sun 5pm-11pm; no Amex.*
Food: *till 10.30pm.* **DJ:** *Wed-Sun.*

Capital Hotel SW3
22-24 Basil St   7589 5171   5–1D
*As you might hope, this luxurious small hotel a short walk from the back door of Harrods has a cocktail bar which has been done out in the best possible taste. However, though it's a comfortable and extremely civilised spot, it's really too small to be hugely atmospheric. Good cocktails, though (and a fair selection of malts and cigars). / **Website:** www.capitalhotel.co.uk* **Food:** 11am-11pm.

Capitol SE23
11-21 London Rd   8291 8920   1–3D
*Originally an Art Deco Egyptian-style cinema (1929) and previously a bingo hall, this is now a part of the Wetherspoons chain and one of the grander ones at that. The huge Grade II listed building has been attractively converted, and many original features restored although it can feel slightly anonymous. / **Details:** no-smoking area.* **Food:** *till 10pm.* **Happy hour:** *all day Mon.*

The Captain Kidd E1
108 Wapping High St   7480 5759   11–1A
*This Wapping riverside tavern looks every bit an ancient inn (complete with a cute courtyard entrance and exterior wooden staircase). It is, in fact (in the nicest way) a complete sham as it's only about ten years old (and named after a famous pirate, who was hanged nearby). A large Samuel Smiths pub, it has two bars and a large terrace, overlooking the river, with barbecues in summer. The upstairs restaurant ('The Gallows') is run separately from the bar operation. / **Details:** no-smoking area in restaurant.* **Food:** *L & D.*

Cardinal SW1
23 Francis St   7834 7260   2–3B
*Is it a guide book's job to regret? If so, this potentially wonderful Edwardian corner site – presumably built at about the same time as the nearby Westminster (R.C.) Cathedral – is as good an object for regret as any. Samuel Smith's recent refurbishment has done nothing to bring out the charm of what is a soaringly elegant building, and we could spot hardly any real ales on tap! A real opportunity missed. / **Details:** no-smoking area at lunch.* **Food:** *L till 3pm, D till 9pm.*

Cargo EC2

83 Rivington St   7739 3440   9–1D

A kind of bigger Cantaloupe (same owners), these large converted railway arches are a perfect industrial-look setting for this sizeable venue. Vast queues on the best nights testify to its position as one of Shoreditch's most popular scenes.
The smallish restaurant (leading onto an outside terrace) and large bar are each in separate arches from that containing the entertainment – and attractions in themselves – but you still have to pay whatever entrance the particular night requires to get in. / **Website:** www.cargo-london.com **Details:** Mon-Thu 12.45pm-1am, Fri 12.45-3am, Sat 6pm-3am, Sun 1pm-midnight. **Food:** till 11pm. **DJ:** nightly. **Live music:** bands Fri. **Happy hour:** all day till 7pm (20% off all drinks).

Carlton Tower SW1

2 Cadogan Pl   7235 1234   5–1D

This plush hotel does comfort very well, and its small ground-floor cocktail bar – which overlooks a swanky Grill Room – doesn't let the side down. It's a surprisingly pleasant space to visit on a sunny day, when the shadows from the bold Venetian blinds add a touch of exotic character which seems some way from Knightsbridge. / **Website:** www.carltontower.com **Details:** Mon-Sat 12.30pm-3pm & 6.30pm-11.30pm, Sun 12.30pm-3pm & 7pm-10.30pm. **Food:** L till 2.45pm, D till 10.30pm.

Carpe Diem W1

28 Paddington St   7935 0556   3–1A

Although serving some traditional bitters, this seems to be mainly a wine bar for the commuter crowd – an idea reinforced by the stripped pine look and blackboard lists of wines available. Food (a tad pricey) is available at both lunch and dinner. / **Details:** Sat till 10pm, Sun till 5pm; no-smoking area at lunch and on weekends. **Food:** till 9pm.

The Castle SW11

115 Battersea High St   7228 8181   10–1B

From the street, this Battersea backstreet pub looks rather unpromising. Inside it's been pleasantly revamped, but it's the unusually nice pretty garden at the back which makes it worth a bit of a journey on a sunny day. Most drink lager, wine or Young's bitter, and the food isn't at all bad.
/ **Website:** www.thecastle.co.uk, www.youngs.co.uk **Details:** no Amex. **Food:** L till 3pm, D till 9.45pm.

Castle Free House N1

54 Pentonville Rd   7713 1858   8–3D

*No disrespect to the Pentonville Road, but it's a surprise to find somewhere on it that's as nice as this newly revamped boozer. With its striped wallpaper and low lights, it's old-fashioned and comfortable in a way that's a touch surprising in trendy Islington. A rooftop terrace (with marquee for colder times) is a particular attraction. / **Details:** no Amex. **Food:** L till 2.30pm, D till 9.45pm.*

The Cat & Canary E14

1-24 Fishmerman's Walk   7512 9187   11–1C

*There's not much in Canary Wharf that isn't run by Big Business Inc., and sadly this is just another corporate chain pub, this time a Fuller's. Still, it has a prime location (just off Cabot Square) and a great terrace (overlooking West India Quay) making it a useful place to rendezvous with your Docklands pals in summer. / **Website:** www.fullers.co.uk **Details:** closed Sun; no-smoking area. **Food:** till 10pm.*

Catch E2

22 Kingsland Rd   7729 6097   9–1D

*A cool bar on two levels, in the ever-more trendy Shoreditch strip, where you can while away the time over a game of pool or pinball. Or, if you prefer to concentrate on drinking (mostly draft lager) seek out one of the US-style booths at the front. DJs and up-and-coming live acts feature regularly upstairs and down. / **Website:** www.thecatchbar.com **Details:** Tue &Wed 5pm-midnight, Thu-Sat 5pm-2am, Sun 5pm-1am (closed Mon); no credit cards. **DJ:** nightly (non-commercial). **Live music:** bands nightly.*

Cava N16

11 Albion Rd   7923 9227   1–1C

*Opened in autumn 2002, this modern bar/restaurant fronts on to Newington Green. A chic modern interior attracts a local, trendy crowd who sit lounging around quaffing a variety of tipples, from cava to cocktails. There's also a restaurant area which serves a modern European menu. / **Website:** www.cavabar.com **Details:** Mon-Wed noon-11.30pm, Thu-Fri noon-midnight, Sat 10am-midnight, Sun 10am-11.30pm; no Amex. **Food:** till 10:45pm.*

Cave Austin SE3

7-9 Montpelier Vale   8852 0492   1–3D

*Pastel suede sofas and striking Deco-esque lighting make this cocktail bar/restaurant a stylish Blackheath destination. The tiny, but gloriously foliage-filled, rear terrace is a highlight and has a barbecue area for summer days. The place is also well geared up for functions. / **Details:** Fri & Sat till 1am; no Amex. **Food:** L till 3pm, D till 10pm, Fri-Sun till 10pm.*

Cecconi's W1

5A, Burlington Gdns   7434 1500   3–3C

*Mayfair-chic doesn't come much more elegantly understated than this recently-relaunched Italian bar/restaurant, a stone's throw from Savile Row. It's stylishly somber interior is an ideal place for a cocktail to kick off a night in the West End or – at a price – you could just stay for dinner. / **Website:** www.cecconis.co.uk **Details:** Mon-Sat 10am-11pm, Sun 10am-10pm. **Food:** L till 3pm, D till 11pm.*

Cellar Gascon EC1

59 West Smithfield   7796 0600   9–2B

*Unusual regional wines and tapas-style 'dégustations' from south-western France are just two of the reasons to visit this small but very stylish, Smithfield bar. As at its sibling – the famed Club Gascon restaurant next door – veggies (and geese-lovers) should steer clear of many of the bar snacks (which tend to feature foie gras, foie gras and a bit more foie gras). / **Details:** Mon-Fri noon-midnight, closed weekends. **Food:** till 11.30pm.*

Centuria N1

100 St Paul's Rd   7704 2345   8–2D

*It's the food operation which wins high popularity for this noisy Highbury gastropub, where the Mediterranean scoff comes highly recommended. That's not to say it's a bad place for boozing too, though, with some comfy sofas on which people typically sip on lager or vino. / **Details:** Mon-Fri from 5pm; no Amex. **Food:** till 10.45pm.*

The Chandos WC2
29 St Martin's Ln 7836 1401 2–1C
Just off Trafalgar Square, this large, rambling Samuel Smiths pub is well known as a convenient West End rendezvous. It is certainly handy (especially for the Coliseum), if rather anonymous. / **Details:** *no-smoking area.* **Food:** *till 7pm, Fri-Sun till 6pm.*

Chapel N1
29A Penton St 7833 4090 8–3D
Bit of an odd one this – if you like the idea of a drink in a low-lit panelled space, broken up by ecclesiastical-style arches, this Islington bar might well be just the place for you. Slightly off the main drag, it attracts quite a grown-up following, by local standards. A terrace is a summer attraction. / **Details:** *Mon-Thu from 3pm, Fri & Sat noon-1am, Sun noon-11pm; no Amex.* **Food:** *Sun only.* **DJ:** *Fri-Sat.* **Happy hour:** *Mon-Sat 4pm-7pm (1/3 off RRP).*

The Chapel NW1
48 Chapel St 7402 9220 6–1C
Just down from Edgware tube, this traditional-looking boozer conceals a trendy gastropub interior. Good pub fodder is on offer, and there is a selection of board games to while away a rainy afternoon. In the evenings, it can get very busy. / **Food:** *L till 2.30pm, D till 10pm.*

Charlie Wright's International Bar N1
45 Pitfield St 7490 8345 9–1D
A notably diverse crowd – in both age and style – is attracted to this large, darkly-lit bar on the Hoxton/Islington fringe. Attractions include pool tables, a mirror ball, TV, some perfectly OK Thai food and – last but not least – a late licence. / **Details:** *Mon-Wed noon-1am, Thu-Fri noon-2am, Sat & Sun 5pm-2am; no Amex.* **Food:** *L till 3pm, D till 10.30pm.* **DJ:** *Thu-Sun.* **Happy hour:** *till 8pm (pint £2.50).*

Charterhouse 38 EC1
38 Charterhouse St 7608 0858 9–1B
Don't be fooled by the fact that this Smithfield bar seems to be only as wide as its doorway – it gets wider, and in fact ends up on two floors. Late opening (and DJs) at weekends help make it quite a trendy destination. / **Website:** *www.charterhouse-bar.co.uk* **Details:** *Mon-Thu noon-11pm, Fri noon-2am, Sat 10am-2am, Sun 10am-midnight; no Amex.* **Food:** *till 9pm.* **DJ:** *Fri-Sun.*

Che SW1

23 St James's St   7747 9380   2–2B

Not many cocktail bars have quite such an interesting building (from the outside anyway) as the '60s landmark inhabited by this plush St James's bar/restaurant. While the first-floor restaurant is a bit corporate and business-y, the swish downstairs bar is one of the most popular in the area and – being quite small – often feels full. The Cuban theme for which the place is named is by-and-large pretty invisible, other than the photos (of Sr. Guevera), and a smoking room with a magnificently stocked humidor. / Details: Sat 3.30pm-11pm, closed Sun. Food: till 10.30pm.

The Chelsea Ram SW10

32 Burnaby St   7351 4008   5–3B

This smart and comfortable Chelsea backstreet boozer – on the way to the Lot's Road power station – has made quite a name for itself in recent times with the quality of its cooking. Whether you're eating or not, it's certainly one of the most pleasant places to sink a pint hereabouts.
/ Website: www.chelsearam.com, www.youngs.co.uk Details: no Amex. Food: till 10pm (Sun 12.30pm-3.30pm).

China White W1

6 Air St   7343 0040   3–3D

Is it still 'A'-list? is it going out? That some people still care as it approaches its fifth birthday says something for the staying power of this large and exotic subterranean den, near Piccadilly Circus, decked out on a lavish Indonesian theme. It's members only on Wednesdays, Fridays and Saturdays, so your chances of entry are (somewhat) higher on other nights. The guys on the door can be pretty harsh though. / Website: www.chinawhite.com Details: Mon-Sat 8pm-3am, closed Sun. Food: till 2.30am. DJ: nightly.

Chintamani SW1

22 Jermyn St   7839 2020   3–3D

'Groovy' and 'Turkish' aren't usually mentioned in the same breath, but this very glossy restaurant and bar south of Piccadilly Circus – which opened in late 2002 – aims to break the mould. It certainly ain't cheap (especially in the restaurant) but the décor is kinda cool (they've spent a fortune) and the cocktail bar seems to be establishing itself with the Gucci classes. / Details: Mon-Sat 11am-4pm & 6pm-12.30am, Sun 6pm-12.30am. Food: 4.30pm-11.30pm. DJ: Fri & Sat.

Churchill Arms W8

119 Kensington Ch St   7727 4242   6–2B

The renown of this Fuller's hostelry a couple of minutes' walk from Notting Hill Gate has little to do with the beer. At the back of a rather ordinary bar, a pretty and airy conservatory is to be found, whose very good, and very cheap Thai food is legendary. Oddly for a pub, you can book – a good idea as it's always packed. / **Website:** *www.fullers.co.uk* **Food:** *L till 2.30pm, D till 10pm.*

Ciao SW6

222 Munster Rd   7381 6137   10–1A

Since the late '80s, this archetypal Fulham hang-out has been something of a rite of passage for younger locals. Much of the operation is as a brasserie, but drinkers at the small bar (which also does bar snacks) aren't made to feel too incidental and get the benefit of the cheery hubbub throughout. Wine seems to be the house tipple of choice. / **Food:** *till 10.30pm.*
Happy hour: *5.30pm-7.30pm (£1 off house wine & beer).*

Cicada EC1

132-136 St John St   7608 1550   9–1A

One of the epicentres of Clerkenwell life, this funky bar/restaurant is invariably packed with a fearsomely trendy local crowd. The quality oriental food on offer is an attraction in its own right, and there's also a good cocktail list (as well as trendy lagers). The Red Room downstairs (available for private hire only) is decorated in an opulent, 'opium den' style that's strikingly at odds with the concrete bar and leather banquettes above. / **Website:** *www.cicada.nu* **Details:** *Sat 6pm-11pm, closed Sun; no-smoking area.* **Food:** *till 10.30pm.*

Circle

317 Battersea Park Rd, SW11   7627 1578   10–1B
348 Clapham Rd, SW9   7622 3683   10–1C

With its vending machines dispensing sweeties, rustic furniture and candle-lit (in the evening) interior, the Stockwell original of this mini-chain (on an uninteresting stretch of road) has become a popular venue for local Claphamites, whiling away the time over table football and a pint of lager (Stella, Carlsberg or Lowenbrau). It also has the plus of a newly-extended garden. A couple of years ago it spawned a Battersea sibling run on similar lines. / **Details:** *Mon-Sat 11am-11pm, Sun noon-10.30pm; no Amex.* **Food:** *L&D & bar snacks.* **Happy hour:** *SW11 Mon-Fri 5pm-7pm, SW9 Tue 6pm-8pm.*

Circus W1

1 Upper James St   7534 4000   3–2D

Apart from the fact that it's quite slick and expensive-looking, there's not much to say about the minimalistic styling of the ground floor restaurant at this Soho fixture near Golden Square – a favoured schmoozing spot for local media moguls.
Even those who think upstairs is anonymous, though, think the basement bar has great vibes and it delivers a quality list of cocktails (till late at night at weekends).
/ **Website:** www.circusbar.co.uk **Details:** Mon-Wed noon-1am, Thu-Sat noon-3am, closed Sun. **Food:** L till 3pm, D till 11.45pm. **DJ:** Thu-Fri from 9pm.

The Cittie of Yorke WC1

22 High Holborn   7242 7670   9–2A

Complete with large overhead wine butts, wooden booths and a vaulted ceiling, this cavernous Samuel Smiths pub, next to Grays Inn, is better endowed with historical fixtures and fittings than perhaps any other pub in the capital. It makes an atmospheric, if not particularly cosy, watering hole.
/ **Details:** closed Sun. **Food:** till 9pm.

The City Barge W4

27 Strand on the Green   8994 2148   1–2A

If Scottish & Newcastle tried a bit harder, this rambling pub (dating in parts from 1484) in pretty Strand-on-the-Green could be one of the best in town. The top bar offers great views over the Thames, and the downstairs bar (complete with waterproof door for high tides) is cosy and quaint. Subdued staff and a general feel of neglect, though, mean it's primarily recommendable for supping ale in summer out on the towpath.
/ **Details:** no-smoking area. **Food:** till 9.30pm.

City Food Ale and Wine House EC3

1 Lombard St   7929 6611   9–3C

City locations don't come much more central than Soren Jessen's bar/brasserie/restaurant, bang opposite the Bank of England. With its airy converted banking-hall setting, it's a favourite venue for serious business wining and dining, but the bar is also favoured by finance types for an after-work bevvy. Not a huge amount of space is dedicated to the bar (in the centre of the room), but in the evenings some tables are set up for drinkers. / **Website:** www.1lombardstreet.com **Details:** Mon-Fri 7.30am-11.30pm, closed weekends. **Food:** L till 3.30pm, D 5.30pm-midnight.

City Limits E1
16-18 Brushfield St   7377 9877   9–2D
*For off-duty bankers and brokers tired of the loud and anonymous watering holes of the City, this cosy, independently owned wine bar – in ground floor Victorian premises near Spitalfields Market (and with a cellar bistro) – offers a nice change. There are a few bottled lagers, but regulars seem to stick to the vino. / **Details:** closed weekends. **Food:** L till 3pm, D till 9pm.*

The City Page EC4
2a, Suffolk Ln   7626 0996   9–1D
*The Pages are generally rather superior drinking places, and this outpost in the lanes near Cannon Street station is a more than usually comfortable cellar wine bar. There are lots of niches, making the place ideal for quiet conversation. / **Website:** www.frontpagepubs.com **Details:** Mon-Fri 9am-11pm, closed weekends. **Food:** till 8pm.*

The Clachan W1
34 Kingly St   7494 0834   3–2C
*Proximity to Liberty's ups the tone at this tucked-away, early 19th century Nicholson's pub (and in days past it was actually owned and run by the store). Its interior still has a number of period features and provides a quiet, more-than-usually civilised retreat from the West End. / **Food:** till 9pm.*

The Clarence SW1
53 Whitehall   7930 4808   2–2C
*In the heart of government, physically at least, this unadorned panelled and beamed pub has lots of tables for weary tourists in the day, and attracts an after-work, older crowd in the evenings. It's a pleasant space, but often too noisy to be relaxing. / **Food:** D only, bar snacks all day.*

Claridges Bar
Claridges Hotel W1

55 Brook St   7629 8860   3–2B

It's not often that a grand hotel goes hip with as much assurance as Claridges has achieved with the creation of this new, wonderfully glamorous, Deco-ish bar (complete with its own street entrance). For somewhere attached to royalty's favourite hotel in the middle of stuffy old Mayfair, it has an it-could-be-Manhattan pizzazz that sets it apart, and makes it a great choice for a special occasion… or, maybe you drink Champagne cocktails every night? (In the heart of the hotel, there is also the Macanado Fumoir – a tiny but lavishly furnished room dedicated to cigar smokers.)
/ **Website:** www.savoygroup.com **Details:** Mon-Sat noon-1am, Sun 4pm-midnight. **Food:** till 12.45am Mon-Sat (Sun 11.45pm).

Clerkenwell House EC1

23-27 Hatton Wall   7404 1113   9–1A

A classic Clerkenwell lounge bar, attracting the local media and designer types. Not perhaps the world's most inspired destination, but comfortable enough if you secure a seat in one of the rather well worn armchairs. / **Details:** Mon-Fri noon-11.30pm, Sat 6pm-11.30pm. **Food:** L till 2.45pm, D till 9.45pm. **DJ:** Fri.

The Clifton Hotel NW8

96 Clifton Hill   7372 3427   8–3A

Is this the most civilised pub in London? Discreetly located in the middle of a street of grand St John's Wood houses, it has the most modest of signs and a location that seems to have been chosen to avoid anything so vulgar as passing trade. (Perhaps this is why Edward VII is reputed to have chosen to conduct his liaison with Lillie Langtry here.) Its charming, intimate, woody interior make it well worth seeking out, and, for the summer, there's a pretty terrace. / **Details:** no smoking at bar. **Food:** till 10pm (9.30pm Sun).

The Coach SE10

13 The Mkt, Greenwich   8293 0880   1–2D

On the southern corner of Greenwich's covered market (and with an outside, heated terrace in the market itself), this clean, modern pub is predictably mobbed at weekends. An open fire adds to its charms at any time. / **Details:** no Amex. **Food:** L till 3.30pm, D till 10pm (weekends L&D).

The Coach & Horses W1

29 Greek St   7437 5920   4–2A
*The fame of this Soho pub is boosted both by its celebrity and journalistic associations (the staff of Private Eye have held a fortnightly lunch in the upstairs room here since the paper was founded). It is an atmospheric, packed watering hole, whose pinkly-lit décor has changed little since the war, and attracts a completely mixed clientèle. / **Details:** no Amex; no-smoking area. **Food:** L&D. **Happy hour:** Sun-Fri 11am-4pm (pints £2.30).*

The Coal Hole WC2

91 Strand   7379 9883   2–1D
*A few doors down from the Savoy, this large, high-ceilinged Nicholson ale house is a well known standby for a drink in Theatreland, and draws a diverse crowd. Mock-Tudor styling may not be all the rage nowadays, but here it works surprisingly well. Downstairs, there is also a cosier basement bar (which is open at busy times). / **Details:** Sun noon-6pm. **Food:** till 5pm.*

The Cock Tavern W1

27 Gt Portland St   7631 5002   3–1C
*This Samuel Smith's establishment near Oxford Circus – marked by four huge exterior lanterns – is a decent, un-mucked-about-with boozer by West End standards, offering a range of well-kept beers, a few cosy booths and tables outside in summer. (History anoraks note: it is thought the pub may be built on what was the largest cock pit in London). / **Details:** no Amex. **Food:** L till 2.30pm, bar snacks 6pm-8.30pm.*

Cock Tavern EC1

East Poultry Ave, Central Markets   7248 2918   9–1B
*One of the few London pubs with a licence permitting ale to be served from dawn (for the meat-traders of Smithfield) – this establishment is literally underneath the market. Breakfasts (and also lunch) are a feature and, as you might hope, fry-ups are the speciality. The place is a bit of an institution but – though the setting has a certain homely, checked-tablecloth charm – the décor would win few prizes for style. / **Details:** Mon-Wed 6am-3.30pm, Thu-Fri 6am-9.30pm, closed Sat & Sun. **Food:** B Mon-Fri, L till 3.30pm, D till 8.30pm (Thu&Fri only). **Happy hour:** Thu-Fri 5.30pm-9.30pm (3 pt lager £5, large spirit & mixer £2).*

Cockpit EC4

7 St Andrews Hill   7248 7315   9–2B

*Listed in the Guildhall as having been the venue for the last legal cock fight in the City – the sign over the door at this funny little free house (in the back lanes near Cannon Street station) is now one of the few reminders of what used to be one of the most popular spectator sports in town. It's the sort of unchanging local of the type they don't make 'em like anymore (down to the game of shove ha'penny). / **Details:** Sat 11am-early evening, closed Sun. **Food:** L till 2.30pm, D till 9pm.*

Cocomo EC1

323 Old St   7613 0315   9–1D

*A hip, slightly hippy crowd cram into this funky small hang-out (a coffee shop by day) – which has become a linchpin of the strip of bars along the road from Shoreditch Town Hall. The decoration in the ground floor bar is cosy, eclectic and vaguely chintzy – a bit like a Christmas party in a boudoir. Downstairs, the red-decorated basement has a louche, vaguely clandestine feel to it. Most of the punters go for cocktails, though Red Stripe is available on draft. There are DJs nightly. / **Details:** Mon-Sat noon-midnight, Sun 5pm-11.30pm. **Food:** till midnight. **DJ:** nightly. **Happy hour:** Sat-Thu till 8pm, Fri till 7pm (cocktails £3.50).*

The Coleherne SW5

261 Old Brompton Rd   7244 5951   5–3A

*Even in the days when gay pubs seemed much more riské than they do today, this large Earl's Court boozer was well-known, even in the 'straight' community, as the Most Famous Gay Pub in the World. The place used to attract a crowd largely clad in impressive amounts of leather, but the scene has mellowed in more recent years – it's younger, and there are sometimes even women! / **Details:** no-smoking area. **Happy hour:** Wed (all drink £1.50).*

The Collection SW3

264 Brompton Rd   7225 1212   5–2C

A truly impressive space – and there aren't many of those around South Kensington (not in use as bars anyway) – has made this popular Eurotrash rendezvous one of the ongoing success stories of south west London's drinking scene. There's a mezzanine restaurant too, but it's only really of interest as a vantage point from which to watch the goings-on in the bar. International socialites Paris Hilton and Ivanka Trump have recently bought in to the management, so look out for a relaunch in 'Manhattan style' (whatever that means). / **Website:** www.the-collection.co.uk **Details:** Mon-Fri from 5pm. **Food:** D till 11pm. **DJ:** nightly.

The Common Room SW19

18 High St   8944 1909   10–2A

Like the nearby Fire Stables, this laid-back lounge bar on the main drag imports some clean modern style into cutesy Wimbledon Village. It's smaller and more low key than its rival, but a useful option for a quieter occasion. / **Details:** no-smoking areas until 4pm. **Food:** till 10pm (weekends 9.30pm).

The Common Rooms SW11

225 St John's Hill   7207 1276   10–2B

Up the hill from the main Battersea 'action', this sleek, chilled, darkly-decorated bar – jazzed up by the occasional pink neon flash running along the wall – has set its sights at a slightly older (and richer) clientèle than many place hereabouts, and has succeeded in becoming something of a local 'beautiful people' destination. / **Website:** www.thecommonrooms.com **Details:** Fri & Sat till 1am; no Amex. **Food:** till 10.30pm (weekends 1am). **DJ:** Thu-Sun. **Live music:** funk bands 4pm-8pm Sun. **Happy hour:** Mon-Fri 6pm-8pm, Sat-Sun 5pm-7pm (cocktails from £3.95).

Connaught Bar W1

Carlos Pl   7499 7070   3–3B

By the crusty standards of the former régime, the style at the Connaught – the Mayfair hotel which used to be thought of as London's grandest – is a bit over-relaxed nowadays. That's not a bad thing in everyone's book, and as a comfy, quite glamorous location for a cocktail or glass of bubbly, many like this Nina-Campbell-designed bar adjoining 'Menu' (the restaurant run by Gordon Ramsay). For traditionalists, there's also the old-fashioned American Bar (though it too may be revamped some time soon). / Details: Mon-Sat 11am-midnight, Sun 11am-10.30pm. Food: till 11pm.

(Aquasia Bar) Conrad Hotel SW10

Chelsea Harbour   7823 3000   5–3B

If you can't get away to Monaco for the weekend, a sunny-day trip to this hotel overlooking Chelsea marina is about as close as London gets to feeling like the Riviera. Grab a spot outside if you can for the best views of the water and yachts – otherwise there are floor to ceiling windows by which you can sip a cocktail or a glass of wine. / Website: www.conradhotels.com Details: no-smoking area. Food: till 10.30pm. Happy hour: Fri 5pm-9pm (50% discount on all drinks).

Coopers' Arms SW3

87 Flood St   7376 3120   5–3C

The understated charms of this sparsely furnished Young's pub, in a Chelsea backstreet, give something of the impression of a slightly distressed gentlemen's club, and it's a popular refuge from the King's Road mêlée. Though it's had its ups and downs over the years, the quality of the food tends to be quite a plus, too. / Website: www.thecoopers.co.uk, www.youngs.co.uk Food: L till 3pm, D till 9.30pm.

Le Coq D'Argent EC2

1 Poultry, City   7395 5000   9–2C

On a hot summers day in the City, there's no nicer place to be than sipping something refreshing at this impressive sixth-floor complex (owned by the Conran group), overlooking the Bank of England. It has an excellent rooftop terrace, plus 'garden' tables. Inside, the drinking area segues into the large (and somewhat anonymous) dining room. / Website: www.coqdargent.co.uk Details: Sat 6:30pm-10pm, Sun noon-3pm. Food: L till 3pm, bar snacks 5pm-10pm.

Cork & Bottle WC2

44-46 Cranbourn St   7734 7807   4–3B

Nestling besides a sex-shop, this cramped basement near Leicester Square has been a reliable West End retreat for two decades now, and still has a great reputation as a pre-theatre rendezvous. It certainly isn't cheap, but the outstanding wine list reflects the enthusiasm of owner/connoisseur Don Hewitson. Solid, if not exciting, wine bar fodder is also available.
/ **Website:** www.donhewitsonlondonwinebars.com **Details:** no-smoking area at lunch. **Food:** till 11.30pm (Sun 10.30pm).

Corner Store WC2

33-35 Wellington St   7836 2944   4–3D

Part of Massive Pubs (the owners of the Tups) – this Covent Garden corner gastropub is very handy for a pre/post-theatre drink or snack. With its dark, antiqued, mismatched furniture, quite bright and airy setting and leather seats, it's more stylish than most corporately-backed offerings.
/ **Website:** www.massive.com **Food:** till 10pm.

Corner & Barrow

16 Royal Exchange, EC3   7929 3131   9–2D
9 Cabot Sq, E14   7512 0397   11–1C
1 Ropemaker St, EC2   7382 0606   9–2C
111 Old Broad St, EC2   7638 9308   9–2C
12 Mason's Ave, EC2   7448 3700   9–2C
19 Broadgate Circle, EC2   7628 1251   9–2D
5 Exchange Sq, EC2   7628 4367   9–2A
1 Leadenhall Pl, EC3   7621 9201   9–2D
2b Eastcheap, EC3   7929 3220   9–3C
37 Jewry, EC3   7680 8550   9–2D
3 Fleet Pl, EC4   7329 3141   9–2A
44 Cannon St, EC4   7248 1700   9–3B

Despite its long history – and, as a wine merchant, Royal Appointment – this is the only quality wine bar chain in London which has made a real break with olde-worlde style. All its branches are a symphony of white walls, bleached wood and halogen down-lighters. Its stronghold is the City – its sole former West End branch now having closed – and probably its best-known branch occupies an impressive location, overlooking Broadgate ice rink. / **Website:** www.corney-barrow.co.uk **Details:** closed Sun. **Food:** L&D & bar snacks.

Couch W1

97-99 Dean St   7287 0150   3–1D

As modern chain pubs go, this big corner-site is at the more refined end of the breed, with big antiquey rustic tables, brown and cream décor and gilt mirrors. It's an option worth knowing about in Soho, though it can get packed with local workers who've finished their 9-5. / **Food:** *till 9pm (no D Fri).* **DJ:** *Sat 8pm-11pm.*

Cow W2

89 Westbourne Park Rd   7221 0021   6–1B

Physically in Bayswater but spiritually in Notting Hill, Tom Conran's boozer has enjoyed continuing success. The very small public bar manages a pretty good approximation to rural Ireland (if you ignore the crowds of trustafarians, that is), and the seafood dishes (oysters and so on) are very good. Upstairs, there's a cosy dining room, managed separately. / **Details:** *no Amex.* **Food:** *L till 4pm, D till 11pm.*

Cranks

36 Southwick St, W2   7402 7539   6–1C
48 Lower Marsh, SE1   7928 8778   1–2C

Fresh fruit rum (or tequila) cocktails and late night salsa music at weekends (plus classes in W1 on Mon & Sun) are guaranteed to help the party go with a genuine Cuban swing at these Latino-themed dance bar/restaurants, in Paddington and Waterloo. Cuban tapas or full meals will help to soak up some of the margaritas, coladas and daiquiris. / **Details:** *W2 Mon-Fri noon-midnight, Sat 6pm-midnight, Sun 11.30am-10pm; SE1 Mon-Thu noon-midnight, Fri noon-1am, Sat 6pm-midnight.* **Food:** *SE1 L noon-3pm, D 5pm-11.30pm, tapas till 12.30am.* **Happy hour:** *SE1 5pm-6.30pm; W2 Mon-Sat 5pm-7.30pm, Mon-Wed 10pm-midnight (cocktails 2 for the price of 1).*

The Cricketers TW9

Maids Of Honour Rw, The Green   8940 4372   1–3A

There are lots of pubs that bear the name, but not many in London suburbs which still overlook charming leafy cricket pitches. This 19th-century hostelry (owned by Greene King) is one of the few with a picture-book location overlooking Richmond Green. It's cosy and characterful enough inside, but it's in summer when you can take your pint on to the grass (or in to their courtyard) that it really comes into its own. / **Details:** *no Amex; no smoking at bar.* **Food:** *till 8.45pm (weekends 6pm).*

Crocker's Folly NW8
24 Aberdeen Pl   7286 6608   8–3A
*This wonderful Victorian gem was built by one Mr Crocker in the mistaken belief that he had divined the future site of the London railway terminus (which was in fact later erected at Marylebone). This explains the otherwise puzzling location of this enormous palace of a pub, stuck in the middle of a residential street near Lord's. It is impressive both in its scale and in the quality of its furnishings and boasts a particularly wide range of real ales. / **Details:** no Amex; no-smoking area. **Food:** L till 3pm, D till 9pm (Sat 8pm). **Happy hour:** Sun-Thu 5pm-9pm (2 for 1 on bottles).*

Crooked Billet SW19
15 Crooked Billet   8946 4942   10–2A
*In summer, the crowds from this Young's hostelry and its neighbouring twin (the Hand in Hand) crowd out the green after which the pub is named (or perhaps it's vice-versa?). It does have other attractions however – the interior is very characterful and cosy, and they serve a good variety of pub grub (and of wines by the glass). / **Website:** www.youngs.co.uk **Details:** no-smoking areas. **Food:** L till 2.30pm (Sun till 4pm), D till 9.30pm.*

Cross Keys SW3
1 Lawrence St   7349 9111   5–3C
*It something of a surprise in the backstreets of Old Chelsea to come across this trendified boozer, which was substantially jazzed up (and had an impressive dining-conservatory added) a few years ago. It has a really buzzy atmosphere, though, and is a very popular destination with younger locals. / **Website:** www.thexkeys.co.uk **Food:** D till 11pm & Sun L.*

Cross Keys WC2
31 Endell St   7836 5185   4–2D
*If you think the facade if this foliage-covered Covent Garden-fringe pub is ornate, wait until you get inside. The modestly-scaled interior houses a cornucopia of ornaments, mirrors, pictures, horse brasses, road signs, brass pots, and even the odd stuffed fish. To top it all off, there's a small collection of Beatles memorabilia, and a napkin signed by none other than Elvis Presley. / **Food:** till 2.30pm.*

Crosse Keys EC3

9 Gracechurch St   7623 4824   9–3C

Not everyone is a fan of JD Wetherspoon, but it's hard not to be wowed by this conversion of an enormous and majestic '20s banking hall in the heart of the City. Its capacity runs well into the high hundreds and with its large columns and lanterns and stucco ceiling, the vast space provides a setting unlike any other in town. Unusually for a Wetherspoons, an added attraction is a wide selection of guest ales. / **Details:** *Sat 11am-7pm, closed Sun; no-smoking area.* **Food:** *till 10pm.*

The Crown SW3

153 Dovehouse St   7352 9505   5–2C

This brashly modernised Chelsea boozer has some aspirations to 'gastropub' status. It's never exactly become a 'destination', but it's handy enough as a stopping-off point between Brompton Cross and the Chelsea 'Beach'. / **Details:** *no Amex.* **Food:** *till 9pm.*

The Crown E3

223 Grove Rd   8981 9998   1–1D

It's really as a dining destination that this massive East End boozer — whose upstairs dining room has an excellent view over Victoria Park — is most worth knowing about. It's an all-organic (Soil Association-approved) operation, and it's especially popular at weekends, when it's open for breakfast from 10.30 am. That's not to say they leave drinking out of the equation — there are six organic varieties of beer (including 'Eco Warrior') and an organic wine list. / **Website:** *www.singhboulton.co.uk* **Details:** *Mon from 5pm; no-smoking areas.* **Food:** *L&D.* **Happy hour:** *Mon pm (half-price wine with every meal).*

Crown & Anchor WC2

22 Neal St   7836 5649   4–2C

This useful airy corner pub in north-Covent Garden arguably looks more like a wine bar (though it serves a good range of bitters and lagers), with drinkers who tend to spill onto a large pedestrianised area in summer. It's useful as a meeting place or standby for a shopping lunch, but not really a destination in its own right. / **Website:** *www.markettaverns.co.uk* **Food:** *till 5.30pm.*

Crown & Goose NW1
100 Arlington Rd   7485 2342   8–3B
This agreeable, revamped boozer in a Camden Town side street is worth seeking out to escape the mayhem of the main drag. Bitters include London Pride and John Smith and the usual range of lagers are also on offer. It's an ideal place for a drink and a chinwag. There's also a function room that can be hired for a small fee. / **Details:** *no Amex.* **Food:** *till 9.30pm.*

The Crown & Greyhound SE21
73 Dulwich Village   8299 4976   1–3D
Recently refurbished and under a change of management, this huge listed Victorian pub is situated in the heart of leafy Dulwich Village and caters to a crowd of all ages. With its original Victorian fittings, huge rear beer-garden and not-bad food, its no surprise that its treasured locally (and not just because pubs are thin on the ground hereabouts). / **Details:** *no-smoking area.* **Food:** *L till 2.30pm, D till 10pm.*

The Crown & Sceptre W12
57 Melina Rd   8746 0060   7–1A
If you like pubs that still feel like pubs, yet don't want to put up with the pub standards of yesteryear, this backstreet Shepherds Bush boozer is for you. Despite some nice bits of trendification (and offering some good, well priced gastropub fare), it still feels every bit a local, with a fair range of bitters and lagers on tap. It has a nice terrace, too. / **Details:** *no Amex; no-smoking area.* **Food:** *L till 3pm, D till 10pm.* **Happy hour:** *(50% off all food - lunchtimes Mon-Fri (not indefinate but 1/3rd off will replace it and be in place for forseeable future)).*

The Crown & Two Chairmen W1
31 Dean St   7437 8192   4–2A
This well-known Taylor Walker pub – permanently packed with a youngish local media crowd – is a perennial Soho success story, though its style – all wood floors and sandy walls – is fairly unremarkable. / **Details:** *Sat noon-11pm, Sun 5pm-10.30pm.* **Food:** *till 3pm, Wed-Fri till 6pm.*

The Crown Tavern EC1

43 Clerkenwell Greenn   7253 4973   9–1A

This Victorian pub on a corner overlooking Clerkenwell Green has been made over recently in a simple modern style, with muted colours and low-key lighting. It's a comfortable place with a very reasonable selection of lagers (Hoegaarden, Leffe, Grolsch, Staropramen, Carling) and bitters (TT Landlord, London Pride, Adnams). / **Details:** *no smoking at bar.* **Food:** *till 9.30pm.*

Crutched Friar EC3

39-41 Crutched Friars   7264 0041   9–3D

Georgian origins and an unusual, almost baronial entrance helps imbue this large pub with a fraction more character than is the norm for the City. A nice terrace at the rear is a further attraction. / **Details:** *closed weekends; no-smoking area.* **Food:** *L till 3.30pm, D till 9pm.*

Cuba W8

11-13 Kensington High St   7938 4137   5–1A

Though it is a dependable "fun" choice at most times, the greatest strength of this crowded Kensington bar is that it is open late, and is lively until the wee hours. Downstairs there's a dance floor where regular samba classes are a fixture. / **Details:** *Mon-Sat noon-2am, Sun from 2pm.* **Food:** *till 1am.* **DJ:** *nightly.* **Live music:** *live band every other Fri.* **Happy hour:** *Mon-Sat till 7.30pm, all day Sun (half-price beer & cocktails, wine £5).*

Cuba Libre N1

72 Upper St   7354 9998   8–3D

An ever-popular Cuban bar-restaurant in Islington done out in slightly OTT, muralled style. Its lively atmosphere wins it many fans – dancing in the bar is not unknown – as does late opening. The South American food may help make the place an all-round party destination, but it's not an attraction in its own right. / **Details:** *Mon-Thu 11am-midnight, Fri & Sat 11am-2am, Sun noon-10pm; no Amex.* **Food:** *till 11pm, Fri-Sat till 11.30pm, Sun till .* **Happy hour:** *Mon-Fri 5pm-8pm, Sat noon-8pm, Sun noon-10pm (2 for 1).*

The Cutty Sark Tavern SE10
4-6 Ballast Quay   8858 3146   1–2D
*Not actually located near its namesake, this well-established free house ("listed, 1675") is slightly off the beaten track, and attracts a mainly local crowd. With its outside tables and benches, right by the river, it makes a great get-away-from-the-crowds destination on a weekend trip to Greenwich. / **Food:** L till 5pm, D till 9pm.*

CVO Firevault W1
36 Great Titchfield St   7636 2091   3–1C
*The showroom of a company that specialises in designer fireplaces that are more like art installations provides the unlikely setting for this dark and slightly mysterious basement bar/restaurant. Prices – sustained by popularity with the trendier elements of the local rag trade, perhaps – are surprisingly high, but this is certainly a destination with a difference. / **Details:** Mon-Fri 9.30am-10.30pm, Sat noon-5pm, closed Sun. **Food:** till 10.30pm.*

Cynthia's Cyberbar SE1
4 Tooley St   7403 6777   9–3C
*The Cynthia in question is a robot waitress – and, yes, she can serve drinks. The futuristic chrome-and-mirrors interior of these rooms underneath London Bridge makes it a favourite for a younger crowd, who lap up the long list of themed cocktails – Space Bender and Alien Vomit, for example – with glee. The fun atmosphere is boosted by good-value happy-hour offers, and DJs (and dancing) most nights. / **Website:** www.cynbar.co.uk **Details:** Tue-Wed from 5pm, Thu-Fri from 4pm; no credit cards. **Food:** D till 10pm. **DJ:** nightly from 10pm. **Happy hour:** Mon-Fri till 8pm (beer & alcopops £2, wine £6.50, champagne £17).*

Dacre Arms SE13
11 Kingwood Pl   8244 2404   1–3D
*It's a bit out on a limb (in a residential area between Lee and Blackheath), but this black-painted pub is well worth knowing about. The attractive, comfortable interior is fairly traditional with half-panelled booths and decked out with a cosy clutter of junk. There is a beer garden at the back. / **Details:** no credit cards.*

Dartmouth Arms NW5

35 York Rise   7485 3267   8–1B

*Good, honest simple fare makes this Dartmouth Park gastropub
– in very stripped-down style – a true local drop-in destination.
A pleasant place to rendezvous if you're in the area.* / **Details:** no
Amex. **Food:** till 10pm.

Davy's

3 Brewers Gn, Buckingham Gt, SW1   7222 0561
Crown Pas, Pall Mall, SW1   7839 8831
10c Hanover Sq, W1   7499 7569
4 Gt Portland St, W1   7636 5287
50-54 Blandford St, W1   7486 3590
Hand Ct, 57 High, Holborn, WC1   7831 8365
Off Bury Pl, Bloomsbury, WC1   7404 5338
17 The Arches, off Villiers St, WC2   7930 7737
27 The Mkt, WC2   7836 1415
5 William IV St, Strand, WC2   7836 9839
27 Spring St, W2   7723 3351
Unit 2 Euston Tower, Regents Pl, NW1   7387 6622
161 Greenwich High Rd, SE10   8853 0585
1-3 Tooley St, SE1   7403 8343
42 Tooley St, SE1   7407 9189
48-50 Tooley St, SE1   7403 5775
31-35 Fisherman's Walk, Cabot Sq, E14   7363 6633
1 St Katharine's Way, E1   7480 6680
2-3 Artillery Pas, E1   7247 8215
190 City Rd, EC1   7608 0925
53-60 Holborn Viaduct, EC1   7248 2157
2 Exchange Sq, EC2
2-12 Wilson St, EC2   7377 6326
33 Foster Ln, EC2   7606 2110/8721
63 Worship St, EC2   7377 1574
7 Moorfields High Wk, EC2   7588 4766
91-93 Moorgate, EC2   7588 2581
91-93 Moorgate, EC2   7920 0857
1 St Mary at Hill, EC3   7283 4443
120 Fenchurch Ct, EC3   7623 3251
Friary Ct, Crutched Friars, EC3   7481 1131
Lower Thames St, EC3   7621 0619
10 Creed Ln, EC4   7236 5317

Davy's (continued)
*With around 50 branches, Davy's can claim to be the big
daddy of the London wine bar world. A few modern ventures
aside, most of their branches come in a pretty much Identikit
olde-worlde style – complete with sawdust on the floor – which
suits many of their ancient-cellar locations very well. Their very
predictability makes them a kind of default rendezvous for
many City slickers, and many branches also have (perfectly OK)
dining rooms. / Details: all branches closed all or part of weekend.
Food: L&D & bar snacks.*

De Hems W1
11 Macclesfield St   7437 2494   4–3A
*"Rough, noisy and central", as it was described to us – the only
Dutch bar in London is a large, cavernous pub on the northern
fringe of Chinatown. Those who hate crowded and smokey pubs
will loathe it – for serious drinkers of Dutch ales, though, this is
the place, and the range extends to Belgian and wheat beers.
Live music nightly. / Details: Mon-Sat noon-midnight, Sun noon-10.30pm.
Food: till midnight (Sun till 10.30pm).*

Denim WC2
4a Upper St Martin's Ln   7497 0376   4–3B
*With its vast glazed front and massed banks of video screen,
it's hard to miss this bar in the heart of Theatreland.
The external appearance is certainly impressive, and there's
more to it than meets the eye, with much of the space in the
large basement bar. Even so, there's a sense that being so
obvious it's prone to attracting a pretty undiscerning 'West End'
crowd. / Details: Mon-Sat 5pm-1am, Sun 5pm-11pm; no Amex. Food: till
1am. DJ: Fri-Sat. Happy hour: 6pm-8pm (beer £2.50, half-price cocktails).*

Detroit WC2
35 Earlham St   7240 2662   4–2C
*One of London's earlier design-led bars, this north Covent
Garden venue has lasted well (in spite of its hidden-away
basement location), and its combination of a maze-like cave
setting and 'Blakes 7'-style decorations have stood the test of
time. An intimate place, with lots of nooks and crannies, it's at
its best as a pre-clubbing venue (and serves some OK food).
/ Details: Mon-Sat 5pm-midnight, closed Sun. Food: till 10.30pm.
DJ: Thu-Sat.*

Dial
Mountbatten Hotel WC2

20 Monmouth St   7836 4300   4–2B
This large windows of this hotel bar (and restaurant) overlooking Covent Garden's Seven Dials mini-roundabout help make it a great people-watching venue. Mock-croc pouffes, leather chairs and dark wood surrounds create quite a chic setting, if one whose fairly conservative charms make it something of a business venue. / Details: Mon-Sat 10am-11pm, Sun 10am-10pm. Food: till 11.30pm. DJ & Live music: bands and DJ's occasional.

The Dickens Inn E1

St Katharine's Way   7488 2208   9–3D
For an 'away-from-it-all' waterside location that's just a few minutes walk from the City, this mega-scale establishment near Tower Bridge has got an awful lot to recommend it. As the name suggests, however, you're talking serious touristville, but the outside terraces, with views over the marina, are really quite pleasant. / Food: bar snacks Mon-Fri noon-3pm, Sat-Sun noon-4.40pm.

District E8

19 Amhurst Rd   8985 8986   1–1D
Next to Hackney Central BR, this recently-established DJ bar plays music with a diverse range of styles – funk, soul, break beats, house, ... The décor is wooden and retro, the lighting low and volume generally on the high side. Drinks include spirits, John Smith for bitter drinkers and quite a selection of lagers. / Details: Mon-Thu 5pm-1am, Fri 4pm-1am, Sat 2pm-1am, Sun noon-1am; no Amex. Food: till 8pm. DJ: Wed-Sun. Happy hour: 4pm-8pm (cocktails 2 for 1).

ditto SW18

55 East Hill   8877 0110   10–2A
This relaxed, slightly Bohemian spot has established itself as a key rendezvous for the local Wandsworth thirtysomethings. The restaurant is on quite a scale, but the bar – with its comfortable sofas – is an attraction in its own right. / Details: no Amex. Food: L till 3pm, D till 11pm.

Dixie's Bar & Grill SW11

25 Battersea Rs   7228 7984   10–2B

Most people do seem to eat, but surely it can't be the quality of the Tex-Mex fare which keeps Battersea's younger souls coming back to this basic roadhouse? The busy but mellow vibe – and the margaritas and Mexican beers – must have more to do with it. / **Details:** *Mon-Fri from 4pm.* **Food:** *till 10.30pm (Sun 9.30pm).* **Happy hour:** *Mon-Sun 6pm-8pm (25% off all drinks).*

Dog & Bell SE8

116 Prince St   8692 5664   11–2C

Opposite what remains of the Deptford dockyard, this is a regular CAMRA local pub-of-the-year winner (with regular guest beers) and attracts a wide-ranging crowd. The interior is fairly standard, with a TV that seems invariably tuned to horse-racing. There is a large rear terrace, and parents take note: the pub is next to a very large adventure playground. / **Details:** *Sun noon-3.30pm & 7pm-10.30pm; no credit cards.* **Food:** *L till 2.30pm, D till 9pm (Mon-Fri only).*

The Dog & Duck W1

18 Bateman St   7437 4447   4–2A

A very atmospheric, cramped and cosy Nicholson's Soho pub, complete with a wonderful Edwardian tiled and mirrored interior. It's very popular with the younger locals, and, in summer, the pavement outside makes a good vantage point from which to watch the world going by. / **Details:** *Sat 4pm-11pm, Sun 5pm-10.30pm.* **Food:** *L&D.*

The Dog House W1

187 Wardour St   7434 2116   3–1D

Just a doorway and a yellow sign announces the presence of this brightly-decorated basement bar – a long-running Soho favourite. Grab a seat in one of the cosy alcoves, or hang around at the bar drinking happy-hour cocktails or bottled beers. Nightly DJs spinning a wide range of tunes give the place a party atmosphere that attracts a young and relatively unpretentious crowd. / **Details:** *Mon-Fri from 5pm, Sat from 6pm, closed Sun.* **Food:** *till 10.30pm.* **DJ:** *Fri 8pm-11pm.* **Happy hour:** *Mon-Fri 5pm-7.30pm (half-price cocktails, bottle wine £8, £1 off spirits).*

Doggetts Coat & Badge SE1

1 Blackfriars Bridge Rd   7633 9057   9–3A

*If it wasn't on the Thames, it would have very few charms at all – this vast three-floor pub, with a great outside terrace, is a sad example of how complacent some riverside boozers can be, especially if they have the advantage of being only a bridge away from the City. / **Details:** management declined to provide information.*

Dogstar SW9

389 Coldharbour Ln   7733 7515   10–2C

*One of the first bar-clubs to open in London in the mid-90's, the Dogstar became a byword for hip and happening in cutting edge Brixton. Open till late and full of banging tunes on Friday and Saturday evenings, it also serves a good Sunday lunch with '80s disco afterwards to aid recovery from the night before. / **Website:** www.dogstarbar.co.uk **Details:** noon-2am (Fri & Sat 4am); no Amex. **Food:** Sun L only. **DJ:** nightly, dancing. **Happy hour:** Fri-Sat 7pm-9pm (half-price cocktails).*

Dorchester Bar
Dorchester Hotel W1

53 Park Ln   7629 8888   2–2A

*This sumptuous Mayfair hotel boasts the ultimate in glitzily glamorous cocktail lounges – how appropriate that the mirror-covered piano here used to belong to Liberace. Delicious snacks are available (payment may require the removal of arms and legs), and, if you take one of these, you can drink here until midnight, while listening to the pianist or (on three nights a week) a jazz band. / **Website:** www.dorchesterhotel.com **Food:** till 11.45pm (Sun 10.30pm).*

Dove W6

19 Upper Mall   8748 5405   7–2A

*It has a great location, but that's not the only selling-point of this Dickensian Fullers tavern – the classiest of the many traditional pubs by the river at Hammersmith. It's a particular favourite for Sunday lunch, and it is as difficult in summer to get a seat on the small, riverside terrace as it is in winter to nab a spot by the fire. Other claims to fame include an entry in the Guinness Book of Records for the country's smallest public bar, and as the place where James Thompson penned 'Rule Britannia'. Children are not welcome. / **Food:** till 8.30pm.*

Dove E8

24-26 Broadway Mkt 7275 7617 1–1D

This eccentric bar, in artsy Broadway Market, is chock-full of plants on the window sills. It has a cosy feel to it and serves a selection of Belgian beers and two draught bitters to a mainly local crowd. Basic pub fare is also available. / **Details:** *Mon-Tue 11.30am-11pm, Thu-Sat 11.30am-10pm, Sun noon-10.30pm, closed Sun; no Amex; no-smoking area.* **Food:** *till 10pm.*

Dover Castle W1

43 Weymouth Mews 7580 4412 3–1B

This Sam Smith's boozer, in a cobbled mews near Portland Place, offers more than usual in the way of character. If you're looking for a place to drink near the West End with – how can one put it? – mature appeal, this may well be it. / **Details:** *closed Sun.* **Food:** *L till 2.30pm, D till 9pm.*

Dover St Wine Bar W1

8-9 Dover St 7629 9813 3–3C

Cheap it ain't, but this Mayfair bar-nightclub stalwart remains (in the face of surprisingly little oppo') one of the best places in town for dinner and a boogie (with fair-good mingling opportunities for those on the pull). This is mainly a group-dinner venue, but you can just drink (though not, Fri & Sat, before 10 pm). Live bands alternate with the DJ, playing a mix of jazz, blues, Latin and soul. (Note: there are entrance charges some times/days.) / **Website:** *www.doverst.co.uk* **Details:** *Mon-Thu noon-3pm & 5.30pm-3am, Fri & Sat noon-3pm & 7pm-3am, closed Sun.* **Food:** *till 2am (closed Sat L & Sun).* **DJ & Live music:** *nightly.*

The Dovetail EC1

9 Jerusalem Pas 7490 7321 9–1A

By far the best of London's (admittedly small) crop of Belgian beer halls, this hidden-away Clerkenwell spot offers 101 different Low Land brews. Draught options range from the mainstream to the obscure, and the sheer variety of bottled beers (Trappist, Lambic, Geueze, white, fruit and pilsners, to name but a few types) is mind-boggling – luckily, there are tasting notes, and staff are happy to offer samples. The eccentric décor (think kitsch Gothic monastery) and the food recommends the place to non-beer lovers, too. / **Website:** *www.belgianbars.com* **Details:** *closed Sun; no Amex; no-smoking area.* **Food:** *L till 3pm, D till 10pm.*

Dragon Bar EC2
5 Leonard St   7490 7110   9–1D
*If not advertising your presence is the sign of cool, few places
are hipper than this longstanding member of the 'Sosho' set.
Its anonymous dark grey exterior (in an unpromising side
street) only adds to its beatnik, speakeasy charms. DJs are a
regular fixture, and upstairs – not part of the bar – there's an
art space (whose décor helps explain the name).*
/ **Website:** www.dragonbar.co.uk **Details:** Mon-Thu noon-11pm,
Fri noon-midnight, Sat 2pm-midnight, Sun 2pm-10.30pm; no Amex. **DJ:** nightly
from 8pm (hip hop). **Live music:** occassionally live music.

Drapers Arms N1
44 Barnsbury St   7619 0348   8–3D
*An unusually pretty Islington side street provides the setting for
this newly-launched gastropub, which has quickly established a
reputation as one of the best places of its type – be prepared,
though, for cooking (and prices) of restaurant standard.
The décor – stripped back to an almost Georgian sobriety –
is quite unusual, too.* / **Details:** no Amex. **Food:** L&D.

Drawing Room & Sofa Bar SW11
103 Lavender Hill   7350 2564   10–2B
*Perhaps inevitably, given the name, sofas seem to be in rather
short supply at this rather haphazard-seeming Battersea
operation. The candlelit bar is a sort of eccentric, fairytale girly
delight, with pink walls and lots of gilt, and an odd collection of
clocks. Drinkswise, it's a mix of bottled lager, wine and
cocktails.* / **Details:** Mon-Fri from 5pm; no Amex. **Food:** 6.30pm-11pm.

The Duck SW11
110 Battersea Rise   7228 0349   10–2B
*No longer the Dog & Duck – this cavernous pub received the
'Changing Rooms' treatment a year or so ago, to emerge with
pink and chartreuse walls and an assortment of oddly shaped,
retro furniture in co-ordinating colours. An open kitchen with
wood-fired pizza oven adds interest to the scene (and there's
an eating area separated from the main bar).* / **Food:** L&D.
DJ: Fri-Sun. **Happy hour:** Mon & Thu (£1 off cocktails & double shots).

Duke of Cambridge SW11
228 Battersea Bridge Rd   7223 5662   10–1B
*Sunday lunch is the forte of this large Battersea gastropub –
decorated in colonial/wine bar style – but it's a popular and
relaxed venue at any time. Quite extensive outside seating
(covered and heated in winter) makes it a particularly popular
sunny-day destination.* / **Website:** www.geronimoinns.co.uk **Details:** no
Amex. **Food:** L till 2.30pm (weekends till 4pm), D will 9.45pm, .

The Duke of Cambridge N1
30 St Peters St   7359 3066   1–1C
*Undoubtedly in Islington, but a world away from the tourist
delights of Upper Street, this back street boozer – apparently
furnished from a junk shop – is something of a cult destination
among organic food fans in particular. It's one of the few places
to eat (of any type) that's actually approved by the Soil
Association and that goes for the wine and beers too.*
/ **Website:** www.singhboulton.co.uk **Details:** Mon from 5pm; no smoking in
restaurant. **Food:** Tue-Sat L till 3.30pm, D till 10.30pm.

Duke of Devonshire SW12
39 Balham High Rd   8673 1363   10–2B
*From the front, it may be nothing out of the ordinary,
but there's certainly more than meets the eye to this popular
Young's local. The huge Victorian interior, the sizeable beer
garden (great for kids), and the late weekend licence all draw a
mixed crowd, from Balhamite yuppies to old faithfuls.*
/ **Website:** www.youngs.co.uk **Details:** Wed, Thu & Sat till midnight, Fri & Sat
till 2am; no Amex. **Food:** L&D.

Duke of Edinburgh SW9
204 Ferndale Rd   7924 0509   10–1C
*From the outside this modern pub looks small and sterile, but it
hides the largest and most surprising beer-garden in these
parts, where barbecues are often a feature. Indoors,
the atmosphere is relaxed, and there is a pool table too.*
/ **Details:** no Amex. **Food:** L&D. **DJ:** Mon-Sun from 7pm.

The Duke of Wellington W11
179 Portobello Rd 7727 6727 6–1A
Prominently situated on a corner, this Young's pub had its five minutes of fame in 'Notting Hill'. As the area gets ever-more trendy (if that's possible), this cheerful, unreformed boozer is one of the few locally not to have received the 'Changing Rooms' treatment and it's popularity doesn't seem to have been dented as a result. Attractions include board games, big screen TV and – on the first Thursday of each month – a talent competition. / **Website:** www.youngs.co.uk **Food:** L only.

The Duke's Head SW15
8 Lower Richmond Rd 8788 2552 10–1A
A huge bay window overlooking the Thames is one of the prime features of this impressive, panelled Victorian Young's pub, one of the most spacious and civilised traditional boozers in town. When the weather is fine you can take your drink outside (though there are no seats). It's also one of the key spectators pubs on Boat Race day (it's right by the start). / **Website:** www.youngs.co.uk **Details:** no Amex. **Food:** till 11pm.

Dukes Hotel Bar SW1
35 St James's Pl 7491 4840 2–2B
Now the Connaught's gone all hip (well, relatively speaking), this smart and discreet St James's establishment is one of the few central hotels which still exudes a proper and truly old-fashioned (in the best sense) charm, and the martinis have quite a reputation. Note that gentlemen are required to wear a jacket and tie in the evening. / **Website:** www.dukeshotel.com **Food:** till 4.30pm.

Dulwich Wood House SE26
39 Sydenham Hill 8693 5666 1–3D
Recently refurbished, this large and airy pub (housed in a Victorian gatehouse) between Crystal Palace, Forest Hill and Sydenham is worth knowing about in a thin area. It's owned by Young's, so you can be assured of well-kept ales and similarly good wines with its list of 18 bottles, almost all available by glass. There are a number of bars (including a no-smoking one), with quite a large garden at the back. Decent fare, too, at reasonable prices. / **Website:** www.youngs.co.uk **Details:** no-smoking area. **Food:** till 9.30pm.

The Durell SW6
704 Fulham Rd 7736 3014 10–1A
As new modern pubs go, this large, rambling venture near the Munster Road may be a mite anonymous, but it's been done out with a reasonable eye for style. Attractions include a large 'playroom' at the back with a couple of pool tables and a large projection screen. / **Food:** *till 10pm.*

(The George Bar) Durrants Hotel W1
26-32 George St 7935 8131 3–1A
This quintessential English hotel first opened in 1790, and it has been in its current private ownership for over 80 years. As you'd hope, the bar is very much in the traditional vein. The panelled mahogany décor, leather furnishings and hushed atmosphere provide a welcome relief after a hard day's graft, or shopping in nearby Oxford Street.
/ **Website:** *www.durrantshotel.co.uk* **Details:** *Mon-Sun 11.30am-2.30pm & 5.30pm-11pm.* **Food:** *L&D.*

Dusk W1
79 Marylebone High St 7486 5746 3–1A
A former boozer on a Marylebone corner has been made over into a sort of superior All Bar One – a Style in the City bar, with all the clichés to match. That's not to say that its slightly anonymous charms don't make it a thoroughly handy place in a part of town that's still rather short of airy, modern drinking space, especially if you're looking for some fairly substantial food at the same time. / **Website:** *www.thespiritgroup.com* **Details:** *9.30am-11pm (Sun 10.30pm).* **Food:** *breakfast, L & D.* **DJ:** *Fri.*

Dust EC1
27 Clerkenwell Rd 7490 5120 9–1A
An unusually chic exterior, complete with potted box hedges, signals the existence of this large Clerkenwell bar. Workers in the sewing factory – which these premises once were – might be rather surprised by the 'art' road signs ('No God for 2 miles' etc) which now adorn the large space inside. For all that the place offers a fairly standard take on the lounge bar experience, including food on a Mediterranean theme and DJs at weekends. / **Website:** *www.dustbar.co.uk* **Details:** *Mon-Wed noon-midnight, Thu-Fri noon-2am, Sat 7pm-2am, closed Sun.* **Food:** *till 10pm.* **DJ:** *Thu-Sat.*

E&O W11

14 Blenheim Cr   7229 5454   6–1A

In no time at all, Will Ricker's modernistic 'Eastern and Oriental' bar and restaurant has become the new linchpin of the Notting Hill set (and a star-spotter's paradise, to boot). The restaurant is an attraction in itself, but the sophisticated-looking bar is no second best, offering a fantastic buzz as well as a good range of cocktails. / **Website:** www.eando.nu
Details: Mon-Sun noon-midnight. **Food:** till 10.30pm.

The Eagle EC1

159 Farringdon Rd   7837 1353   9–1A

This is the pub that broke the mould – it was the first (in 1991) to throw off the shackles of the past, and to combine quality, contemporary cooking and a good range of both wines and beers. Though many places now ape its 'gastropub' style, the constant scrum of would-be diners confirms it still retains its position at the head of the pack. / **Details:** Sun till 5pm; no Amex.
Food: L till 2.30pm (weekends till 3pm), D till 10.30pm.

Eagle Bar Diner W1

4-5 Rathbone Pl   7637 1418   4–1A

A burger-diner just north of Oxford Street somehow doesn't sound the trendiest destination, but cynics may be confounded when they visit this cool new spot. The burgers are pretty good, but it's the cocktails and the vibes which draw the evening crowds. / **Website:** www.eaglebardiner.com **Details:** Mon-Fri 8am-11pm, Sat 10am-11pm, Sun 11am-5.30pm. **Food:** till 10:45pm. **DJ:** Thu-Sat.
Live music: occasional bands.

Ealing Park Tavern W5

222 South Ealing Rd   8758 1879   1–2A

This large South Ealing pub was once the kind of uninviting old boozer which didn't invite further investigation. It's just been transformed though (by the people who also own St John in Archway) into one of the best gastropubs in town. There's a very good-sized bar, and a sparse but atmospheric, and very lofty dining room with the kitchen fully on display. / **Details:** Mon from 5pm. **Food:** till 10.30pm.

East Dulwich Tavern SE22

Lordship Ln 8693 1316 1–3D

*In the old days, this was very much a bog-standard boozer but it's been given an airy and modern look of late, including huge "look-at-me-looking-at-you" windows. It's a large place, but it can get quite crowded especially at weekends. Upstairs used to have comedy nights, but these have recently been replaced by a restaurant. / **Details:** Thu-Sat till midnight, Sun noon-10.30pm; no Amex. **Food:** from 6pm.*

Eclipse

113 Walton St, SW3 7581 0123 5–2C
158 Old Brompton Rd, SW5 7259 2577 5–2B
108-110 New King's Rd, SW6 7731 2142 10–1A
186 Kensington Park Rd, W11 7792 2063 6–1A
57 High St, SW19 8944 7722 10–2A

*It's not often – in fact it's pretty much unknown – that one bar chain grabs the attention of beautiful people in many of the top postcodes in town. That's exactly what Matt Hermer seems to be doing with his chain of cosily swish bars, which has expanded from his mega-popular, five-year-old Walton Street to South Kensington, Fulham, Notting Hill… even sleepy old Wimbledon. / **Details:** vary. **Food:** bar snacks only. **DJ:** SW5 Thu-Sat. **Live music:** W11 & SW19 bongo player, .*

Edgar Wallace WC2

40 Essex St 7353 3120 2–1D

*Edgar Wallace was a prolific thriller-writer at the beginning of the last century – over 160 of his books have been made into films, and he was working on the screenplay for King Kong when he died. This attractive Victorian pub (his former home) was named after him on the centenary of his birth in 1975, and displays memorabilia from his life. Legal beagles from the Inns of Court and the local law firms provide much of the place's custom. / **Details:** closed weekends; no Amex. **Food:** L till 3pm.*

The Edge W1
11 Soho Sq 7439 1223 4–1A
Spilling into the square on sunny afternoons, and heaving at weekends, this is one of the longest-running Soho success-stories, catering to a mainly gay crowd. Three floors offer a range of music styles, with DJs nightly. Start an evening here and you could easily find yourself staying all night (not least because the crush often makes it difficult to move around). / **Details:** Mon-Sat noon-1am, Sun noon-10.30pm; no Amex. **Food:** till 8pm. **DJ:** nightly. **Live music:** pianist or singer, nightly.

Eight Bells SW6
89 Fulham High St 7736 6307 10–1A
This small Georgian tavern near Putney Bridge tube claims to be the oldest in Fulham, having occupied this site since the late 17th-century. It's a characterful, tightly-packed panelled place, with a U-shaped bar that feels very much a civilised local. It's uninspiring location and small size, though, prevent it from being a major destination. / **Food:** L till 3pm, bar snacks till 10.30pm.

El Paso Club EC1
350-354 Old St 7739 4202 9–1D
The basement club – which features some interesting fringe music and poetry events as well as disco nights and the like – drives the scene at this bar/venue near Shoreditch town hall. The woody ground-floor bar, complete with mezzanine, looks a bit like a misplaced Tex/Mex restaurant, and its staples are draft lagers and a selection of shooters. / **Details:** Mon-Wed till 1am, Thu till 2am, Fri & Sat till 3.30am, Sun 11am-midnight; no Amex. **Food:** till midnight (Mon), 1am (Tue), 2am Thu-Sat, 11.30pm (Sun). **DJ:** Tue, Fri-Sat (disco). **Happy hour:** Mon-Fri 11am-7pm (all beers & wines £2).

El Vino's
30 New Bridge St, EC4 7248 5548 9–3A
47 Fleet St, EC4 7353 7541 9–2A
6 Martin Ln, EC4 7626 6876 9–3C
Old-fashioned, but in a particularly attractive and welcoming way, these famous City wine bars remain extremely popular with pinstripes of all types. The Martin Lane branch (which trades under the name Olde Wine Shades, see also) is the oldest wine house in the City – but it's the famous Fleet Street branch which is like stepping into a time machine. They all offer simple but satisfying cooking (with the option of restaurant service). / **Details:** Mon-Fri 8.30am-10pm, closed Sat & Sun. **Food:** noon-3pm.

Elbow Room

103 Westbourne Grove, W2   7221 5211   6–1B
89-91 Chapel Mkt, N1   7278 3244   8–3D
135 Finchley Rd, Swiss Cottage, NW3   7586 9888   8–2A
97-113 Curtain Rd, EC2   7729 5051   9–1D

Flock wallpapered walls, neon lights and purple-felted tables have helped make these pool bars funky places to hang out. The original (W2) branch is the calmest – all the other venues are DJ bars. Sink a few beers and American-style snacks (burgers, nachos, etc) while waiting for a table to be vacated (at peak times there are long queues, and you're limited to an hour's play). The company (slogan 'the rebirth of pool') is intent on serious expansion, so look out for new openings.
/ **Website:** www.elbow-room.co.uk **Details:** vary. **Food:** L&D. **DJ:** N1 nightly.

Electric Brasserie W11

191 Portobello Rd   7908 9696   6–1A

Adjoining the landmark Electric Cinema in the beating heart of Notting Hill, this newly redeveloped venue (by the team from Soho House) slugs it out with nearby E&O for the hearts and minds of the local trustafarians. There a small members' club, as well as the ground floor bar and brasserie, where eating is the major part of the operation. The bar, however, is regularly heaving with hip local residents and assorted hangers-on.
/ **Website:** www.the-electric.co.uk **Details:** Mon-Sat 8am-midnight, Sun 8am-11pm. **Food:** till 10pm.

Elephant & Castle W8

40 Holland St   7368 0901   5–1A

A cute location, in a backwater just off Ken' High Street, adds to the appeal of this cosy, traditional Georgian boozer. When it's busy (which is often), it can be a bit of a squeeze, at which times many prefer to drink in the street outside (assuming the three tables have gone on the pub's miniscule terrace). / **Details:** no Amex; no-smoking area. **Food:** L till 3pm (Sat till 5pm).

Elephant Royale E14
Westferry Rd   7987 7999   11–2C
Although the Thai restaurant operation dominates at this newish outfit at the tip of the Isle of Dogs, there is also quite a sizeable bar operation. The interior design is a bit tacky (well actually it's very tacky), but on a summer's day you can drink on the nice riverside terrace which has a magnificent view of Greenwich over the water. In the evenings, arrive early if you want to bag a table. / **Details:** *till 10.30pm.* **Food:** *till 10.30pm.*

Elysium
Café Royal W1
68 Regent St   7439 7770   3–3D
In the cellars of the Café Royal, this lavishly designed cocktail and Champagne bar has quickly become a member of the (self-consciously) 'elite' set of cool crowd club/bars near Piccadilly Circus. (They certainly charge enough for entry: £15 in the week and £20 at weekends) It's made up of a maze of different chambers, and they've really gone for it when it comes to the flamboyant Moroccan-inspired look, including some enormous banquettes for lounging. See also Ku de Ta. / **Website:** *www.elysiumlounge.co.uk* **Details:** *Wed-Sat 10.30pm-3am.*

Ember EC1
99-100 Turnmill St   7490 3985   9–1A
A tiny rear conservatory and a wooden bench with carved-out seats add quirky charm to this recent sibling to Battersea's Babel. Both the spacious ground floor and private basement room (subEmber) are decorated in fiery tones, as the name suggests. A handy location (opposite Farringdon tube) and late-night opening towards the end of the week look set to ensure continuing popularity. / **Website:** *www.faucetinn.com* **Details:** *Thu till 1am, Fri & Sat till 2am, closed Sun.* **Food:** *L till 3pm, D till 10pm.* **DJ:** *Sat.*

The Endurance W1
90 Berwick St   7437 2944   3–2D
Berwick Street, with its fruit market, is one of the more characterful thoroughfares in central London. The team behind Bloomsbury's Perseverance have recently relaunched an old boozer in the middle of the street as a gastropub, but its whole approach – in accordance with the Soho location – is fairly down-to-earth. A good place if you want to eat, or if you just want to down a pint or two.

The Engineer NW1
65 Gloucester Ave 7722 0950 8–3B
This legendary Primrose Hill establishment can claim to have helped found the gastropub revolution and – with its stylish but earthy approach, cool bar, atmospheric restaurant and dependable cooking – it continues to draw a glamorous and trendy crowd from far and wide. Get there early if you want a seat, especially in the great garden in summer.
/ **Website:** www.the-engineer.com **Details:** Mon-Sat 9am-midnight, Sun 9am-11pm; no Amex. **Food:** L till 3.30pm, D till 9.30pm.

Enterprise NW3
2 Haverstock Hill 7485 2659 8–2B
You can't really miss this large and strikingly-decorated Victorian boozer near Chalk Farm tube, which has long had a reputation as one of the nicest pubs in the immediate area. Part of the main room has had the 'library' treatment – the approach can seem so naff, but here it's fitted in very well. / **Details:** no credit cards. **Happy hour:** till 7.30pm (doubles of vodka, gin, whisky £2.50).

The Enterprise SW3
35 Walton St 7584 3148 5–2C
A 'feel-good' ambience has helped make this clubbily comfortable pub-conversion near Harrods – half bar/half bistro – a long-running success-story with a well-heeled local crowd. The food's no big deal, but that doesn't mean you may not have to wait for a table – you can always sink a bottle of bubbly while you wait. / **Website:** www.sparkjumbo.co.uk **Food:** L till 2.30pm (weekends till 3pm), D till 10.15pm.

Evangelist EC4
33 Blackfriars Ln 7213 0740 9–3A
Something of a surprise in this pretty City back lane, this large modern gastropub has an interesting layout, with lots of comfortable seating (and some nice alcoves, for those who get there early). It's got a good reputation for its grub, though as the week goes on it seems there's more emphasis on drinking and less on eating, as full meals give way to bar snacks.
/ **Details:** closed weekends. **Food:** till 8pm.

Exhibit SW12

Balham Station Rd   8772 6556   10–2B

Fish tanks in the wall and seriously low-slung sofas complete the modernistic, Scandinavian-style décor at this cool Balham bar, whose name is apposite – it's definitely a place for posing. The outside tables, with fine views of Sainsbury's car park, are very popular in summer. Food is available in the bar, and there's also a restaurant upstairs.
/ **Website:** www.theexhibit.uk.com **Details:** Fri & Sat till midnight; no Amex. **Food:** L only (bar snacks Mon-Thu pm only).

Falcon SW4

33 Bedford Rd   7274 2428   10–2C

Just round the corner from Clapham North tube, on an unpromisingly busy road, this large and attractive boozer makes a good 'find'. A pleasantly stripped-down interior and beer gardens front and rear help secure its position as one of the most popular places in the area. Most people are drinking draft lager or wine, and it's one of a small group of similar pubs locally doing OK Thai grub. / **Details:** no Amex. **Food:** L till 3pm, D till 10.30pm, all day weekends.*

Ferry House E14

26 Ferry St   7537 9587   11–2C

At the very tip of the Isle of Dogs stands a boozer that lays claim to being the oldest pub on the 'island'. It's on the Thames Path, but lacks a river view, perhaps explaining why it remains largely the preserve of the locals. / **Details:** Mon-Fri from 2pm.

Fiction SW11

47 Northcote Rd   7228 6240   10–2B

A catchy-looking mosaic fascia advertises the vaguely wacky charms of this small Battersea café/bar. If you're looking for somewhere slightly more intimate than the many other throbbing joints in the neighbourhood, this could be the place. / **Details:** Tue-Sun 9am-11pm (closed Mon). **Food:** Tue-Fri 9am-2pm, D 7pm-11pm, weekends 9am-6pm.

Fifteen NW1
15 Westland Pl 7251 1515 9–1C
Seen the TV program, want to check out Jamie Oliver's new place, but can't get a booking in the restaurant? You can always try the upstairs bar which is already packing 'em in. The sleek modern styling throughout the whole of this warehouse conversion has won nothing but raves – similarly the cocktail list which is well out of the ordinary. As for the food, the word is that it's not bad but a bit pricey. / **Website:** www.cheekychops.org
Details: Mon-Sat 11am-midnight, closed Sun.

The Fifth Floor
Harvey Nichols SW1
Knightsbridge 7235 5250 5–1D
Long famed as a pick-up joint par excellence, this elevated bar – part of a complex which also includes a restaurant and food hall, above the Knightsbridge department store – has recently had a major refurb'. Unlike the neighbouring dining room, however, its walls are sadly not programmed periodically to change colour, and – unless your on the pull – the place's soulless attractions seem rather limited (especially if the poisonous attitude we encountered at the door is typical).
/ **Website:** www.harveynichols.com **Details:** Sun noon-6pm. **Food:** till 4pm.

Film Café SE1
South Bank, Waterloo Rd 7928 5362 2–2D
The canteen-like café/bar of the National Film Theatre is a useful meeting point for visitors to any of the cultural spots along the South Bank. The wooden outside seating, although underneath Waterloo Bridge, is great in summer, and made even more pleasant by the bustle of the second-hand book market and the occasional busker. / **Website:** www.bfi.org.uk
Details: no-smoking area. **Food:** L till 3pm, D till 9pm, weekends till 9pm.
Happy hour: Mon-Thu 5pm-7pm.

Filthy McNasty's EC1
68 Amwell St 7837 6067 9–1A
A sinister character on the huge 'Whiskey Café' sign advertises the presence of this rather scruffy-looking spot, in the wasteland between Clerkenwell and Islington. Despite a healthy focus on Guinness and whiskeys, it's by no means your standard Irish theme bar, though – its attractions include literary readings, live music and hearty grub. / **Details:** Sat noon-midnight,
Sun noon-10.30pm. **Food:** L & D. **DJ:** Wed & Sun.

Fina Estampa SE1

150 Tooley St   7403 1342   9–3C

*An unexpected gem in the area between London and Tower Bridges, this low-lit Peruvian tapas bar is a stylish venue for drinks (cocktails and South American wines) and a nibble (there's also a restaurant upstairs). Decorated with an intriguing mixture of designer leather armchairs and native musical instruments, it would make a good destination for those with romance in mind. / **Website:** www.finaestampa.co.uk **Details:** Mon-Fri noon-2.30pm & 6.30pm-10.30pm, Sat 6.30-10.30pm, closed Sun. **Food:** L & D.*

Finch's SW10

190 Fulham Rd   7351 5043   5–3B

*It always seems a touch anonymous, but this large and airy Victoria boozer has long been a useful destination on this stretch of road known to local trendies as the Chelsea 'Beach'. It remains the best place of its type in the immediate vicinity. / **Website:** www.youngs.co.uk **Food:** L till 2pm (Sun L till 4pm), D till 8pm.*

The Fine Line

77a Kingsway, WC2   7405 5004   2–1D
236 Fulham Rd, SW10   7376 5827   5–3B
31-37 Northcote Rd, SW11   7924 7387   10–2B
182 Clapham High St, SW4   7622 4436   10–2C
10 Cabot Sq, E14   7513 0255   11–1C
1 Monument St, EC3   7623 5446   9–3C
124-127 Minories, EC3   7481 8195   9–3D
1 Bow Churchyard, EC4   7248 3262   9–2B

*One of the newer 'trendy wine bar' brands (est. 1998), this time from Fuller's. Deliberately targeting female drinkers (with big open windows, pale furniture and comfortable sofas), its branches offer tolerable snacks and a decent wine list. / **Website:** www.fullers.co.uk **Details:** vary. **Food:** L&D. **DJ:** EC2.*

The Fire Stables SW19

27-29 Church Rd, Wimbledon Village   8946 3197   10–2A
When this large, strikingly-designed bar/restaurant was opened a couple of years ago, it was just the kind of trendy destination sleepy old Wimbledon Village needed. It still has few rivals hereabouts and gets pretty crowded with a crowd who come as much to eat as to drink – both in the rear restaurant and also on the bare wooden tables at the front.
/ **Website:** www.thespiritgroup.com **Details:** no-smoking area. **Food:** L till 3pm (Sat L till 4pm), D till 10.30pm.

Fishmarket
Great Eastern Hotel EC2

Bishopsgate   7618 7200   9–2D
Amongst all the various watering holes around Liverpool Street station, this extremely swish and lofty champagne and seafood bar is arguably the best (and certainly, in our book, it's the one bit of Conran's Great Eastern Hotel empire that truly deserves the word 'glamorous'). You enter through a lobby in which there's a restaurant of the same name, which has all the atmosphere of a, er, lobby. / **Website:** www.fish-market.co.uk
Details: Mon-Fri till 10.30pm, closed weekends. **Food:** L till 2.45pm, D till 10.45pm.

5B Urban Bar E14

27 Three Colt St   7537 1601   11–1B
Once an ordinary working man's pub (called the Five Bells & Blade Bone), this Docklands boozer has been given a trademark makeover by the Urban Bar company. That is, its exterior is now zebra-striped, it has a neo-Gothic interior which houses – safely contained, of course – a large python. Oz and Kiwi flags and the TNT advert in the window hint at the clientèle. You have been warned. / **Details:** Mon-Tue 5pm-midnight, Wed-Sun noon-midnight; no Amex. **Food:** till 1am.

The Flask NW3

14 Flask Walk   7435 4580   8–1A
Not to be confused with the possibly even more famous Flask in Highgate, this serious beer-drinkers' Victorian pub, bristling with CAMRA awards, is conveniently located on a quiet, pedestrianised lane in the centre of Hampstead. The front bars, divided by a charming, original screen, are more characterful than the new rear conservatory. / **Website:** www.youngs.co.uk
Details: no Amex. **Food:** L till 3pm (Sat L till 4pm), D till 8.30pm (Sat D till 9pm).

The Flask N6

77 Highgate West Hill   8348 7346   8–1B

Idyllically located in the prettiest part of Highgate, this multi-roomed, coaching inn (owned by Taylor Walker) is early-18th century in origin and feels almost as if it were deep in the country. On a sunny day, its fame ensures that the large yard is full to overflowing. There's a good selection of bitters (and guest ales) and quite a wide range of food available at most times. / **Details:** no Amex; no-smoking area. **Food:** L till 3pm, D till 10pm.

Fluid EC1

40 Charterhouse St   7253 3444   9–1B

A neat retro-Japanesey theme (incorporating old arcade games) adds interest to this diminutive bar in Smithfield, with Kirin on tap and sushi available all day. During the week it's packed with a mixture of urban trendies and suits, while at the weekends the lack of natural light means it's a natural for pre-Fabric clubbers. Also at weekends, the tiny dance floor downstairs is itself home to a resident DJ. / **Website:** www.fluidbar.com **Details:** Mon-Wed noon-midnight, Thu-Fri noon-2am, Sat 7pm-2am, closed Sun. **Food:** till 10pm. **DJ:** Thu-Sat from 10pm. **Happy hour:** noon-2pm, 6pm-7pm (2 for 1).

The Founders Arms SE1

52 Hopton St   7928 1899   9–3B

Location, location and location. Those are the three prime virtues of this comfortable but basic pub, overlooking the Thames (which used to be located next to a power station, and now finds that the power station has been converted into The Tate Modern). Plenty of outside seating ensures the summer crowds are well accommodated. / **Website:** www.youngs.co.uk **Details:** no-smoking area. **Food:** till 8.30pm (7.30pm Sun).

Foundry EC2

84-86 Great Eastern St   7739 6900   9–1D

Is it a bar or is it an installation? You never quite know what you're going to find at this grungily-sited former bank branch (which still features a safe in the basement). It's a laid back, studenty place, but offers a fair range of booze, and remains popular. / **Website:** www.foundry.tv **Details:** Tue-Sat 4pm-11.30pm, Sun 4pm-11pm (closed Mon); no credit cards. **DJ:** Tue-Sat.

Fox & Anchor EC1

115 Charterhouse St   7253 5075   9–1B

*In a dead-end side-street (if you're driving) by Smithfield Market, this Nicholson's boozer (which has a superb tiled exterior) is the most famous – and the nicest – of the local ale houses. It's famous for its breakfasts (invariably full English, with all the trimmings) and is one of those places where, thanks to a local variation in the licensing laws, you have long been able to enjoy an early morning pint. / **Details:** Mon-Wed 7am-4pm, Thu 7am-7pm, Fri 7am-9pm, closed Sat & Sun. **Food:** Mon-Fri B 7am-2pm.*

The Fox & Hounds SW1

29 Passmore St   7730 6367   5–2D

*For an escape from Sloane Square, you won't do much better than this pocket-handkerchief-size establishment, which benefits from a cute but hidden corner location, making it very much a locals' haunt. It used to be known for its anachronistic licence that prevented it serving spirits, but these days a G&T is yours for the asking. / **Website:** www.youngs.co.uk **Details:** Mon-Sun 11am-3pm & 5.30pm-11pm; no Amex. **Food:** L till 2.30pm.*

Fox & Hounds SW11

66 Latchmere Rd   7924 5483   10–1B

*A Mediterranean gastropub just off Lavender Hill (about 10 minutes' walk from Clapham Junction), which comes complete with the usual plain, rustic décor, and whose attractions include a good wine list. It's very popular with local thirtysomethings, with Sunday lunch particularly popular. / **Details:** Mon from 5pm, Tue-Thu noon-3pm & 5pm-11pm; no Amex. **Food:** L till 3pm, D till 10pm.*

The Fox & Pheasant SW10

1 Billing Rd   7352 2943   10–1A

*For once the name does not lie – this sweet little Greene King pub, (situated in a villagey area between Chelsea and Fulham which estate agents like to call "The Billings") does feel just like an unpretentious country tavern. It's on an intimate scale, with two rooms, decorated with stuffed creatures and sporting prints. / **Details:** no Amex. **Food:** L till 2.30pm.*

Fox Dining Room EC2
28 Paul St   7729 5708   9–1C
A year on from opening, one of the founders of the legendary Eagle has not – yet – quite 'done it again' at this characterful Shoreditch boozer. That's not to say that the small circular downstairs bar isn't a good choice for a superior snack with a glass of wine or a pint, nor that the upstairs dining room isn't an atmospheric spot serving good value food. / **Details:** *Mon-Fri noon-11pm, closed weekends; no Amex.* **Food:** *D till 10pm.*

Fox Reformed N16
176 Stoke Newington Church St   7254 5975   1–1C
A sweet, well-established wine bar offering simple fare and located near the Clissold Park end of Stoke Newington Church Street. Games, especially backgammon, are a crucial element of the atmosphere, and there's a tiny garden for the summer. / **Details:** *Mon-Fri 5pm-midnight, weekends noon-midnight; no-smoking area.* **Food:** *till 10.30pm.*

Franklin's SE22
157 Lordship Ln   8299 9598   1–3D
Looking rather like a French-style café, this East Dulwich wine bar (with restaurant behind) is a popular destination with local thirty- and fortysomethings who are looking for a civilised spot to down a bottle of vino (or lager). Authentically enough, it can get quite crowded and smokey. / **Details:** *Mon 5pm-midnight, Thu-Sat noon-midnight.* **Food:** *D till 10.30pm (no L Mon).*

Freedom W1
60-66 Wardour St   7734 0071   3–2D
This trendy Soho spot was one of the first modern bars to hit the area, and remains as popular as ever with a youngish 'polysexual' crowd (thanks in part to a recent, much-needed, revamp). Cocktails in the pink-and-orange-lit bar are a fine way to kick off an evening in the West End, or chill out during the day on low sofas. Downstairs, entertainments include cabaret and DJs. / **Details:** *Mon-Wed noon-midnight, Thu noon-2am, Sun 2pm-10.30pm; no Amex.* **DJ:** *Thu-Sat.*

Freedom Brewing Company WC2
41 Earlham St   7240 0606   4–2C
Freedom is one of London's few (but expanding number of) microbreweries, and this Covent Garden basement bar is a congenial place in which to sample its well-reputed brews (including Pilsner, Traditional Pale Ale and Soho Red). The original bar/restaurant formula and post-industrial décor have recently been scrapped in favour of a more loungey, retro-look bar, with clear orange Perspex chairs and Mondrian-esque carpet. / **Website:** *www.freedombrewery.com* **Food:** *till 10pm.*

The Freemason's Arms WC2
81-82 Long Acre   7836 3115   4–3C
Barely off the beaten track of touristy Covent Garden, this large pub – appropriately named, given the proximity of the Masonic Grand Temple – is decorated in a simple but traditional style. Greene King ownership may account for an unusually strong 'regular' following. / **Food:** *L till 3pm, D till 8.30pm.*

French House W1
49 Dean St   7437 2477   4–3A
This small and atmospheric free house's place in history was secured during WWII, when it became a favourite watering hole of de Gaulle and the Free French. It retains a decidedly Gallic air and serves a wide range of aperitifs and a good selection of wines. In recent years the cosy, upstairs dining room has developed quite a reputation in its own right. / **Food:** *till 3pm.*

Freud's WC2
198 Shaftesbury Ave   7240 9933   4–1C
This perennially buzzy cellar bar – established in 1986, and one of London's first style bars – has always felt like a 'find'. It barely advertises its presence – look for the fire-escape stairs in front of the shop of the same name. The décor makes extensive use of concrete, but once you've had a few of the (lethal) cocktails – from the blackboard list over the bar – you'll be incapable of feeling discomfort or, indeed, much else.
/ **Details:** *no Amex; no-smoking area.* **Food:** *L till 4.30pm, bar snacks 6pm-11pm.*

The Fridge Bar SW2
I Town Hall Pde, Brixton Hill   7326 5100   10–2C
*Next to the famed (related but separate) club of the same
name, this long and narrow bar/club has a dance-floor
downstairs. It's a lively place and DJs play a range of music
from hip-hop to house on different nights so attracting a diverse
and trendy crowd. Late opening is a key attraction (sometimes
until the next day), but there are admission charges.*
/ **Website:** www.fridge.co.uk **Details:** Mon-Thu 6pm-2am, Fri-Sun 6pm-4am.
DJ: Tue, Sun & Sat. **Live music:** occasional. **Happy hour:** Mon-Thu
6pm-9pm (half-price spirits & draught beer).

Friendly Society W1
79 Wardour St   7434 3805   4–3A
*A hidden location (down some stairs, in an alley behind a
branch of Ann Summers) lends an air of exclusivity to this
oddly-proportioned venue. A camp crowd stand around, or hang
out on the white leather sofas in a white-walled space done out
with a few kitsch touches (such as Barbie and Ken dolls and
fish tanks). Many use it as a springboard to a night's clubbing,
but there's also a regular DJ (often in the form of owner Maria).*
/ **Details:** Mon-Fri from 4pm, weekends from 2pm; no Amex. **DJ:** nightly.

Frog & Forget-me-Not
204 Dawes Rd, SW6   7610 2598   10–1A
60 Selkirk Rd, SW17   8672 6235   10–2A
32 The Pavement, SW4   7622 5230   10–2C
*This relaxed group does not go in for the latest in interior
design, and that's its main attraction. If you're looking for a
comfy and unpretentious place where you can collapse on
slightly knackered sofas reading the Sunday papers
(and perhaps enjoying a good Sunday roast), then its branches
are worth seeking out.* / **Details:** Mon-Sat noon-11pm (SW17 Mon-Fri
4pm-11pm), Sun noon-10.30pm; no Amex. **Food:** SW4 & SW17 L&D,
SW6 snacks only.

Front Page SW3
35 Old Church St   7352 2908   5–3C
*Charmingly located on an Old Chelsea corner, this Victorian pub
– revamped a few years ago, but without destroying its
character – is ideally located for refreshment before a visit to
the King's Road UGC cinema. It makes a pleasant hang out in
its own right, too (and if you want to eat there's some perfectly
competent Thai food available).* / **Website:** www.frontpagepubs.com
Details: closed Sun. **Food:** till 10pm.

Fuego EC3

1a Pudding Ln   7929 3366   9–3C

A tacky tapas bar near the Monument, whose redeeming feature for its fans is in providing a lively venue that's slightly 'different', by the standards of the Square Mile.
/ **Website:** www.fuego.co.uk **Details:** Mon-Fri 11am-2am, closed weekends. **Food:** L till 4pm, D till 10pm. **DJ:** Tue-Fri. **Happy hour:** 5pm-7pm (beer £1.25, house wine £6, spirit & mixer £2.50).

The Fulham Tup SW10

268 Fulham Rd   7352 1859   5–3B

This distant-end-of-Chelsea outpost of the popular chain of modern boozers has become quite a spiritual home for the local rugby-shirt-wearing classes (except on the days when they're displaced by the crowd off to the footie at nearby Stamford Bridge). / **Website:** www.massivepub.com **Food:** L till 3pm, D till 10pm. **DJ:** Fri-Sat. **Live music:** jazz Sun.

Funky Munky SE5

25 Camberwell Church St   7277 1806   1–2C

The name pretty much says it all about this lively and clubby Camberwell bar – perhaps more welcoming than some places of its type – which keeps the locals happy with its nice but simple food, its regular DJs and, most of all perhaps, its late licence. / **Details:** Mon 5pm-midnight, Tue-Sat noon-2am, Sun noon-midnight. **Food:** L till 4pm (weekends 5pm). **DJ:** Thu-Sun. **Happy hour:** 5pm-7pm (cocktails 2 for 1).

G E Club
Great Eastern EC2

Liverpool St, City   7618 7076   9–2D

It's not helped by its low ceilings and conference room proportions, but this soberly decorated cocktail bar on the first floor of the Great Eastern Hotel (famously revamped à la Conran) has made a fair stab at creating a trendy enclave in the City. After 6pm you have to be a member, but prior to that it's open to all. / **Website:** www.geclub.co.uk (password protected) **Details:** Mon-Fri 11am-6pm (members Mon-Fri 11am-2am, Sat 8pm-2am). **Food:** L till 4pm, D till 10.30pm. **DJ:** Wed-Sat 10pm-2am.

G-A-Y Bar W1

30 Old Compton St   7494 2756   4–2A

Like its predecessor, Manto Soho, this newly-refurbished 'video bar' offers the standard Soho formula of heavily marked-up beers, beefy bar staff and standing-room only at weekends. Unlike Manto's, however – which, at quieter times, could be quite a stylish and comfortable place to hang out – this new incarnation has all the high-octane campness of its sibling club night at the Astoria. / Happy hour: Thu-Sun (selected drinks £1.50).

Garlic & Shots W1

14 Frith St   7734 9505   4–2A

A true oddity, this Soho bar (whose parent is in Stockholm) is gloriously Gothic-styled and 'decorated' with spiders and skulls. The music is usually heavy metal; and Vodka shots – choose from over 100 – are the house speciality. In the restaurant there's pretty good food, but everything, ice-cream included, comes laced with garlic (there's even beer with garlic). / Website: www.garlicandshots.com Details: Mon-Wed 5pm-midnight, Thu-Sat 6pm-1am, Sun 5pm-11.30pm; no Amex. Food: till 11.15pm, Fri & Sat till 12.15am.

The Gate EC1

St John St   7336 6099   9–1B

With a sea-green exterior, terracotta walls, wooden floors and leather sofas, this Smithfield bar looks for all the world like an All Bar One, if one with the colour turned up. Adnams on draught and Bitburger on tap, DJs (on Fri) and some decent happy hour offers set it apart from the ubiquitous chain, however, and make it a comfortable place to spend an evening. / Details: Mon-Thu noon-11pm, Fri 11am-1am, closed weekends. Food: till 9pm. DJ: Fri. Happy hour: 5pm onwards (2 for 1 Becks, 6pm-8pm 2 for 1 vodka & Red Bull).

George
Great Eastern EC2

Liverpool St   7618 7300   9–2D

A Conran make-over has done little to detract from this impressive, traditional bar near Liverpool Street, with its thick glass, huge oils, and dark wood panelling. His influence is more on evidence in the dining room at the side (done out in a rather characterless modern style), serving simple British dishes. / Website: www.great-eastern-hotel.co.uk Food: L till 12.30pm, D till 9.30pm, Sat & Sun brunch noon-5pm.

George II (GII) SW11

339 Battersea Park Rd   7622 2112   10–1B

This vast Battersea gastropub may not be exactly inspired on the décor front, but that does nothing to dent its enormous local popularity – be prepared to shout. Part of the appeal is food that's well above the usual standards. / **Details:** *no Amex.* **Food:** *L till 3pm, D till 10pm, all day weekends.* **DJ:** *Fri-Sat from 8pm.*

George Inn SE1

77 Borough High St   7407 2056   9–3C

London's sole surviving galleried 17th-century coaching inn, off a cobbled courtyard near London Bridge, is owned by the National Trust, and leased to the Laurel Pub Company. The warren of bars and panelled drinking rooms were allegedly haunts of both Samuel Johnson and Shakespeare – as well as being mentioned by Dickens in Little Dorrit – so expect a crush of tourists most of the year. / **Website:** *www.georgeinn-southwark.co.uk* **Details:** *no-smoking area at lunch.* **Food:** *L till 3pm (weekends 4pm), D till 10pm.*

The Gipsy Moth SE10

60 Greenwich Church St   8858 0786   1–2D

This is the nearest public house to Greenwich's Cutty Sark and, although the exterior is rather unprepossessing, the interior is actually rather nice (and attracts a good following of locals, as well as tourists). There is a large and attractive garden, and the grub isn't at all bad, considering. / **Details:** *no-smoking area.* **Food:** *till 9.30pm.*

The Globe W11

103 Talbot Rd   7727 9559   6–1B

Seemingly styled after a Prohibition speakeasy, this offbeat joint is something between a bar and a club (you'll probably have to pay an entry charge of about a fiver), and best-known as a place to head after hours. An eclectic crowd pack into a no-frills, cramped setting and try to make themselves heard over the loud music. / **Details:** *late licence.*

Globe WC2

37 Bow St   7379 9896   4–2D

*An attractive Covent Garden pub whose unfussy but traditional, décor only hints at its Big Brewery ownership. Despite being sited directly opposite the ROH delivery entrance, it's something of an oasis of calm in this busy and touristy area. / **Food:** till 10pm.*

Goat In Boots SW10

333 Fulham Rd   7352 1384   5–3B

*Long before anyone christened the strip of road it occupies the 'Beach', it was trendy for younger folk to hang out – or, more especially, outside – this Chelsea boozer. New owners took over in 2002, but spiritually nothing's really changed – especially at the weekend or an warm evenings, this remains the place to join the younger locals at play. / **Food:** till 3pm, Sun all day. **DJ:** Fri-Sat. **Happy hour:** 5pm-7pm (changes daily).*

Golborne House W10

36 Golborne Rd   8960 6260   6–1A

*To most people, it's an ugly block of flats in a grotty (if up-and-coming) location, but to architecture-anoraks North Kensington's Trellick Tower is a masterpiece of 20th-century design. Whatever your viewpoint, this revamped boozer at its foot – decked out in a colourful, bare style – is well worth knowing about, and attracts a funky crowd. The cooking has quite a reputation. / **Website:** www.golbornehouse.co.uk **Details:** Fri & Sat noon-midnight; no Amex. **Food:** L till 3.45pm, D till 10.15pm.*

Goodge W1

62 Goodge St   7436 9448   3–1D

*This small cocktail bar – long and thin, and with a few tables outside – is one of the more pleasant rendezvous off the Tottenham Court Road, and is popular with the local media types for after-work drinks. The décor is more functional than anything else but it's attractive all the same. On Fridays, DJs spin funk and soul. / **Details:** Sat 6pm-11pm, closed Sun; no Amex. **Food:** L till 4pm, D till 10.30pm. **DJ:** Fri.*

The Goose & Firkin SE1

47-48 Borough Rd   7403 3590   9–3C

This incongruous-looking Southwark corner boozer was actually the original of the eccentric Firkin microbrewery company. It was set up in 1979, and avoided being sold into prostitution at the hands of the big breweries who rolled out the Firkin 'concept' so aggressively in the '80s and '90s. It is now owned by the estimable Shepherd Neame brewery, and there are plans to refurbish – and possibly re-name – the pub as we go to press. / **Website:** www.shepherd-neame.co.uk **Details:** Sat 6pm-11pm, closed Sun. **Food:** till 8.30pm. **DJ:** Sat.

Gordon's Wine Bar WC2

47 Villiers St   7930 1408   2–1D

London's oldest wine bar – in wonderfully gloomy candlelit cellars near Embankment tube – is accessed via an anonymous doorway, down a set of rickety stairs. It offers a good range of wines (and sherries, ports and Madeiras, but nothing else) at tolerable prices, plus rather expensive hot dishes and plates of bread and cheese. In summer, arrive early to bag one of the prized tables on what is one of the nicest terraces in the centre of town. / **Details:** no Amex. **Food:** till 10pm.

Goring Hotel SW1

15 Beeston Pl   7396 9000   2–3B

For an elegant experience in the environs of Victoria station, it's impossible to beat the bar of this quality hotel that's now heading for a century in the ownership of the same family. A walk on the wild side this is not, but if its comfort and civilisation you're after, few place's in town equal its calm and attention to detail. / **Website:** www.goringhotel.co.uk **Details:** no-smoking area. **Food:** till 11pm.

Grand Central EC2

93 Great Eastern St   7613 4228   9–1C

Anyone expecting architecture in the style of the NYC railroad station will be sorely disappointed by this groovily-decorated corner site in Shoreditch (formerly a bank). Its many local supporters, however, find it a great place to kick back, and down a beer or a cocktail. Food is available but, except on Sundays, it seems rather incidental. / **Website:** www.grandcentral.org.uk **Details:** Mon-Fri 7.30am-midnight, Sat 6pm-midnight, Sun 11am-5pm. **Food:** L&D (closed Sat L). **DJ:** Thu-Sun. **Happy hour:** Mon-Sat 5pm-7pm (varies).

Grand Union W9

45 Woodfield Rd   7286 1886   6–1B

*One of the newer Notting Hill's trustafarians' hang-outs, this very barely refurbished boozer – which makes quite a lot of its honest English cuisine – is in fact just 'over the canal', in Maida Hill. It seems to derive much of its alleged trendiness from the fact that it's under the same ownership as Woody's, the adjoining night club. Few would knock the attractions of its outside terrace in summer, however. / **Details:** no Amex. **Food:** L till 3pm (Sun 4pm), D till 10pm.*

La Grande Marque EC4

47 Ludgate Hill   7329 6709   9–2A

*A grand (and listed) Victorian bank building (with an impressive interior more evocative of Vienna than London) provides the setting for this superior wine bar, just down the hill from St Paul's. Champagne is quite a house speciality, but this doesn't mean they don't understand the concept of a bargain pricing – a bottle of '93 Dom Perignon, for example, will set you back a mere £99. (Beer drinkers don't despair – there's Bitburger on draft.) / **Details:** closed weekends. **Food:** L only.*

Ye Grapes W1

16 Shepherd Market   7499 1563   2–2B

*Cutesy Shepherd Market is arguably the most attractively higgledy-piggledy part of Mayfair (in general a rather stultifyingly grand part of town), and has a slightly racy reputation as a centre for high class prostitution. A location on its corner creates a characterful setting for this traditional and atmospheric Victorian boozer, which attracts a clientèle ranging from local suits to tourists. / **Details:** no Amex; no-smoking area.*

The Grapes E14

76 Narrow St   7987 4396   11–1B

*For our money the nicest of the historic East End riverside taverns – this quiet, characterful little pub (established 1583, rebuilt 1720) is a nice, no-nonsense place whose remote location (near the Limehouse Link) thankfully takes it off the tourist trail. Fish 'n' chips in the bar would be a great accompaniment to a pint of Adnam's. Or eat in the more formal seafood restaurant upstairs, which boasts impressive river views. / **Details:** Mon-Fri noon-3pm & 5.30pm-11pm. **Food:** till 9.15pm.*

Great Eastern Dining Room EC2

54-56 Great Eastern St   7613 4545   9–1D

Though (as the name hints) food is a main part of the operation, here, it's really its attractions as a groovy bar which put Will Ricker's (he of the increasingly-famous E&O) original venue on the map. It attracts a mature crowd by local standards, drawn by a combination of sophisticated styling and original cocktails (plus food that's not half bad). Downstairs in 'Below 54', the music is louder and the style more clubby.
/ **Website:** www.greateasterndining.co.uk **Details:** Mon-Fri noon-midnight, Sat 6pm-midnight, closed Sun. **Food:** till 10am-10.30pm. **DJ:** Thu-Sat.

The Grenadier SW1

18 Wilton Rw   7235 3074   5–1D

A storybook-perfect mews location contributes to the enormous popularity of this cute and ancient tavern, a stone's throw from Hyde Park Corner. It's in all the tourist guides and often packed to the rafters, but somehow manages to retain its charm. If you want to eat, there is a tiny and overcrowded restaurant, but those in the know settle for a Bloody Mary and a sausage (for both of which the place has quite a reputation). / **Food:** L till 2pm, D till 9pm (weekends L&D).

Ground Floor W11

186 Portobello Rd   7243 8701   6–1B

When Notting Hill was starting to turn trendy at the end of the '80s, this sofa-strewn lounge bar was one of the first to be converted from a terrifying gritty boozer into a cool hang-out for the growing ranks of Notting Hillbillies. You'd be hard pressed to tell it from many other modern bars these days, but vestiges of its glamorous past linger. And, yes it was in The Film. / **Details:** no credit cards. **Food:** L till 4pm, D till 11pm.

The Grouse & Claret SW1

14 Little Chester St   7235 3438   2–3B

Family-owned brewers Hall & Woodhouse are the proprietors of this smart backstreet boozer. Its modern building lacks the charms of some of its Belgravian competitors, but if you're looking for a quiet spot for a pint of Badger, it has much to recommend it. The Cellar Bar makes a reasonably atmospheric venue for a smaller party (and is handily located, a few minutes walk from Victoria). / **Details:** closed weekends; no Amex. **Food:** L till 2.30pm.

The Grove W6

83 Hammersmith Grove   8748 2966   7–1B

This large corner pub, on one of Hammersmith's nicer roads, received a bright modern makeover a few years ago. It's a favourite neighbourhood hang-out for a thirtysomething crowd, drawn by its airy, relaxed setting and a few nice outside tables in summer (plus good organic grub). Happy hour here is very civilised, with a deal on champagne in the early evening.
/ **Website:** www.groverestaurants.co.uk **Details:** Mon-Sat 11am-midnight, Sun 11am-10.30pm; no Amex. **Food:** L till 3pm, D till 11pm, bar snacks 4pm-6pm. **Happy hour:** 5pm-7pm (£10 off champagne).

The Guinea W1

30 Bruton Pl   7409 1728   3–2B

The tail wags the dog a bit at this Young's tavern (hidden away in a pretty Mayfair mews) – the bar is dwarfed in scale by the restaurant. Still, it makes a characterful, traditional spot for a pint of ale – if you have a big appetite and a gold card, the steaks served next door are pretty good too.
/ **Website:** www.youngs.co.uk **Details:** Sat 6.30pm-11pm, closed Sun. **Food:** L till 2.30pm, D till 10.30pm.

Ha! Ha!

43-51 Gt Titchfield St, W1   7580 7252   3–1C
6 Villiers St, WC2   7930 1263   2–1D
390 Muswell Hill Broadway, N10   8444 4722

These may be more of your classic 'female-friendly' chain-bars, but they have some handy locations (near Charing Cross and Oxford Circus), and are in our view preferable to the 'Pitchers' and 'Slugs' which infest the West End. Decent-enough grub, too.
/ **Website:** www.hahaonline.co.uk **Details:** Mon-Sat 11am-11pm, Sun 11am-10.30pm – N10 opens at 10am Sat & Sun – W1 closed Sat & Sun. **Food:** L&D. **DJ & Live music:** N10 most weekends.

(Ling Ling Bar) Hakkasan W1

8 Hanway Pl   7907 1888   4–1A

Despite its ultra-grungy location, off Tottenham Court Road, this beautifully-designed oriental basement bar/restaurant has been a smash hit with a chic (and decidedly prosperous) thirtysomething crowd. The cocktail bar is only a small part of the operation, but still makes a cool spot to hang out, and you can dine from the (relatively) inexpensive bar menu.
/ **Details:** Mon-Wed & Sun noon-1am, Thu-Sat noon-2am. **Food:** L till 3.00pm. **DJ:** nightly from 9pm.

Half Moon E1

213-223 Mile End Rd   7790 6810   1–1D

Formerly a theatre (and before that a chapel), this large Stepney Green site has been impressively refurbished by Wetherspoon's. Students from the local Queen Mary College form a large part of the clientèle, attracted by the decently-priced beers (all the usual suspects) and, in summer, the patio garden. / **Food:** *till 10pm.* **Happy hour:** *Mon pm (special offers).*

Half Moon SW15

93 Lower Richmond Rd   8780 9383   10–1A

A ten-minute walk from Putney Bridge, this large, agreeably seedy Young's pub is one of the better-known music pubs in the capital (having, in their day, hosted Van Morrison, The Stones, U2, Kate Bush, and so on…). Performances take place in the grotty rear room, but there's also quite a lot going on in the characterful front bar, which attracts a mix of students, musicians, and local Arthur Daley types (well the Winchester Club is just down the road). / **Website:** *www.halfmoon.co.uk, www.youngs.co.uk* **Details:** *no Amex.* **Food:** *till 9pm.*

The Halkin
Halkin Hotel SW1

5 Halkin St   7333 1234   2–2A

Nahm, a swanky Thai restaurant with an (undeserved, we think) Michelin star has been the main 'news' item of recent time at this discreet Belgravia hotel, not far from Hyde Park Corner. It has an elegant (if quite brightly-lit) bar, however, which is a useful spot for a chic cocktail if you're in these parts. / **Website:** *www.halkin.co.uk* **Details:** *Mon-Sat noon-midnight, Sun noon-11pm.* **Food:** *till 11pm.*

Hamilton Hall EC2

Liverpool St Stn   7247 3579   9–2D

If you want to drink in the environs of Liverpool Street while avoiding the Conran style (and pricing) of the many options at the Great Eastern Hotel, this large Wetherspoons – in a listed building, originally a ballroom – may be the place for you. Unsurprisingly, it gets regularly mobbed as the City drones head for home and notwithstanding its fine architecture can feel a bit soulless. / **Details:** *no-smoking area.* **Food:** *10am-10pm.*

Hand & Shears EC1

1 Middle St 7600 0257 9–2B

*The site of this classic Smithfield boozer dates its history back to the medieval Cloth Fair (hence the name), but the current building is a mere 450 years old. Today, it's a quiet spot, with an atmosphere from the days when pubs were men's territory, and had décor to match. / **Website:** www.hand&shears.com* **Details:** *closed weekends.* **Food:** *L till 3pm.*

Hare & Billet SE3

1A Hare & Billet Rd 8852 2352 1–3D

*Blackheath's oldest pub may not officially have a beer garden, but that has never stopped people pouring out onto the heath (just across the road) on a hot day. It's owned by Hogshead, but Belgian beers and classic pub grub make it a popular place with locals and visitors alike. / **Details:** no-smoking area.* **Food:** *till 7.30pm.*

Harringay Arms N8

153 Crouch Hill 8340 4243 8–1C

*This small and quiet early-Victorian Hornsey pub may have seen better days, but its lived-in appearance is part of its cosy charm, and there's a patio at the rear. It offers a fairly standard range of bitters (Directors, Courage Best, J Smiths) and lagers (Stella, Kronenbourg, Carlsberg). / **Details:** no credit cards.*

Hartfield's Wine Bar SW19

27 Hartfield Rd 8543 9788 10–2A

*Lost on a corner, in the middle of Wimbledon Town's one-way system (not far from the BR station), this cheerful, low-key wine bar is one of the few watering holes of any quality in the area. It defies its grotty location with a fair selection of vinos and some decent snacks and more substantial food. / **Website:** www.hartfields.com* **Details:** *Mon-Thu noon-11pm, Sat 6pm-midnight, closed Sun.* **Food:** *L till 2.30pm (Mon-Fri), D 6pm-10pm.*

Harwood Arms SW6

Walham Grove 7386 1847 10–1A

*It's a welcome surprise to find this cheerful backstreet boozer – lost in the maze of roads north of Fulham Broadway, which has been tarted up in contemporary style, but remains quite a cosy place. It serves Young's bitters, and a reasonable range of lagers. / **Details:** no Amex.* **Food:** *L till 2.45pm, D till 9.45pm.*

Havana

17 Hanover Sq, W1   7629 2552   3–2B
490 Fulham Broadway, SW6   7381 5005   10–1A

A loud, brash Latino chain (of which the Fulham outpost has just had a major refit), whose attractions include happy hour, salsa tuition most nights (modest charge), late opening and fairly inexpensive cocktails. After your tuition, you can strut your stuff until the wee hours. / **Details:** *W1 5pm-2am, Fri & Sat 5pm-3am, Sun 6pm-1am – SW6 11am-2am, Sun noon-12.30am.* **Food:** *L&D, tapas after midnight.* **Happy hour:** *5pm-7.30pm (half-price jugs of cocktails, £5 off bottle of wine).*

The Havelock Tavern W14

57 Masbro Rd   7603 5374   7–1B

The obscure location in an Olympia backstreet is inversely proportional to the enormous popularity of this excellent gastropub. Despite its foodie credentials, though, this is still a good place for a pint, with Boddingtons Bitter and a wide range of lagers on tap. Arrive early if you want a table.
/ **Website:** *www.thehavelocktavern.co.uk* **Details:** *no credit cards.* **Food:** *L till 2.30pm, D till 10pm.*

The Head of Steam NW1

1 Eversholt St   7383 3359   8–3C

Close to Euston station this modern pub attracts – hardly shock news this – mainly a commuter crowd (and is suitably decorated with railway memorabilia). It has its attractions, though – the mezzanine area is non-smoking, and there's an unusually large range of bitters and some good lagers on draught. / **Details:** *no Amex; no-smoking area.* **Food:** *L till 2.30pm, D till 8pm.*

Heeltap & Bumper

Off Bury Pl, Bloomsbury, WC1   7404 7404
White Hart Yd, Borough High St, SE1   7407 2829
2 Paul St, EC2   7247 3319
2-6 Cannon St, EC4   7248 3371

This small, City-based chain of shiny 'concept bars' is brought to you by Davy's wine merchants. The Borough branch has outside seating within the splendid courtyard of the historic George Inn (see also), and the St Paul's branch (EC4) has great views of the Cathedral. None of the locations are open at weekends.
/ **Website:** *www.davy.co.uk* **Details:** *11am-11pm (EC2 Mon & Tue 9pm), closed Sat & Sun.* **Food:** *L&D & bar snacks.*

Heights Bar
St George's Hotel W1
Langham Pl   7580 0111   3–1C
While the vista falls short of being truly amazing, there's only so little you can see from the 15th floor of a central London building, and it lends a sense of occasion to a trip to this cocktail lounge (atop a '60s hotel by Broadcasting House). Some people quite like the interior (revamped a few years ago) – others suggest you keep your eyes firmly fixed on the horizon. / **Food:** till 10pm. **Happy hour:** 8-9pm (wine, beer & cocktails half-price).

Henry J Beans
195 King's Rd, SW3   7352 9255   5–3C
273 Camden High St, NW1   7482 0767   8–3B
Beer, burgers and cocktails on a Mexican theme are what this chain of bars is all about. The Chelsea branch listed is of particular note – not because of the interior (which is typically theme-y), but because it has a huge, attractive (and completely unexpected) garden, which draws a crowd on sunny days. / **Website:** www.henryjbeans.com **Details:** vary. **Food:** L&D. **DJ:** Fri-Sun. **Happy hour:** Mon-Fri 5pm-8pm, Sun 5pm-close (house spirits £1, bottle of wine £7.50).

Highgate NW5
79 Highgate Rd   7485 8442   8–2B
This large and loud new gastropub – once a carpet showroom – has been a big hit, up Kentish Town way, and its ground floor bar is busy pretty much every evening. The basement restaurant offers the opportunity to sample much of the atmosphere – and a bit less of the noise – which you consume some good (and substantial) grub. / **Details:** Mon-Fri noon-11pm, Sat noon-midnight.

The Hillgate Arms W8
24 Hillgate St   7727 8543   6–2B
Hillgate Village – as estate agents call the little enclave just south of Notting Hill Gate – is, in its quiet way, one of the cutest spots in town. At its heart, this pretty traditional boozer is one of those rare civilised traditional pubs, and it's regularly crowded with well-heeled locals, cinema-goers and so on. There are a couple of tables and benches on the pavement outside. / **Website:** www.massivepub.com **Details:** no Amex. **Food:** till 10pm.

Hobgoblin

272 New Cross Rd, SE14   8692 3193   1–2D
95 Effra Rd, SW2   7738 4959   10–2C
Students and footie fans are two key elements of the target market for this national chain of largish, friendly pubs which major in big screen TVs and special offers for four-pint pitchers of ale. Of the two south east London branches listed, both have good gardens (New Cross especially, which also benefits from a large conservatory). Their draft bitters include IPA, Bombardier and Pedigree – for lager lovers there's Stella, Fosters and Kronenbourg. / **Details:** *SW2 Mon-Thu 2pm-midnight, Fri & Sat noon-2am, Sun noon-11pm; SE14 Mon-Sat 11am-11pm, Sun noon-10.30pm; SE14 no Visa, SW2, no Amex.* **Food:** *SE14 Mon-Fri till 8.30pm, Sat till 4.30pm, Sun till 4pm.* **Happy hour:** *SE14 Mon-Fri 2pm-8pm (20% off for students only).*

Hodgson's Wine Bar WC2

115 Chancery Ln   7404 5027   9–2A
In the slightly desolate part of the legal quarter, by Fleet Street, this cellar wine bar is a local favourite. Tables are widely spaced by wine bar standards, making it a good place for people who want to be able to talk (or gossip). The bar food is quite substantial (and the pretty restaurant upstairs offers a relatively inexpensive menu in the evenings). / **Website:** *www.115.uk.com* **Details:** *closed weekends.* **Food:** *till 10.50pm.*

Hollands W11

6 Portland Rd   7229 3130   6–2A
This small old-fashioned restaurant-cum-wine bar, just off leafy Holland Park Avenue, is generally something of a locals' delight. It's a also a popular destination for those seeking a reasonable smart, but not too pricey, venue for an informal party. / **Details:** *Mon-Sun noon-12.30am; no-smoking area.* **Food:** *L till 3pm, D till 11pm.* **Happy hour:** *noon-7pm (£2 off wine & champagne).*

The Holly Bush NW3

22 Holly Mount   7435 2892   8–1A
This 18th-century tavern, owned by Taylor Walker, is pretty much unchanged to the present day (well ok, the gas-lighting has been adapted to electric lighting) and enjoys one of the most picturesque locations in London – in a warren of streets and walkways, up a stone staircase from Hampstead's Heath Street. On a summer day, you can stand on the pavement outside. / **Details:** *no Amex.* **Food:** *L till 4.30pm, D till 10pm.*

Holy Drinker SW11

59 Northcote Rd, Clapham Junction 7801 0544 10–2B
*Intimate lighting, chilled music, candles and a brace of open
fires contribute much to the atmosphere of this Battersea bar,
which has been very successful in attracting the local would-be
Bohemian crowd. The array of drinks is impressive: sixteen ales
and lagers (including organic and microbrewery beers),
five vodkas, ten rums, seven malts (the list goes on) and a
carefully picked selection of wines and Champagnes.*
/ **Details:** Mon-Fri from 4.30pm, Sun 1pm-10.30pm; no Amex.

Home EC2

100-106 Leonard St 7684 8618 9–1D
*When it opened (then just in the basement) this funky
bar/restaurant – spacious, and with lots of sofas – was about
the coolest thing ever to have hit Shoreditch. It's now expanded
– with a stylish ground-floor restaurant (good scoff) –
and settled into a fun and still-fashionable stride.*
/ **Website:** www.homebar.co.uk **Details:** Mon-Fri 5pm-midnight,
Sat 6pm-midnight, closed Sun; no-smoking area. **Food:** 6pm-10pm. **DJ:** Fri-Sat.

The Hoop & Grapes EC3

47 Aldgate High St 7265 5171 9–2D
*You haven't drunk too much! – the windows at the front of this
ancient building, just about the only timber-framed City building
to survive the Great Fire – really are at a crazy angle.
The place is not perhaps as hugely atmospheric as the
description of its ancient heritage might lead you to believe
(not helped by a very trafficked location), but it's a characterful
traditional boozer nonetheless.* / **Details:** closed weekends; no smoking.
Food: L till 3pm.

Hop Cellars SE1

Southwark St 7403 6851 9–3C
*Set within the cellars of the characterful 19th-century Hop
Exchange, this Southwark wine bar offers an extensive wine list.
The cosy premises – handy for Tate Modern – have the
trademark scrubbed appeal of many Balls Brothers
establishments, with low, barrelled ceilings and stone floors.
Gourmet sandwiches and light bites are available.*
/ **Details:** Mon-Fri till 10pm, closed weekends. **Food:** till 8.45pm.

Hope W1

15 Tottenham St   7637 0896   3–1D
*Just round the corner from Goodge Street tube, this attractive
pub is a good traditional all-rounder, serving a range of ales,
and dishes such as the 'sausage of the week' range.*
/ **Details:** *Sun noon-6pm; no Amex.* **Food:** *till 6pm.*

Hope & Anchor N1

207 Upper St   7354 1312   8–2D
*DJs and live musicians provide music nightly at this darkly-
revamped Greene King Islington boozer (where many of the big
names of New Wave and Punk – The Clash, The Stranglers,
The Cure – cut their musical teeth in years gone by). Upstairs,
you have the option of playing pool or table football.*
/ **Details:** *Mon-Sat noon-1am, Sun noon-midnight; no Amex.* **Food:** *till 4pm
(weekends 7pm).* **DJ:** *Fri-Sat.* **Live music:** *bands nightly.*

Hope & Sir Loin EC1

94 Cowcross St   7253 8525   9–1B
*Being in the environs of Smithfield Market, this famous boozer
has long been able – thanks to the local licensing laws to serve
alcohol from early in the day. It's a perfectly pleasant place at
any time, but it's for a fry-up with a pint – served in the first-
floor dining room – that it's of particular note.* / **Details:** *Mon-Fri
7am-4pm, closed weekends.* **Food:** *L only.*

The Horniman at Hay's SE1

Hays Galleria, Tooley St   7407 1991   9–3C
*This large, high-ceilinged bar near London Bridge, occupies the
Thames-side frontage of atmospheric Hay's Galleria and enjoys
a view of HMS Belfast. Office workers (from, among others,
the funky new GLA building) and riverside walkers seem to
make up the majority of customers.* / **Details:** *no-smoking area.*
Food: *L till 5pm, bar snacks till 9pm.*

Horse SE1

124 Westminster Bridge   7928 6277   2–2D
*The area around Lambeth North tube is not especially rich in
nice places to drink, so this oddly-named relaunch of an
atmospheric old boozer is good news locally. With its open
kitchen, the place has some pretensions to gastropub status,
but it's of just as much interest to those simply looking for a
pleasant place to sink a pint or a glass of wine.* / **Details:** *Sat
6pm-11pm, closed Sun; no Amex.* **Food:** *L till 3pm, D till 10.30pm.*

Horse & Groom SW1

7 Groom Pl 7235 6980 2–3A

*Pubs don't come much more storybook-perfect that this charming, villagey-feeling boozer in a Belgravia mews, owned – appropriately enough – by Shepherd Neame (which claims to be England's oldest brewery). In spite of its charms, it seems well off the tourist beat – just as well as its (rather brightly-lit) interior is on the compact side. / **Details:** closed weekends. **Food:** L till 3pm.*

Hoxton Square Bar & Kitchen N1

2-4 Hoxton Sq 7613 0709 9–1D

*It's not just a location on the square itself which makes this large bar a key Hoxton destination. Bare concrete décor is softened by subdued lighting and a cool crowd lounging on the plentiful supply of sofas. The sound system puts out anything from Reggae to Metal, but usually at a volume where conversation is feasible. Other attractions include a good selection of spirits and draft lagers (for example Erdinger or Afdelingen), plus simple snacks. The pleasant outside terrace is a prime summer posing spot. / **Details:** Mon-Sat 11am-midnight, Sun 11am-10.30pm. **Food:** till 10pm.*

100 Pub SW4

100 Clapham Park Rd 7720 8902 10–2C

*On the Clapham/Brixton borders, a woodily-furnished, trendy but relaxed pub that attracts a friendly, local, young crowd. For the most part, they're larger drinkers to a man (or woman), with the selection offered including Stella, Heineken, Grolsch, Hoegaarden and Staropramen. On a sunny day the outside tables are especially popular. / **Website:** www.100pub.com **Details:** Mon-Fri from 4.30pm; no Amex. **Food:** Sun noon-7pm. **Happy hour:** Mon-Fri 4.30pm-7pm (cocktails £1).*

Hush W1

8 Lancashire Ct 7659 1500 3–2B

*Part-ownership by Roger Moore's son has done no harm at all to the PR profile of this expensively trendy bar (plus brasserie and restaurant) discreetly located just off, er, Bond Street. Given the St Tropez/Verbier crowd the place attracts, 007 would indeed feel right at home. They don't do a bad Martini either. / **Website:** www.hush.co.uk **Details:** closed Sun. **Food:** L&D.*

ICAfé SW1

The Mall   7930 3647   2–2C

Situated in an imposing building near Admiralty Arch, this pleasant café/bar is well worth knowing about as an alternative to the nearby tourist-traps with the added bonus that is it open until 1am Tue-Sat. You will have to take out day membership of the ICA (£1.50 on weekdays and £2.50 at weekends), but you are quite likely to get a table. You can always combine your visit with a look at their latest cutting-edge modern art installations, but go before you've had a drink so you know what you're seeing owes nothing to alcohol.
/ **Website:** www.ica.org.uk **Details:** noon-1am (Mon 10.30pm); no-smoking area. **Food:** Tue-Sat 5pm-11pm, Mon-5pm-10.30pm, Sun brunch noon-4pm. **DJ:** Sun & Mon. **Live music:** bands Thu.

Ifield SW10

59 Ifield Rd   7351 4900   5–3A

It doesn't have the very best location – off one of west London's busiest roads – but this comfortable corner gastropub is one of the nicer places to hang out on the Earl's Court/Chelsea fringes, whether or not you're intending to sample the simple but good cooking. / **Details:** Mon-Thu from 5pm. **Food:** L&D.

Iguacu SW6

486 Fulham Broadway   7381 2372   10–1A

New to Fulham Broadway, this cosy café (at the back) and bar (at the front) is a mellow place. Candles in bottles, and painted bricks create a wine bar ambience, but its South American inspirations and focus on world music (with the odd live DJ) helps create a slightly 'different' atmosphere. There's quite a range of booze – beer, wines, spirits and cocktails – and also a full restaurant service. / **Details:** management declined to provide information.

The Imperial Arms SW6

577 King's Rd   7736 8549   10–1A

Funkily converted, this Fulham boozer – with its red walls and Chesterfield sofas – benefits from a warm and welcoming ambience (in spite of some slightly bizarre nautical murals). Other reasons to know of it include a pleasant courtyard; some quite substantial food; and a fair range of bitters and lagers. / **Details:** no Amex. **Food:** L till 2.30pm (weekends till 3pm), D till 9.30pm. **Happy hour:** 3pm-7pm (beer £2.50, spirits reduced).

The Independence N1
235 Upper St   7704 6977   8–2D
Recently converted, this panelled Islington boozer towards the top end of Upper Street – a sibling to Bloomsbury's popular Perseverance – makes a virtue of uncompromising plainness. If you go for that spare look, though, it's a congenial location, and offers a range of good, simple cooking, plus a range of brews that's stronger on lager than bitter. / **Details:** *Mon-Tue 4pm-midnight, Wed-Fri 4pm-2am, Sat noon-2am, Sun noon-1am.* **Food:** *L till 4pm, D till 10pm.* **DJ:** *Thu-Sun.*

Inigo SW8
642 Wandsworth Rd   7622 4884   10–1B
With a style that's both funky (there's a bean bag corner) and cosy, this Clapham bar has been quite a hit with local twentysomethings. Chunky dark-wood furniture, candles and a real fire contribute the atmosphere. Lager is probably the drink of choice (though there's also a fair degree of cocktail consumption). / **Details:** *Mon-Fri 6pm-2am, Sat & Sun noon-2am; no Amex.* **DJ:** *nightly 8pm-2am (house).* **Happy hour:** *before 9pm (shooters £1).*

The Interval WC2
14-15 Irving St   7925 1801   2–1C
Drinking (and eating) round Leicester Square tends to be such a naff experience that it's difficult to believe that this smart, spacious and loungey bar/restaurant is for real. It's rapidly established itself as a really useful West End rendezvous, whether you're intent on a night's clubbing, or just going to the flicks. / **Food:** *11am-9pm.* **DJ:** *Fri-Sat.*

The Intrepid Fox W1
97-99 Wardour St   7494 0827   3–2D
It helps to have a liking for heavy metal, if you plan on dropping in to this atmospheric, well-known boozer in central Soho, famed as a hang out for Goths and Metal freaks and whose décor looks a bit like cast off lots from a horror movie. If you're not into body art, you can pay closer than usual attention to a pint of Worthingtons or Grolsch. / **Website:** *www.intrepidfox.com* **Details:** *Sun from 3pm; no credit cards.*

Ion Bar W10

161-165 Ladbroke Grove   8960 1702   6–1A

Ownership by the Mean Fiddler group helps explain both the importance of music and the sleekness of the styling at this rather unexpected venue – underneath the Westway by Ladbroke Grove tube. It's on two floors, though the mezzanine operates as a restaurant (except at busier times, when it is annexed by drinkers and clubbers). DJs put the emphasis on soul, funk and disco. / **Website:** www.meanfiddler.com **Details:** *Mon-Sun noon-midnight.* **Food:** *bar snacks all day, D 6pm-11pm.* **DJ:** *nightly from 8pm.* **Happy hour:** *Mon-Fri noon-6.30pm (20% discount on all drinks).*

The Islington Tup N1

80 Liverpool Rd   7354 4440   8–3D

If you're familiar with the Tup formula you'll pretty much know what to expect at this corner boozer, which has a handy location not far from Chapel Street market chain. It's bright, stripped-down corner premises, however, make it one of the nicer boozers in a congenial group. / **Website:** www.massivepub.com **Food:** *L till 3pm, D till 10pm (Sat 9pm).*

Isola SW1

145 Knightsbridge   7838 1044   5–1D

Is this the plushest drinking space in London? With its imposing, chrome columns, it seems almost like a cathedral to the god of alcohol, enjoying much more success as a glossy Knightsbridge cocktail bar than it ever did during its short-lived stint as a dining room (its original purpose, when it was built in the late '90s). In the basement an Italian eatery is done out in more '60s style – or at least how they might have done things then if there had been as much money sloshing about. / **Details:** *Mon-Sat 6pm-midnight, closed Sun; no-smoking area.* **Food:** *L till 2.45pm, D till 10.45pm.*

Itsu SW3

118 Draycott Ave   7584 5522   5–2C

This popular branch of the smart sushi-conveyor chain is a well-known destination for a light bite, or for a pleasant respite from shopping at nearby Brompton Cross. What's perhaps rather less well known is that, upstairs, there's a small stand-alone bar – a comfortable venue for a discreet cocktail. / **Website:** www.itsu.co.uk **Details:** *Mon-Fri from 6.30pm, Sat 12.30pm-3pm & 6.30pm-11pm, Sun 6.30pm-11pm.* **Food:** *till 11pm.*

Jamaica Wine House EC3

St Michael's Alley   7626 9496   9–2C

Traditionalists were nervous at the recent makeover of this back alley bastion of olde London (on the site of what was the City's first coffee house), but they needn't have sweated. The revamp (by the 'Tup' people) is in good taste, and if the lighting around the bar wasn't so slick it might be hard to work out that anything had changed. There's a good range of lagers and bitters (which, on a good day, you can drink outside), and also quite an emphasis on wine. / **Website:** www.massivepub.com **Details:** *closed weekends; no Amex.* **Food:** *till 3pm.*

Jamie's

58-59 Poland St, W1   7287 6666
74 Charlotte St, W1   7636 7556
50-54 Kingsway, WC2   7405 9749
28 Westferry Circus, Canary Wharf, E14   7536 2861
10 Whitechapel High St, E1   7265 1977
43-44 Cloth Fair, EC1   7600 7778
64-66 West Smithfield, EC1   7600 0700
155 Bishopsgate, EC2   7256 7279
54 Gresham St, EC2   7606 1755
107-112 Leadenhall St, EC3   7626 7226
119-121 Minories, EC3   7709 9900
13 Philpot Ln, EC3   7621 9577
The Pavilion, Finsbury Circus Gdns, EC3   7628 8224
34 Ludgate Hill, EC4   7489 1938
5 Groveland Ct, EC4   7248 5551

This City-based chain of wine bars make useful – if often bland – destinations. Notable branches include the Pavilion (in a quirky hut overlooking a bowling green at Finsbury Circus), Canary Wharf, (which has great river views) and the diminutive Cloth Fair site (near Bart's) is quite charming, too. The 2002 take-over by the Hartford Group (Canyon, Dakota etc) may shake things up a bit. / **Website:** www.jamiesbars.co.uk **Details:** *11am-11pm, some branches closed at weekends.* **Food:** *L&D & bar snacks.*

Jerusalem W1

33-34 Rathbone Pl   7255 1120   3–1D

A bit of a surprise in the street by the Royal Mail sorting office, just north of Oxford Street, this candlelit basement bar has a thoroughly ecclesiastical feel, with long tables and old church pews. In business for a few years, it remains quite trendy destination, thanks in part to DJs, playing – depending on the night – a mixture of dance, house & Latino funk.
/ **Website:** www.thebreakfastgroup.co.uk **Details:** Thu-Sat noon-1am, closed Sun. **Food:** till 9.30pm.

The Jerusalem Tavern EC1

55 Britton St   7490 4281   9–1B

The sole London outpost of a highly respected Suffolk brewery – St Peter's – this tiny Clerkenwell bar (dating back to 1720) is an ale-lover's paradise, and a charming spot in which to while away a few hours. All of the company's (excellent) cask and bottled ales are available, from the light Golden Ale to the old-style Porter. Bar snacks are available at lunchtime.
/ **Details:** closed weekends. **Food:** L only.

Jorene Celeste N1

153 Upper St   7226 0808   8–3D

This large former pub in Islington has been done out in a style presumably designed to evoke the Rive Gauche, circa 1950. The flaw in the logic – Parisians never having 'got' the pub concept – is obvious, but, especially at quiet times, this makes for a comfortable place for a tête-à-tête.

Jugged Hare SW1

172 Vauxhall Bridge Rd   7828 1543   2–3B

A former bank building provides the impressive setting for this ornately decorated Fullers pub. It's not the best boozer in the world, but if you were looking for the best pub in the world, you'd probably give the Pimlico/Westminster borders a wide berth. It is, however, a congenial-enough rendezvous, within a few minutes' walk of Victoria station. / **Website:** www.fullers.co.uk **Details:** no-smoking area. **Food:** till 10pm (Sat 9pm, Sun 8pm).

Julie's Bar W11
135 Portland Rd   7727 7985   6–2A
With its lavish, eclectic décor, this long-established Holland Park wine bar (next to Julies restaurant) is one of the most enduringly popular in town. It's a comfortable and characterful place with a nice outside terrace, all of which helps to justify its rather hefty prices (especially for the food). Wine, and especially champagne, is the tipple of choice, but there's also a selection of cocktails. / **Website:** www.juliesrestaurant.com **Details:** Mon-Sat 9am-11.30pm, Sun 9am-11pm. **Food:** L till 2.45pm, D till 10.30pm (Sun 9.30pm).

Just Oriental SW1
19 King St   7930 9292   2–2B
Apart from the style of the bar snacks, there's not really much oriental about this St James's basement cocktail bar. It is, however, well worth knowing about as one of the more spacious and comfortable bars around St James (and younger in appeal than many of the places in the area). / **Website:** www.juststjames.com **Details:** Sat 6pm-11pm, closed Sun. **Food:** till 11pm.

Kettners W1
29 Romilly St   7734 6112   4–2A
This grand Soho landmark (founded in 1867 by the ex-chef of Napoleon III) has had a chequered recent history as a grand pizzeria. However, it's now been purchased by PizzaExpress, who look set to restore its former glory (decoratively speaking at least). The atmospheric small Champagne bar to the left of the entrance has quite a following, and there is also a wine bar. A pianist adds much to the charm of the place. / **Details:** Mon-Sun 10am-midnight. **Food:** L&D.

The King's Arms WC1
11 Northington St   7405 9107   4–1C
A nice plain boozer, just north of Gray's Inn, that's cheered by red velvet curtains, a real fire in winter, and some proper bitters (which can be accompanied by simple pub grub). It's a popular destination with those who work locally. Upstairs, there's a non-smoking bar. / **Details:** closed weekends; no-smoking area. **Food:** L till 3pm.

King's Head N1

115 Upper St 7226 0364 8–2D

Very fine and very Victorian, this superbly unmucked-about-with hostelry is an unchanging fixture in Islington's ever-changing pub scene. The lofty ground-floor bar has regular live music and a pleasant, slightly studenty feel. Drinks are served until midnight. To the rear, what is claimed to be London's first pub-theatre (tel 7226 1916) puts on performances of some note.

/ **Details:** no credit cards. **Food:** L till 3pm.

King's Head SW6

4 Fulham High St 7736 1413 10–1A

It's for the live music nightly that you'd seek out this studenty-feeling pub near the end of the Fulham Road (which boasts Jimmy Page, Sting, and Toploader as amongst its "discoveries"). The competing attractions in its brightly-lit side bar include pool, darts and pinball. / **Details:** no credit cards.

The Knights Templar WC2

95 Chancery Ln 7831 2660 9–2A

The main banking hall of this former branch of the NatWest now houses a large bar that's part of the ever-expanding Wetherspoon's empire. An impressive Georgian building, it's very popular with the local legal beagles, and can get very busy, especially at lunchtimes. / **Details:** Mon-Fri 10am-11pm, Sat 11am-7pm, closed Sun; no-smoking area. **Food:** till 10pm.

Ku De Ta
Café Royal W1

9 Glasshouse St 7439 7770 3–3D

Entered from behind the Café Royal (but part of the same building), this swankily designed modern bar lives somewhat in the shadow of its better-known basement neighbour Elysium (see also). At least you don't have to pay to enjoy a cocktail here, and if you want to round off the evening with a visit to the club, the bar has its own entrance.

/ **Website:** www.elysiumlounge.co.uk **Details:** Mon-Tue 11am-1am, Wed-Sat 11am-3am, closed Sun. **Food:** L till 4pm, Mon & Tue D till 1am, Wed & Sat D till 3am. **Happy hour:** 5pm-7pm.

Kudos WC2
10 Adelaide St   7379 4573   2–1C
Just north of Trafalgar Square, this chilled gay bar on two levels has attracted a diverse and friendly crowd for over a decade. The ground floor has a glass frontage (which is opened completely during summer) where les boyz check you out checking them out. Downstairs is slightly more intimate with alcoves, low lighting and video screens.
/ **Website:** www.kudosgroup.com **Details:** no-smoking area. **Food:** L only.
DJ: Wed & occasionally Fri-Sat. **Live music:** occasional jazz night.
Happy hour: Mon-Sun 6pm-7pm (Fosters, Red Stripe, Red Square or Fosters Ice £2.50).

Lab W1
12 Old Compton St   7437 7820   4–2A
The London Academy of Bartending, no less. As you'd therefore expect, flashy 'mixology' is taken seriously at this retro Soho spot – there's an impressive tome listing the resulting cocktails, from classics to 'visionaries' (and even 'experiments'). Beyond the tiny, dark ground floor room there's another (equally cosy) bar downstairs that has regular DJs. / **Website:** www.lab-bar.com
Details: Mon-Sat 4pm-midnight, Sun 4pm-10.30pm. **Food:** till midnight (Sun till 10.30pm). **DJ:** Mon-Sat.

The Ladbroke Arms W11
54 Ladbroke Rd   7727 6648   6–2B
This excellent, hidden-away pub, a short walk from Notting Hill Gate, is a cosy and welcoming place, with a particular reputation for its food, and a good choice of wines too. Despite its quiet side-street location, it's busy enough at the best of times, and especially so in summer when the small but very nice terrace is full to overflowing. / **Details:** no Amex. **Food:** L till 2.30pm (weekends till 3pm), D till 9.45pm.

The Lamb WC1
94 Lamb's Conduit St   7405 0713   2–1D
Just south of Coram's Fields in Bloomsbury, this Young's pub is the epitome of a friendly, cosy, traditional, no-nonsense place. As well as a particularly fine Victorian interior, there's an all-year back patio with heaters. / **Website:** www.youngs.co.uk
Details: Sun noon-4pm & 7pm-10.30pm; no Amex; no-smoking area.
Food: till 8.45pm.

The Lamb & Flag WC2

33 Rose St   7497 9504   4–3C
This ancient (late-17th century) and extremely atmospheric Covent Garden tavern couldn't really be much more central, and it's hugely popular as a West End rendezvous. It has a particularly nice small courtyard at the front, which is full to bursting on sunny days. / **Details:** *no credit cards.* **Food:** *L till 3pm.* **Happy hour:** *Mon-Fri 11am-5pm (Courage Best/Youngs £2).*

The Lamb Tavern EC3

10-12 Leadenhall Mkt   7626 2454   9–3D
With a splendid location at the heart of a magnificent covered Victorian market, this is one of the City's better traditional pubs. Inside there are a number of rooms including an elegant first-floor room (one of the few no-smoking bars in the City) and a basement 'Wine bar and Smoking Room', with impressive tiled Edwardian décor. / **Website:** *www.youngs.co.uk* **Details:** *Mon-Fri 11am-9.30pm, closed weekends; no-smoking area at lunch.* **Food:** *11am-2.30pm.*

The Landmark Hotel NW1

222 Marylebone Rd   7631 8000   6–1C
This incredible Victorian building (one of the world's first railway hotels) has in more recent times been given a soaring central atrium, complete with palm trees, that seems a very distant setting from grey old Marylebone. If you're after a grand and relaxing location for a drink, it's hard to better. / **Website:** *www.landmarklondon.co.uk* **Details:** *Mon-Fri 11.30am-midnight, Sat 5pm-midnight, closed Sun; no-smoking area.* **Food:** *till 10pm.*

(The Library) Lanesborough Hotel W1

1 Lanesborough Pl, Hyde Pk Corner   7259 5599   5–1D
The Library Bar of this landmark hotel is arguably its finest room, with the OTT Empire style in which the building is furnished coming off here particularly well – the darkly lit, richly coloured interior has a sumptuousness that puts to shame many a St James's club. If you're really looking to spend, celebrated barman Salvatore Calabrese offers the capital's most comprehensive range of cognacs. / **Website:** *www.lanesborough.co.uk* **Details:** *Mon-Sat 11am-1am, Sun noon-10.30pm.* **Food:** *till 12.30am.*

The Langley WC2

5 Langley St   7836 5005   4–2C

Early in the week, these retro cellars make a funky place for a truly central rendezvous (just a step away from Covent Garden tube). Closer to the weekend, however, you'll have difficulty hearing yourself talk (let alone getting in), as crowds of frenzied office guys and gals apply themselves to the serious task of getting plastered on half-price happy hour cocktails.
/ **Website:** www.latenightlondon.co.uk **Details:** Mon-Sat 4.30pm-1am, Sun 3pm-10.30pm. **Food:** from 5pm. **DJ:** Thu-Sat. **Happy hour:** Mon-Fri 5pm-7pm (all wine (except house) & cocktails half-price, £10 off champagne).

Lansdowne NW1

90 Gloucester Ave   7483 0409   8–3B

Like its nearby rival The Engineer (which it pre-dated by a few months) this chilled Primrose Hill gastropub is a mainstay of hip north London life. The imaginative cooking is every bit as good as down the road (in fact a little cheaper) and its the perfect place for designer-stubbled trendies to ostentatiously work off a hangover. It gets very crowded. / **Details:** no Amex. **Food:** L till 3pm, D till 10pm (Sun 9.30pm).

Latitude SW3

163 Draycott Ave   7589 8464   5–2C

For a drink post-Brompton Cross shopping, locations don't come much handier than this would-be stylish cocktail bar. We've never quite seen the attraction, but it's been in business for a few years now, so we have to assume it's doing something right.
/ **Details:** Mon-Sat 5pm-11.15pm, Members only Tue-Sat 10pm-1am. **Food:** 5pm-10.30pm.

Latymers W6

157 Hammersmith Rd   8748 3446   7–2B

It looks like any other boozer, and for a drink there's no special reason to seek out this large Fuller's pub, on a busy stretch of road near the Hammersmith roundabout. At the back of the saloon, though, is a small Thai dining room, which serves some of the best value oriental scoff in town. / **Details:** closed Sun; no smoking in restaurant. **Food:** L&D.

Laughing Gravy SE1
154 Blackfriars Rd 7721 7055 9–3A
This friendly Southwark wine bar/bistro is somewhat oddly located, a few minutes' walk south of The Cut, but it has attracted a solid local following, thanks to its winning combination of a friendly welcome, good (and inexpensive) wines and decent food – you can eat in the restaurant or, more cheaply, in the bar. The name, as you'll know, comes from a Prohibition-era nickname for alcohol. / **Details:** *Sat 6.30pm-11pm, closed Sun; no Amex.* **Food:** *L&D.*

Lay & Wheeler EC3
33 Cornhill 7626 0044 9–2C
The modern woody style of this City bar may not be instantly distinctive, but the big reputation of the Colchester wine merchants who opened it a couple of years ago has helped make it instantly popular. There's also a decent mezzanine restaurant. / **Website:** *www.lwwinebars.com* **Details:** *Mon-Fri till 10pm, closed weekends.* **Food:** *L till 2.30pm, D till 8.30pm.*

Leadenhall Wine Bar EC3
27 Leadenhall Mkt 7623 1818 9–2D
This attractive City wine bar (benefits from a charming view from the eaves of the wonderful Victorian market) and makes a slightly 'different' City rendezvous, with a good array of tapas-style dishes on offer at lunch (and snacks available in the evening). / **Details:** *closed weekends.* **Food:** *till 10pm.*

Leather Bottle SW17
538 Garratt Ln 8946 2309 10–2A
Summer sees this Earlsfield boozer, opposite Wandsworth cemetery, really come into its own – there's a patio, beer garden, children's playground and regular barbecues. However, the interior is also a suitably cosy space in which to brave the winter months, buoyed up by Young's beers and hearty grub. / **Website:** *www.youngs.co.uk* **Details:** *no Amex.* **Food:** *L till 2.30pm, D till 8pm.*

The Legless Tup SW6

1 Harwood Tce   7610 6131   10–1A
*Near the more distant of the two 'kinks' in the King's Road, this attractive, modernified backstreet boozer draws a local Fulham crowd who sup on a fair range of bitters (Spitfire, Bombardier, Tetleys…) and lagers (Stella, Fosters, Kronenbourg). / **Website:** www.massivepub.com **Details:** no Amex. **Food:** L till 3pm, D till 10pm, Sat till 9pm, Sun till 6pm.*

Leinster W2

57 Ossington St   7243 9541   6–2B
*A good-sized terrace and big-screen TV – such are the principal attractions of this quietly-situated Bayswater pub. It makes a useful destination in a slightly thin area. / **Details:** Mon-Fri noon-3pm & 5pm-11pm, Sat noon-6pm, closed Sun; no Amex; no-smoking area. **Food:** L till 3pm, D till 10pm.*

The Leinster Arms W2

17 Leinster Terrace   7402 4670   6–2C
*This old hostelry is one of the better pubs in a part of Bayswater without too many competing attractions. In keeping with the somewhat transient nature of the area, part of the walls are given over to a photographic 'Hall of Fame' dedicated to United Airlines pilots (the airline's staff use a place nearby for their stop-overs – as they retire their portrait goes up on the wall). / **Food:** till 8pm.*

Lifthouse EC1

85 Charterhouse St   7251 8787   9–1A
*Down the street from Smithfield veteran Smiths, this new three-floor venture has successfully poached some of its neighbour's customers. Formerly the purpose-built HQ of a lift-making company, it incorporates many of the original features into its striking dark-timber décor. Eastern Mediterranean food is available from the ground-floor restaurant, or snack on meze in the first-floor cocktail bar. At night, the whole venue turns into 'L2', a late-night DJ bar. / **Website:** www.lifthouse.co.uk **Details:** noon-midnight, Wed & Thu 1am, Fri & Sat 2.30am; no Amex. **Food:** till 10pm (mezze Sat & Sun L, brunch Sat. **DJ:** Thu-Sat.*

The Light E1

233 Shoreditch High St   7247 8989   9–1D
*Stylishly converted from an electricity station, this airy and buzzy bar/restaurant, just north of Liverpool Street, offers a refreshing change from the ubiquitous chain bars and dark East End boozers in the locality, and is very popular for post-work drinks. School dinner-style bar snacks or a meal in the adjoining restaurant help soak up the booze. / **Website:** www.thelightE1.com* **Details:** *Mon-Fri noon-midnight, Sat 6pm-2am, Sun noon-10.30pm.* **Food:** *till 10.30pm.* **DJ:** *Thu-Sat from 7.30pm.*

Light Bar
St Martin's Lane Hotel WC2

St Martin's Ln, Covent Garden   7300 5599   4–3B
*Like its cousin at the Sanderson (The Long Bar – see also), this Ian Schrager design-hotel – his original London venture – combines groovy Philippe Starck styling with a reputation for being something of a celeb' magnet. Unless you're staying in the hotel, you need to find a way to get yourself on the guest list to have a good chance of making it through the door.
/ **Website:** www.ianschragerhotels.com* **DJ:** *various nights.*

Lime EC2

1 Curtain Rd   7422 0958   9–1D
*We've never actually succeeded in finding many people at this large corner bar just north of the Broadgate centre. Perhaps it's because the would-be trendy décor just seems a bit 'Identikit', or perhaps it's because the food – which is quite a big part of the 'offer' – is nothing to write home about. Either way, the place has been in business for quite a while, so they must be pulling the punters in sometimes – Wednesdays and Fridays are the big deal, apparently. / **Website:** www.limeuk.com* **Details:** *Thu till midnight, Fri till 1am, closed weekends; no Amex.* **Food:** *L&D till 9pm, bar snacks till closing.*

Liquid Lab EC1

20 City Rd   7920 0372   9–1C
*A cool, icy white design (not least the groovy back-lit glass bar), and a vaguely medical theme (X-rays on the walls, for instance) create a cool – but not clinical – atmosphere at this long, thin bar just north of the City. Mixologist 'The Doc' delivers a cocktail selection including such unmissable creations as 'Dead Doc' and 'Blood Clot', but there's also an array of draught lagers and even a draught bitter (London Pride).
/ **Website:** www.liquidlab.co.uk* **Details:** *closed weekends.* **Food:** *till 10pm.*

Living SW9

443 Coldharbour Ln   7326 4040   10–2C

The name may not be inspired – it's decorated Living Room style – but this Brixton sibling to the Dog Star, nearby, has all the funky street cred' of its sibling and attracts a twenty- to thirtysomething crowd, with a music selection centred on house. Upstairs (Fri & Sat), a celebration of '70s and '80s disco brings in a slightly less obviously hip crowd. / **Website:** www.livingbar.co.uk **Details:** Mon-Thu & Sun noon-2am, Fri & Sat noon-4am. **Food:** L & D. **DJ:** nightly (house & 70's/80's).

Living Room

18-26 Essex Rd, N1   7288 9090   8–3D
2 West Smithfield, EC1   7246 0900   9–2A

This stylish duo belong to a well-established Manchester-based chain of restaurant/bars. Both feature the same slick décor of dark wood, cream walls, brown leather sofas and a white grand piano. Be warned that much of the space is reserved for diners only, so the bars can get a little cramped – if you prefer to sip your cocktails in comfort, arrive early.
/ **Website:** www.thelivingroom.co.uk **Details:** vary; no-smoking areas. **Food:** L&D & bar snacks. **DJ:** Fri & Sat. **Live music:** N1 - pianist plays jazz & soul.

The Lock Tavern NW1

35 Chalk Farm Rd   7482 7163   8–2B

Recently opened, this long and thin bar/café – independently owned rather than part of a chain – is a short walk from Chalk Farm Tube and atmospherically decorated with dark wood and ornate mirrors behind the bar. An open kitchen at the rear dispenses food – if the roaring trade they do at lunchtime is anything to go by then it's worth sampling. There's a fair selection of lagers on draft and London Pride for bitter-drinking types. / **Website:** www.thelock-tavern.co.uk **Details:** no Amex. **Food:** L till 3pm (Sun L till 5pm), D till 10pm. **DJ:** Thu-Sun.

Lomo SW10
222 Fulham Rd   7349 8848   5–3B
With its front open to the street on a sunny day, this Chelsea 'Beach' bar has long been a popular perch-on-a-stool-and-watch-the-world-go-by sort of place. Though the style is modern, the tapas dishes – complemented by a good range of Hispanic wines, and sherries – are pretty 'traditional' in style, and consistently of good quality. / **Website:** *www.lomo.com* **Details:** *Mon-Fri 5pm-midnight, Sat noon-midnight, Sun 5pm-11pm.* **Food:** *till 11.30pm.* **Happy hour:** *5pm-8pm (half-price offers).*

The Long Bar
Sanderson Hotel W1
50 Berners St   7300 1444   3–1D
That Kylie had a birthday bash here tells you much of what you need to know about the bar at this hip design-hotel, north of Oxford Street. It follows the mould of most Ian Schrager (yawn, yes he of Studio 54) ventures, where expensively wacky, Philippe Starck design creates a self-consciously wacky environment for self-conscious trendies to hang out in. If your pockets are deep enough it can be great fun (but – unless you have more money than sense – avoid the neighbouring Spoon+ restaurant). / **Website:** *www.ianschragerhotels.com* **Details:** *Mon-Sun 10am-1am.* **Food:** *till 1am.*

The Loop W1
19 Dering St   7493 1003   3–2B
For a hen night or rowdy office party, it might be worth considering this Tardis-like bar/nightclub. Head downstairs to a second bar much bigger than the first, and down again to a nightclub under Hanover Square. / **Details:** *Mon-Wed noon-1am, Thu-Sat noon-3am, closed Sun.* **Food:** *L & D.* **Happy hour:** *5pm-7pm.*

The Lord Palmerston NW5
33 Dartmouth Park Hl   7485 1578   8–1B
Simple but decent cooking, and a reasonable range of wines – and all at moderate prices – is the key appeal of this bare, but somehow quite cosy, gastropub near Archway, which is pretty much always busy. In summer there's a good amount of outdoor space, in the beer garden and patio. / **Details:** *no Amex.* **Food:** *L till 3pm, D till 10pm (Sun 9pm).*

The Lord Stanley NW1

51 Camden Park Rd 7428 9488 8–2C

*From the outside this looks like a very mediocre pub indeed, so the interior comes as a real surprise: decked out with mahogany furniture and candles, and with modern art on the walls. The music studios next door help provide a funkier than usual clientele. / **Details:** Mon from 6pm. **Food:** L till 3pm, D till 10pm.*

Lots Road Pub & Dining Room SW10

114 Lots Rd 7352 6645 5–3B

*Reproaching the architectural eyesore that is Chelsea Harbour, this nice old Victorian pub building stands by the roundabout at the entrance to the complex. It was converted a couple of years ago into a pleasant and airy modern hang out, that's rarely too crowded. An open kitchen offers a range of good but pretty simple fare, at reasonable prices. / **Food:** L till 3pm, D till 10pm, all day weekends.*

(The Lotus Rooms) Bam-Bou W1

1 Percy St 7323 9130 4–1A

*Although it was tarted up a few years ago, this notionally Vietnamese townhouse bar/restaurant still retains something of the louche air of old Fitzrovia (it was, for decades, the White Tower Greek restaurant). On the top two-floors, the Lotus Rooms are decked out in a sumptuous and seductive oriental style and rather beautiful staff (who come complete with an appropriate degree of 'attitude') serve a still-fashionable crowd. / **Website:** www.bam-bou.co.uk **Details:** Mon-Sat 6pm-1am, closed Sun. **Food:** L&D, bar snacks all day.*

Lounge SW12

76 Bedford Hill 8673 8787 10–2B

*This small Balham bar offers a friendly welcome to the gaggle of twenty- and thirtysomethings that gather here. Despite the name, there's only one option for lounging – a large sofa – but it's a cosy place, with regular live music and a restaurant downstairs. / **Details:** Mon-Fri 5pm-midnight, Sat 10am-midnight, Sun 11am-11.30pm; no Amex. **Food:** till 10.30pm. **DJ:** Thu-Sat. **Live music:** Tue & Sun jazz. **Happy hour:** 5pm-7.30pm (£1 off bottled beers).*

Lowlander WC2

36 Drury Ln   7379 7446   4–1C

This stylish café/bar newcomer on the Covent Garden/Holborn fringe is a congenial spot, and especially useful pre-theatre. Unsurprisingly, given the name, Dutch and Belgian beers are the main point – a dozen on draught from the shiny chrome pumps lined up along the bar (plus over 30 bottled varieties), making this one of the better specialist beer halls in London. A decent wine selection is also available. / **Website:** www.lowlander.com **Food:** till 11pm.

Lúnasa SW6

575 King's Rd   7371 7664   10–1A

It may be named after a pagan harvest festival (a time to celebrate and enjoy the fruits of your daily labours, apparently), but this cool hang-out (just over the rail bridge separating Chelsea from Fulham) looks every bit a part of modern London life, complete with projection screen, a very funkily mirrored bar and art on the walls. Cocktails and lager are the orders of the day. / **Website:** www.lunasa.co.uk **Details:** Mon-Sun 4pm-11pm (Sat & Sun match days from noon). **Food:** 6pm-11pm. **DJ:** Thu-Sat (house, garage, hip hop). **Live music:** occasional. **Happy hour:** Mon-Fri noon-9pm (cocktails £3, vodka/mixer £3.50).

The Lyceum Tavern WC2

354 Strand   7836 7155   2–1D

Intimate panelled booths (but only three – get there early to nab one) make this Theatreland pub stand out among the competition. A games area towards the back plus Sam Smith's ales help win it a regular crowd. / **Details:** no Amex; no-smoking area. **Food:** L till 3pm (Sun 4pm), D till 8.30pm.

Mac Bar NW1

102-104 Camden Rd   7485 4530   8–2C

Opposite Camden Town BR, you can't miss this lounge bar, with its purple and orange exterior. It's an attractive place, though, with sofas and a long chrome bar, and changing art exhibitions on the walls. Entertainments include jazz on Wednesdays and other live bands – apparently Blur once played here. / **Website:** www.macbar.co.uk **Details:** no Amex. **Food:** L till 3.30pm, D till 10pm. **DJ:** Fri-Sat.

Maddigans E8
255 Mare St, Hackney   8985 7391   1–1D
*This Irish pub on the main road near Hackney Central BR
attracts a mainly local and commuter crowd. The décor has a
faux-rustic/distressed look to it with gilt mirrors and candles, a
roaring fire adds to the atmosphere and there's a wide selection
of lagers. Not perhaps a destination, but a pleasant place if
you're in the area especially on account of the beer garden with
heaters. / **Details:** no Amex.* **Food:** *L till 3pm (Mon-Fri).*

The Magdela Tavern NW3
2a, South Hill Pk   7435 2503   8–1A
*It's the bullet holes still visible in the sides of the building, rather
than the OK food and the modernified interior, which wins this
pub by Hampstead Heath BR a place in all the guide books.
This is the spot that cheated-on Ruth Ellis shot and killed her
love rat, racing driver boyfriend and became (in 1955) the last
woman in England to be hanged. / **Details:** no Amex.* **Food:** *L till
2.30pm, D till 10pm.*

The Mall Tavern W8
71-73 Palace Gardens Ter   7727 3805   6–2B
*This new gastropub from the team who transformed Kensal
Green's William IV opened, just off Notting HIll Gate, in the
winter of 2002. When it comes to drinks, wine and cocktails
receive as much – if not more – emphasis than beer, and the
food is good. In its early days, the interior was a bit too stark
for its own good – over time let's hope they cosy it up a little.
/ **Food:** till 10.30pm.*

Mandarin Bar
Mandarin Oriental Hyde Pk SW1
66 Knightsbridge   7235 2000   5–1D
*With its imposing late-Victorian façade and the elegantly
marbled halls of its lobby (the whole place was originally built
as a Gentleman's Club), the cocktail bar comes as quite a
surprise at this grand hotel on Knightsbridge. Its hip and its
happening! – thanks to a superb makeover (a couple of years
ago) its one of the sleekest-looking hang outs in town and a hit
with a very chic crowd (who pack it out at peak times).
/ **Details:** Mon-Sun 11am-2am; no switch.* **Food:** *till 1.30am.*

The Maple Leaf WC2

41 Maiden Ln   7240 2843   4–3D

*The "only Canadian bar in England" is in a pretty street, south of Covent Garden market. Copious quantities of Labatt's are consumed, naturally, but otherwise the place seems faithful to the Canadian ideal of being nice-but-a-bit-boring. / **Food:** till 9pm.*

Market Bar W11

240a, Portobello Rd   7229 6472   6–1A

Unlike at the nearby Beach Blanket Babylon, Tony Weller's ground-breaking Gothic design at this once-famous Portobello hang-out seems to have been toned down a little by the passing of the years. Now part of the Massive Pubs group (who own the Tups), it attracts a fairly mainstream crowd nowadays, and is especially popular on Saturdays.
*/ **Website:** www.masivepub.com **Details:** no Amex. **Food:** L till 3pm.*

The Market Place W1

11 Market Pl   7079 2020   3–1C

Vaguely reminiscent of Scandinavia – if only because it's decorated like a sauna and isn't much bigger – this new just-off-Oxford Street attracts a crowd which regularly spills out in to the street. It's a watering hole for the younger end of the local fashion/media set who chew over the day's happenings over a glass of lager (with Löwenbräu and Erdinger on tap).
*/ **Website:** www.marketplace-london.com **Details:** Mon-Wed till midnight, Thu-Sat till 1am, Sun till 11pm. **Food:** till 12.30am. **DJ:** nightly from 7pm.*

The Market Porter SE1

9 Stoney St   7407 2495   9–3C

*One of those rare London pubs where you can pick up a pint on the way to work, as proximity to Borough's wonderfully atmospheric wholesale fruit and veg market permits early-morning licensed opening. And, even better, its independent status means it sells an ever-changing variety of ales. A great spot for breakfast with a beer – but equally worth visiting at any time. / **Details:** Mon-Fri 6am-8.30am & 11am-11pm. **Food:** L only.*

The Marquess of Granby WC2
51-52 Chandos Pl   7836 7657   2–1D
Near the Coliseum, this small old pub is one of the nicer traditional establishments in the environs of Covent Garden in which to sink a pint. There's no outside area, but on a nice day the windows are completely removed, lightening the very Victorian ambience. They get through a real mix of drinks, which includes – at any one time – four guest bitters.
*/ **Details:** no-smoking area. **Food:** L till 4pm, D till 9pm.*

The Marquess Tavern N1
32 Canonbury St   7354 2975   8–2D
*Charmingly situated in a pretty residential quarter of leafy Canonbury, this large, listed mid-19th-century Young's hostelry looks – both inside and out – more like a theatre than a pub. The interior is very elegant and, for a quiet, civilised drink the place makes an excellent choice. / **Website:** www.youngs.co.uk*
***Food:** till 9.30pm.*

The Marylebone Bar & Kitchen W1
74-76 York St   7262 1513   3–1A
*From the same brewery-owned group behind the Lots Road Bar & Kitchen and Wimbledon's Fire Stables, this Marylebone gastropub occupies a former corner boozer site. Somewhat eccentric (but quite dark) décor and unusual draught beers (including Kirin, San Miguel, Wieckse Witte beer and Affligem) are among its attractions. / **Website:** www.spiritgroup.com **Details:** no Amex. **Food:** till 10pm. **DJ:** occasionally.*

Mash W1
19-21 Gt Portland St   7637 5555   3–1C
*Its debatable how good the first-floor restaurant is at this large West End destination, with its huge plate glass windows overlooking the street. The funkily-designed ground-floor bar, though, gets a good rep – wittily decked out in retro, '70s sci-fi style with large brewing vessels on display at the back (the place is also a microbrewery). The home brew comes in four different varieties, but the cocktail menus here are also very well-thumbed. / **Website:** www.gruppo.co.uk **Details:** Mon 8pm-midnight, Tue-Sat 8pm-2am. **Food:** till 11pm. **DJ:** Thu-Sat.*

Mason's Arms SW8

169 Battersea Park Rd   7622 2007   10–1B

*This light and bright gastropub (grottily located next to Battersea Park BR) has a brilliant atmosphere, helped by the ever-changing art displays featured on its walls. It was one of the front-runners in the transformation of London's pub-scene in the mid-'90s, particularly when it came to food (though its former pre-eminence in this area has been under threat in recent times). / **Details:** Mon-Sat noon-3.30pm, 6-10pm, Sun closes 9.30pm. **Food:** till 10.45pm. **DJ:** Sat.*

Match

37-38 Margaret St, W1   7499 3443   3–1C
45-47 Clerkenwell Rd, EC1   7250 4002   9–1A

*This celebrated lounge bar duo epitomise the smooth, understated contemporary style that has crept across town in the last few years. It's not that what they do is remarkable – it's that they've achieved it with a consistency and style that sets them apart from many rivals. The Clerkenwell original has been successfully transported from Exmouth Market to Shoreditch, while the second branch is to be found near Oxford Circus. / **Details:** 11am-midnight. **Food:** EC1 noon-10.30pm, W1 D only till 10.30pm. **DJ:** W1 Fri & Sat (funk/soul).*

Matt & Matt N1

112 Upper St   7226 6035   8–3D

*Friends of the eponymous proprietors can seem to make up a large proportion of the clientèle at this pre-club Islington bar. But all are made welcome at its curiously-proportioned premises, to soak up the "funky progressive house and trance" from the resident DJs. / **Website:** www.mattandmatt.co.uk **Details:** Thu 6pm-1am, Fri 6pm-2am & Sat 8pm-2am; no Amex. **DJ:** nightly. **Happy hour:** Thu & Fri 6pm-8pm (discounts on selected spirits).*

The Mayflower SE16

117 Rotherhithe St   7237 4088   11–1A

*A large, historic, 18th-century Rotherhithe pub (named after a certain ship which once left from here for the New World), whose outside terrace, overhanging the river, affords a wonderful view over the Thames. Its cosy interior attracts a good mix, including businessmen, locals, students and tourists at the end of their riverside walking-tour. / **Details:** Mon-Sat noon-11.30pm, Sun 11.30am-10.30pm; no Amex. **Food:** till 9.30pm.*

Medicine Bar
181 Upper St, N1   7704 8056   8–2D
89 Great Eastern St, EC2   7739 5173   9–1C
With its stripped floors, big leather chairs and sofas, and DJs pumping up the volume, the original N1 branch of what has recently become a mini-chain has long been a linchpin of the Islington going-out scene – particularly for a trendy, twentysomething crowd. The new branch just off Old Street follows a similar formula, though the expensive-looking styling is a bit cooler and less 'raw' than at the Islington original.
/ **Details:** *vary; no Amex.* **DJ:** *Thu-Sun.*

Met Bar
Metropolitan Hotel W1
18-19 Old Park Ln   7447 5757   2–2A
Located at the foot of Park Lane's only trendy hotel (and below the much-fêted Nobu restaurant), this famous bar may no longer be as cutting edge as once it was, but it's been 'in' for an impressive number of years now (over five!). Mortals (ie non-hotel-residents, non-members) are permitted to enter – only till 6pm, though. If you do go, you may wonder what all the fuss is about given that it provides living proof that it's people who make a party – the décor's pretty unremarkable.
/ **Website:** *www.metropolitan.co.uk* **Details:** *Mon-Sat 11am-3am, Sun noon-10.30pm (members and hotel guest from 6pm only).* **Food:** *L&D.* **DJ:** *Wed-Sat.*

Metro SW6
10-12 Effie Rd   7384 1264   10–1A
Done out in classic OTT 'London Spanish' style, this appealing corner site (near Fulham Broadway) manages to be more characterful than you might expect, and it has a very pleasant terrace. At busy meal times they restrict tables just to diners, but 'off peak' it makes a mellow, fun place to hang out with a glass of wine or sangria, or a shot of something with a bit more punch. / **Details:** *Mon-Sun 10am-midnight.* **Food:** *10am-midnight.*

Mezzo W1
100 Wardour St   7314 4000   3–2D
A few too many hen nights and suburban coach parties have, these days, robbed Conran's vast Soho venture of much of the glamour that attached to the place when it opened. But, while it's become fashionable to write it off, there's no getting around its continued popularity, especially at weekends. The pricey basement restaurant has its own bar, but 'Mezzonine' – on the ground floor – is the place for the best bar action. If you take our advice, you'll drink not eat. / **Website:** www.conran.com
Details: *Mon-Fri noon-1am, Sat noon-3am, Sun 5.30pm-11pm.*

Microbar SW11
14 Lavender Hill   7228 5300   10–1B
Burgundy being the house colour, it's tempting to assume that this nicely designed Battersea joint is a wine bar – but in fact quality beers from around the world are the main thing. On draft, then the main offering is Liberty Ale from San Francisco's Anchor Steam brewery, but there's a wide array of bottled beers, many of them Belgian. / **Website:** www.microbar.org.uk
Details: *Mon-Fri from 6pm, weekends from 4pm.*

Mint On Montague SE1
8-10 Borough High St   7089 5710   9–3C
This diminutive bar near Southwark Cathedral isn't especially easy to find but it is particularly atmospheric, occupying stylish basement premises with a crypt-like feel. Impressive mixology accompanies an inventive cocktail list, and bar snacks are simple, but well done. There's a small terrace for the summer. (The bar also has an elder sibling at 182-186 St John St, tel 7253 8368 and – very confusingly – a completely unconnected namesake – at 202 Bishopsgate, tel 7283 5888.)

Mistress P's SW4
29 North St   7622 5342   10–1C
Though the name makes it sound like an S&M dungeon, Patricia Redfern's small corner pub (in an off-the-beaten-track Clapham location) is rather more inviting. With its kitsch, eccentric décor, '70s furniture and fairy lights it's a different take on what is at heart a cosy local. / **Details:** *no credit cards.*
Food: *Sun 4pm-6pm.*

The Mitre W2

24 Craven Terrace   7262 5240   6–2C

Perhaps the only pub in Bayswater that one might describe as a 'destination', this interesting Victorian building – with its dark, rambling, inviting interior and some impressive decorative fixtures – has a slightly Bohemian vibe nowadays. (It actually used to be a bank, and the downstairs bar is in what used to be the vault.) Run by the Laurel Pub Co, it offers a range of lagers (Stella, Heineken, Hoegaarden) and a couple bitters (Boddingtons and London Pride). / Details: no Amex; no-smoking area. Food: till 9.30pm.

Momo W1

25 Heddon St   7434 4040   3–2C

A short while after it opened, this Moroccan-styled den was the talk of the town, after sightings of Tom Cruise with then-wife Nicole Kidman. Those heady days may be gone, but the party hasn't slowed down much – either here or in the hugely atmospheric restaurant above – fuelled by quality cocktails and some great music. The bar is members' only, but diners can drink here before their reservation and – especially early week – if you call ahead they'll generally put you on the guest list. / Details: Mon & Tue 7pm-1am, Wed 7pm-2am, Thu-Sat 7pm-3am. Food: till 11.30pm.

Mono N8

57 Park Rd   8348 4161   8–1C

Open to the public in the early part of the week only, this cool bar/members club – behind a discreet entrance in up-and-coming Crouch End – is well worth seeking out. Inside you find a simple and elegant place, where the vibe is sustained by regular DJs. Bar snacks are available. / Details: Mon from 6pm, Tue-Sat 6pm-1am, Sun 6pm-midnight. Food: Tue-Sat till 12.30am (Sun 11.30pm). DJ: Thu-Sun (dance).

The Montrose NW6

105 Salusbury Rd   7372 8882   1–1B

When it hit the area (under the name The Park) a few years back, the opening of this large, stylish bar/restaurant was a real sign of the up-and-coming nature of Queen's Park. It's never quite lived up to its potential (particularly as a place to eat), but as a place to drink it makes a comfortable, airy place to while away a couple of hours. / Food: L&D.

Mook W11

90 Notting Hill Gate   7229 5396   6–2B

Right by Notting Hill Gate tube, this loungey bar is becoming a deserved success with Portobello Market-hoppers as well as the locals. It's the upstairs that really catches the eye, with its chilled atmosphere, mosaiced walls and sofas. Downstairs is starker, with an open kitchen, and industrial-style lamps hanging low over the tables. / Details: Mon-Wed & Sun noon-11pm, Thu-Sat noon-midnight; no Amex. Food: till 10pm. DJ: Fri-Sun.
Happy hour: Mon-Fri 5pm-7pm (any bottled beer £2, buy 2 glasses of wine & get rest of bottle free).

The Moon & Sixpence W1

185 Wardour St   7734 0037   3–1D

As a Wetherspoon's pub, this light and bright spot in Soho is never going to be a haven for style cognoscenti. With its large windows and chandeliers, however, it's a perfectly pleasant spot for a quick and affordable pint. / Website: www.jdwetherspoon.co.uk Details: no-smoking area. Food: till 10pm. Happy hour: Mon (Fosters £1.39, wine, Smirnoff Ice & Bud £1.09).

The Morpeth Arms SW1

58 Millbank   7834 6442   2–3C

Opposite the MI6 building, and not far from MI5, it's hardly suprising that this small and traditional tavern by the Tate Britain – has something of a reputation as the "spooks' pub". Like many Young's hostelries, it's a cut above average.
/ Website: www.youngs.co.uk Food: till 9pm.

The Mortimer W1

37-40 Berners St   7436 0451   3–1D

With its huge glass front, this Fitzrovia gastropub looks rather sterile and All Bar One-like, but it does some tasty grub and offers good ranges of both bitters and lagers. Its comfy leather Chesterfields are conducive to long afternoon chats and the tables outside are also very popular during the summer months. The place is almost opposite the Middlesex, so it attracts a good number of medics, as well as business folk and shoppers. / Details: closed weekends. Food: till 10pm.

Motcomb's SW1

26 Motcomb St   7235 6382   5–1D

This long-established, clubby, art-filled Belgravia wine bar has that comfortably worn-in feeling, which the presence of many regulars who give the appearance of having been in attendance for decades does nothing to dispel. In the middle of the day, much of the space is taken up with lunchers.
/ **Website:** www.motcombs.co.uk **Details:** *Mon-Sat 10am-11pm, Sun noon-4pm.* **Food:** *L till 3pm.*

Mulberry Bush SE1

89 Upper Ground   7928 7940   1–2C

If everywhere along the South Bank is heaving, head for this (otherwise unremarkable) Young's pub, usefully located just behind London Television Centre and Gabriel's Wharf. No beer garden, but you can stand outside on a sunny day.
/ **Website:** www.youngs.co.uk **Details:** *closed Sun; no-smoking area.* **Food:** *L till 2.30pm (Sat till 4pm), D 5pm-8pm.*

The Museum Tavern WC1

49 Gt Russel St   7242 8987   4–1B

The museum in question is the British Museum, and a location bang opposite the entrance guarantees a pretty touristy crowd here. Not that this is not a fine old Victorian pub, though. Many of the fittings are original and there are some very nice etched glass and mirrors. It's also quite a place if you are into real ale – they have six on tap, guest beers and two festivals a year. / **Food:** *till 10pm.*

MVH SW13

5 White Hart Ln   8392 1111   1–3A

A fantastic setting repays the trip to near Barnes Bridge at this Heaven & Hell themed bar/restaurant for the loos alone, say fans. The small, cosy bar reached up a narrow staircase is Hell (confusingly it's above Heaven, but never mind), but if that's what we sinners have in store for us then things are looking good. Prices are high, but both drinks and nibbles are very superior. / **Details:** *Mon-Sun 5pm-11.30pm.* **Food:** *5pm-11.30pm.*

Mybar
myhotel Bloomsbury WCI

11-13 Bayley St 7667 6000 4–1A
This swanky retro bar – situated in a smart modern Bloomsbury hotel – provides a mixture of sofas and round marble tables where you can lounge about supping a range of delicious cocktails. It's a good choice for a relaxing drink, but – ironically for a place supposedly designed along the principles of Feng Shui – the main drawback is that it's long and thin, so during busy times can get very cramped.
/ **Website:** www.myhotels.com **Details:** Mon-Sun 7pm-11pm. **Food:** L&D.

Na Zdrowie WCI

6 Little Turnstile 7831 9679 2–1D
Just behind Holborn tube, in a tiny alley, this funky, small Polish bar serves over 50 different types of vodka from Luksusowa (potato) to Wyborowa (pineapple), via Ajacoco (coconut), along with four Polish bottled beers, so you can be sure to find a tipple that suits you. A broken glass mosaic on the back wall, low square sofas and small tables complete a great package that's packing 'em in. / **Details:** Mon-Fri 12.30pm-11pm, Sat 6pm-11pm, closed Sun; no Amex. **Food:** till 10pm.

Nadines W1

23-24 Greek St 7734 7006 4–2A
You'd never stumble upon this basement 'night bar' underneath a Soho Moroccan restaurant by accident. Opulently (if inexpensively) decorated in Kasbah style, it comes complete with hubble-bubble pipes, and offers a welcome respite from the hard-edged 'style' bars in this area. A late licence – plus live music and belly dancing at weekends – add to the place's attractions. / **Website:** www.nadines.co.uk **Details:** Mon-Sat noon-3am, Sun noon-midnight. **Food:** till 11pm.

The Nag's Head SW1

53 Kinnerton St 7235 1135 5–1D
A top central choice for a quiet pint: dating from 1777, this venerable Belgravia free house is as rambling and cosy a spot as you might hope to find, and it has an excellent 'villagey' location in a back lane. It is in fact only some five minutes walk from Hyde Park Corner – if you know the way. / **Details:** no credit cards. **Food:** till 9.30pm.

Nam Long SW5

159 Old Brompton Rd   7373 1926   5–2B

A reputation for killer cocktails and louche glamour precedes this well-established bar, long known as an essential rallying point for South Kensington Eurotrash (and in recent times famed for its 'Flaming Ferraris'). A token food order may be required to satisfy licensing regulations (a technicality too small to exclude a place of such dubious eminence), or you can have a proper meal in the Vietnamese restaurant at the back.
/ **Details:** Mon-Sat 6.30pm-11.30pm, closed Sun. **Food:** D till 11.30pm.

Narrow Boat N1

119 St Peter's St   7288 9821   8–3D

On a sunny day, it's the outside terrace overlooking the water which is the special attraction of this agreeable Islington pub, by the Regent's Canal – for a stroll afterwards, descend the spiral stairs down to the towpath. The interior is pleasant, if unremarkable, but the new owner seems to have plans for the place. / **Food:** L till 3pm.

Navajo Joe WC2

34 King St   7240 4008   4–3C

This Mexican bar/restaurant in the centre of Covent Garden boasts one of the largest tequila selections outside of Mexico (over 300), along with 40-plus Cuban rums. From the outside it looks a bit themey, but the design is impressive and it's not just a place for out-of-towners. Quite good food, too. / **Food:** till 11pm. **DJ:** Thu-Sat. **Live music:** jazz Sun. **Happy hour:** 5.30pm-6.30pm.

Nell Gwynne WC2

2 Bull Inn Ct   7240 5579   2–1D

Up an alley off The Strand, this small, traditional boozer is on the site of the Old Bull Inn and is named after Charles II's famous mistress who was born in nearby Covent Garden (and allegedly drank here). It's arguably a bit twee, but at least slightly off the beaten track for somewhere so central.
/ **Details:** closed Sun; no credit cards. **Food:** L till 2.30pm.

New Inn EC2

1 New Inn Broadway   7739 7775   9–1D
For a quiet and cosy take on the Shoreditch experience, seek out this small, tucked-away corner tavern, whose most consistent entertainment is a basket of board games. There's also more lively goings on in the basement some nights – jamming sessions, quizzes, sometimes a band mid week, or open decks on Saturdays. Amongst a familiar array of ales, lagers and spirits there's a selection of speciality German and Belgian bottled beers. / **Details:** *Mon-Fri from 5pm, weekends from 6pm; no Amex.*

Newman Arms W1

23 Rathbone St   7636 1127   3–1D
Off Oxford Street but away from the crowds, this small, traditional pub is reassuringly untouched by the latest trends (it was established in 1730 and retains much of its old character). It's famed for its pies – the pie room is upstairs and you'll probably have to book ahead to get a table. / **Details:** *closed weekends; no credit cards.*

Nicole's W1

158 New Bond St   7499 8408   3–3C
Just gasping for a glass of champagne between Gucci and Donna Karan? Seek out the long and thin basement bar of Nicole Farhi's Mayfair emporium, which has a ringside side to watch the 'scene' in the restaurant. It's most fun in the middle of the day, naturally – later on, the ladies-who-lunch have finished shopping and gone home. / **Details:** *Mon-Fri 10am-10pm, Sat 10am-6pm, closed Sun; no-smoking area.* **Food:** *11.30am-5.30pm.*

19:20 EC1

19-20 Great Sutton St   7253 1920   9–1B
From the mosaic water feature in the window to the colourful pool tables, this Clerkenwell bar/restaurant is a young designer's dream. The main bar (which is made of red leather, naturally) is downstairs – reached via a sweeping circular staircase – where a post-work crowd gather to down inventive cocktails, or Beamish and Kronenbourg on tap. / **Website:** *www.19-20.co.uk* **Details:** *Mon-Fri noon-midnight, Sat 6.30pm-midnight, closed Sun.* **Food:** *L&D.* **DJ:** *Thu-Sat.* **Live music:** *live bands, Wed once a month.*

No 77 Wine Bar NW6

77 Mill Ln   7435 7787   1–1B

The name of this long-established West Hampstead local couldn't really be much more descriptive, and it offers a decent range of wines (plus some bottled beers), plus – if you want it – plain cooking to soak 'em up. / Details: Mon-Tue noon-11pm, Wed-Sat noon-midnight, Sun noon-10.30pm; no Amex. Food: till 10pm.

Noble Rot W1

3-5 Mill St   7629 8877   3–2C

We really like the look and feel of the basement bar of this swanky Mayfair restaurant (and in fact prefer it to the restaurant above). It was one of the earlier places to have been done out in the now ubiquitous Morrocan style, which it carries off very well. By feel, it's naturally a cocktail-y kind of place, but the whole venture makes a feature of wine, and there's a very extensive list. On busy nights, it's sometimes members only, but you're unlikely to have any problems earlier on. / Website: www.noblerot.com Details: Tue-Sun 6pm-3am (closed Mon). Food: till 11pm (bar snacks till close). DJ: Thu-Sat.

Nordic W1

25 Newman St   7631 3174   3–1D

Nordic tourism brochures just inside the entrance add authenticity to this cool Scandinavian venture (in the shadow of the Telecom Tower), where neutral décor is enhanced by glimpses of weird Scandiness. From Red Eric lager to an impressive array of bottled lagers and vodkas – there's an intriguing range of Nordic tipples and a selection of meatballs, herrings, gravadlax and so on to help soften their after-effects. / Website: www.nordicbar.com Details: Sat 6pm-11pm, closed Sun. Food: L till 3pm, D till 10pm. DJ: occasionally. Happy hour: Mon 5pm-7pm & 9pm-11pm, Tue 5pm-7pm, Wed till 8.30pm (Mon-Tue half-price beer & wine, Wed cocktail night, Thu Taittinger champ. £21.50 all night).

North End Dining SW6

308-310 North End Rd   7385 5005   5–3A

This new bar/restaurant occupies a site in the middle of the North End Road market, that was previously the (short-lived) Martini Grill. It's early days, but the décor (acres of sofas and a vibrant colour scheme) is inviting. / Website: www.eskimoflipper.com Details: no Amex. Food: L till 3.30pm, D till 10pm, bar snacks all day. DJ: Thu or Fri.

North Pole W10

13-15 North Pole Rd   8964 9384   6–1A

This revamped old boozer provides some much-needed cheer in the thin environs of White City. Its style is like many others in the Tup group, with bare boards and old school chairs. DJs make an appearance at the weekend. / **Food:** *till 10pm.* **DJ:** *Fri-Sat.*

The Notting Hill Arts Club W11

21 Notting Hill Gate   7460 4459   6–2B

Always busy, this slightly grungy/studenty basement bar and club is a great place to go for a boogie and a drink in relaxed and intimate surroundings. It specialises in a music programme of DJs and bands (as well as art shows) with a dance floor adjoining the bar (which majors in bottled lagers and cocktails). / **Website:** *www.nottinghillartsclub.com* **Details:** *Mon-Wed 6pm-1am, Thu & Fri 6pm-2am, Sat 4pm-2am, Sun 4pm-12.30pm; no Amex.* **Food:** *L&D.* **DJ & Live music:** *nightly.* **Happy hour:** *Mon-Sat 6pm-9pm (beer & wine £2, cocktails £5).*

Numidie SE19

48 Westow Hill   8766 6166   1–3D

This French Algerian spot is a real 'find' in the Crystal Palace desert, with a restaurant on the ground floor level and a bar in the basement. The latter – a long, narrow space – can get very crowded, but the atmosphere is convivial and the crowd friendly. There's just Stella on tap, plus a range of wines and spirits. Every now and again, the chef plays live music with his friends (the instruments are kept on the wall in the restaurant). / **Website:** *www.numidie.co.uk* **Details:** *Tue-Sun 6pm-11pm (closed Mon).* **Food:** *till 10.30pm.*

Nylon EC2

1 Addle St   7600 7771   9–2B

Just south of London Wall at the foot of the ugly Royex House tower is about as nondescript a bit of the City as you might hope to find. It's all the more surprising then to find this enormous, cool, '70s-looking venue. Given its location, the crowd (especially later in the week) includes a fair few bank-slaves winding down after work, but it's much cooler than that sounds and the place gets creative-types too. There's a members' area upstairs for those deemed truly 'in'. / **Website:** *www.styleinthecity.com* **Details:** *Mon-Wed 5pm-11pm, Thu-Fri 4.30pm-1am, Sat 9pm-3am, closed Sun; no Amex.* **Food:** *till 9pm.* **DJ:** *Thu-Fri.*

O'Conor Don W1

88 Marylebone Ln   7935 9311   3–1A

A pint of excellent Guinness awaits at this small, but comfy and homely Irish pub in the heart of Marylebone, which attracts a mainly businessy following (it can get very crowded and smokey). There's a dining room above, which serves some OK hearty grub. / **Website:** www.oconordon.com/ **Details:** closed weekends. **Food:** till 10pm.

O's Bar N8

115 Park Rd, Crouch End   8340 7845   8–1C

The owners of nearby O's Thai Café have also established this swanky, slate-floored minimalist bar (and food is also available here, too). Even though it's at the 'wrong' end of Crouch End, it's a popular destination, especially at weekends. Cocktails seem to be the most popular option, otherwise there are a number of choices for lager drinkers.
/ **Website:** www.oscafesandbars.com **Details:** Mon-Thu noon-midnight, Fri & Sat noon-1am, Sun noon-11.30pm; no Amex. **Food:** 6pm-10.30pm.

O-Bar W1

83-85 Wardour St   7437 3490   3–2D

Prominently-located on a corner in the centre of Soho, this two-level operation is decked out with a plush Gothic theme, and is usually heaving with a mixed crowd of twentysomething lads and ladettes on the pull. It scores high points early evening (for its happy hour) and later on (for its late-licence, at which time you may have to pay for entry). / **Details:** Mon-Sat 5pm-3am, Sun from 4pm. **Food:** L&D. **DJ:** nightly from 9pm. **Happy hour:** 5pm-8pm (spirits with mixer £2).

Oak Bar N16

79 Green Lanes   7354 2791   1–1C

Though it's a mixed gay bar, it's for Lesbians that this Newington Green hang out is one of the most happening scenes in town. A big, bright and slightly tacky retro interior hides rather oddly behind a mock Tudor façade. Lagers (Kronenbourg, Fosters, Stella, Hoegaarden) dominate the list of beers, but wine and alcopops also help fuel the festivities.
/ **Details:** Mon-Thu 5pm-midnight, Fri 5pm-2am, Sat 5pm-2am, Sun 1pm-midnight; no credit cards. **Food:** Sun L 1pm-6pm. **DJ:** Sat-Sun. **Live music:** occasional live band. **Happy hour:** Mon-Fri 5pm-8pm (discounts on cocktails & bottled beers).

Oblivion SW4

7-8 Cavendish Pde, Clap' Com' S'side   8772 0303   10–2C
*Facing the common a stone's throw from Clapham South tube,
this hangar-like joint is most easily identified by the crowds of
twentysomethings hanging out on the large terrace on sunny
weekend afternoons. Antipodeans seem particularly attracted
by its combination of cheesy rock 'n' pop and reasonably-priced
drinks. / **Details:** Mon-Fri from 4pm. **Food:** till 9pm. **DJ:** Thu-Sun.*

Odette's Wine Bar NW1

130 Regents Park Rd   7722 5388   8–3B
*The basement bar of north London's longest-running quality
restaurant success-story. Its dark green décor and gilt mirrors
effortlessly evoke the '70s, but the quality of the wine list –
and a snack if you want one – is bang up-to-date.
/ **Details:** Mon-Sat 6.30pm-10.30pm, closed Sun. **Food:** till 10.30pm.*

Oh! Bar NW1

111 Camden High St   7911 0667   8–3B
*The conversion of Camden Town's drinking spots from grunge
to lounge continues apace. This particular bar's take on the
theme comprises rather garish green and purple décor with
large round tables, and it has succeeded in attracting a mainly
twentysomething crowd. Cool tunes change by the day.
/ **Details:** Mon-Wed & Sun noon-midnight, Thu-Sat noon-2am. **Food:** till 9pm.
DJ: Tue (open deck), Wed (house), Thu (funk/soul/disco), Fri (hip hop & R&B),
Sat (funky house). **Live music:** jazz Mon, African drums Sun.
Happy hour: Mon-Fri 5pm-8pm (2 cocktails for £5).*

Old Bank of England EC4

194 Fleet St   7430 2255   9–2A
*The former Law Courts branch of the Bank of England (which
traded from the late 1800s till 1975) provides a lofty setting of
immense grandeur – albeit one ruined by a horrible carpet –
at this large Fuller's Ale & Pie House. Substantial food is
available – non-smokers may find the small rear dining room
the best setting in which to enjoy it. / **Website:** www.fullers.co.uk
Details: closed weekends. **Food:** till 9pm, Fri till 8pm, Mon-Thu bar snacks
5pm-10pm.*

The Old Bell Tavern EC4
95 Fleet St 7583 0216 9–2A
*It's evident that this ancient City tavern is a cut above the average, so it comes as only a slight surprise that its construction (1670) was overseen by one Christopher Wren. Nowadays it's a pretty straightforward boozer, offering some decent ales. / **Details:** closed weekends. **Food:** L till 3pm.*

The Old Bull & Bush NW3
North End Rd 8905 5456 8–1A
*"Come, come, come and make eyes at me, Down at the old Bull and Bush", so ran the catchy 1920s song. Since a recent refurbishment, a visit to this leafily-located boozer is again an inviting prospect. It's a comfortable place, with low ceilings, exposed beams and deep leather sofas. It's quite spacious, too, and offers solid grub, so it's an ideal destination after a walk on Hampstead Heath. / **Details:** no Amex; no-smoking area. **Food:** till 10pm.*

The Old Coffee House W1
49 Beak St 7437 2197 3–2D
*This traditional corner boozer is one of the very nicest pubs around Soho – just thoroughly cosy and unpretentious, it offers a good range of beers and lagers and attracts a wide-ranging crowd. The name is, of course, completely misleading nowadays – if you like local history, it's all explained in a notice by the door. / **Details:** Sun noon-3pm & 7pm-10.30pm; no Amex. **Food:** L till 3pm.*

The Old Crown WC1
33 New Oxford St 7836 9121 4–1B
*Traditional looking from outside but modern within, this fun and friendly bar attracts a following of local workers. Downstairs can get horrendously crowded, especially on Fridays, but you can escape to the more tranquil lounge bar upstairs. / **Website:** www.lonbestbars.com **Details:** closed Sun. **Food:** L till 3pm, D till 9.30pm. **Happy hour:** daily promotions (Mon half-price wine & cocktails, Thu cocktails £3.95, Fri shots specials, Sat cocktails £1.50).*

The Old Dr Butler's Head EC2

Masons Ave 7606 3504 9–2C

This traditional City pub, in an alley off Moorgate, is owned by quality brewer, Shepherd Neame. Though known for its historical associations (with a 17th-century quack who marketed a brand of medicinal ale), the recent revamp has not left the place with a markedly ancient feel.
/ **Website:** www.shepherd-neame.co.uk **Details:** closed weekends. **Food:** L only.

Old Parr's Head W14

120 Blythe Rd 7371 4561 7–1B

For some good, cheap Thai scoff in a cosy pub environment, it's worth remembering this welcoming, traditional boozer in the backstreets of Olympia. In summer, you can eat (or indeed enjoy a pint) in the small courtyard out back. / **Details:** no Amex. **Food:** L till 2.45pm, D till 10pm.

Old Parr's Head N1

66 Cross St 7226 2180 8–2D

A mixed, vaguely Boho Islington crowd congregate in this attractively revamped ex-boozer on a corner in Islington, which is a very pleasant mix stylewise of old and new. Drinks wise, lager (Stella and Heineken) is probably the most popular choice, (but there's also 6X, Boddingtons, and Abbots on tap, as well as an OK selection of wine and cocktails). There's also Thai food. / **Details:** Mon-Thu from 5pm, Fri 5pm-1am, Sat noon-1am; no Amex. **Food:** D till 9.30pm & Sat L. **DJ:** event nights weekly. **Live music:** band once/month.

Old Queen's Head N1

44 Essex Rd 7354 9273 8–3D

This dark and Bohemian corner boozer (in a style not too different from many others in the environs of Islington Green) has long been one of the areas more popular watering holes. Amongst its distinguishing feature, it numbers table football and a noise level that's high even by the ambitious local standards. / **Details:** no Amex.

Old Red Lion EC1

418 St John St   7837 7816   8–3D

An acting-themed pub with a working theatre upstairs, located opposite Sadler's Wells. Obviously it attracts a fair number of 'thespie' types, but has managed (despite a recent refurbishment) to retain a crowd of locals and a lot of traditional character. A wide range of ales is a further attraction, as well as a few strong euro-lagers on tap. There's a tiny rear beer garden out back. / **Website:** www.oldredliontheatre.co.uk **Details:** no Amex; no-smoking area. **Food:** till 7.45pm.

The Old Ship W6

25 Upper Mall   8748 2593   7–2A

Despite being on the site of one of the oldest inns in Hammersmith, this nautically-themed pub overlooking the river doesn't feel nearly as historic as The Dove (five minutes' walk away). It certainly doesn't want for custom, though – on summer weekends especially (when its large outside terrace and neighbouring grass come into their own) it heaves with a twentysomething crowd which seems to include every Aussie and Kiwi in town. / **Website:** www.oldshipw6.co.uk **Details:** Mon-Sat 9am-11pm, Sun 9am-10.30pm. **Food:** Mon-Sat 9am-10.30pm, Sun 9am-10pm.

The Old Thameside Inn SE1

Clink St   7403 4243   9–3C

This sprawling pub, next to the Golden Hinde – where the South Bank walk takes a diversion along Clink Street – is undoubtedly a bit corporate, but it has a handy location, and is one of the best in the area. / **Details:** no-smoking area. **Food:** L only.

Ye Old White Horse WC2

2 St Clement's Ln   7242 5518   2–1D

A location in the lanes behind the Royal Courts of Justice guarantees a strong legal-land following for this old-fashioned pub. Behind the tiny frontage, there's a red-decorated traditional interior where Breakspears, Flowers, TT Landlord and IPA on tap are the popular tipples. / **Details:** closed weekends; no Amex. **Food:** till 2pm.

Ye Olde Cheshire Cheese EC4
145 Fleet St   7353 6170   9–2A
In Baedeker's 1904 guide, this historic City pub – the local in its time of Dickens and Dr Johnson – was already a recommended London attraction. Since then, little has changed and, especially in winter when the real coal fire is burning, its warren of bars offers one of the best tastes of olde England in town. It attracts a good local following, as well as tourists. The bar grub is in fact quite good, and the restaurant fare perfectly acceptable.
/ **Website:** www.yeoldecheshirecheese.com **Details:** Sat 11.30pm-3pm & 5.30pm-11pm, Sun noon-3pm. **Food:** L till 2.30pm, D till 9.30pm, bar snacks also available.

Ye Olde Mitre Tavern EC1
1 Ely Court   7405 4751   9–2A
When you finally locate this ancient wooden tavern (down a tiny, dank alley off Hatton Garden), it feels like you've stepped back in time – especially in winter, when the outside drinking area is very quiet. There's a couple of connected rooms – the tiny panelled front bar to the comfortable and a cosy back room – in which to enjoy a fair range of ales and lagers.
/ **Details:** closed weekends; no credit cards. **Food:** till 9.15pm.

Ye Olde Red Cow EC1
71 Long Ln   7606 0735   9–1B
Ownership by brewers Shepherd Neame helps this traditional pub – the oldest in Smithfield – stand out in this bit of town. There's a nice private room upstairs, and a restaurant where – as you might expect – steaks from the Market are the speciality. / **Details:** closed weekends; no Amex. **Food:** L only.

Ye Olde Wine Shades EC4
6 Martin Ln   7626 6876   9–3C
A branch of El Vino's (see also); though its Fleet Street sibling is arguably more famous, this one (by Blackfriars Bridge) is rather lighter and airier, and has the distinction of being the oldest wine bar actually within the Square Mile to survive the Great Fire. It otherwise offers a rather similar package – acceptable food and better claret – and is very popular with the local lawyers and other pinstripes. / **Details:** Mon 8.30am-9pm, Tue-Fri 8.30am-10pm, closed Sat & Sun. **Food:** L till 3pm.

Olé SW6

Fulham Broadway   7610 2010   10–1A

*The eye-catching stained glass behind the bar is in sharp
contrast to the modishly minimalist setting at this small new bar
near Fulham Broadway tube. A tapas menu of some distinction
is the real point of the place, but it also makes a nice spot for a
drink. There's a few Hispanic bottled beers, plus twenty or so
Spanish wines. / **Website:** www.olerestaurant.com **Details:** Sun from 6pm.
Food: L till 3pm, D till 10.45pm. **DJ:** Wed.*

On Anon W1

London Pavilion, Piccadilly Circus   7287 8008   3–3D

*On the plus side, this multi-floored West End behemoth was
designed with some imagination and features a whole range of
bars in multivarious improbable styles. On the minus side,
it's hard for a place owned by Big Business and located right
over Piccadilly Circus not to feel a bit naff. The deciding factor
for many is the generous happy hour, which wins it huge
popularity as an after-work hang out.
/ **Website:** www.latenightlondon.co.uk, www.onanon.co.uk **Details:** Mon-Tue
5pm-1am, Wed-Sat 5pm-3am, Sun 5pm-midnight. **Food:** till 3am.
DJ: Wed-Sat from 9pm. **Happy hour:** 5pm-7.30pm (all wine (except house)
& spirits half-price, £10 off champagne, £3 cocktails).*

One SW6

541 King's Rd   7610 9067   10–1A

*The first bar in Fulham – if you're coming from Chelsea, that is
– is this nicely converted former boozer by the hump in the
King's Road. An open fire, lots of red sofas red and subdued
lighting all contribute to a cosy feel. Though this isn't your
classic Antipodean bar, they make a big thing of serving some
of the top Oz beers of choice (VB & Carlton Crown). For the
summer, there's a nice two-level rear terrace.
/ **Website:** www.loadeddog.co.uk **Details:** no Amex. **Food:** L till 3pm, D till
10pm. **Happy hour:** Mon 5pm-11pm, Tue 5pm-close, Wed & Fri
5pm-7.30pm (pint or glass of wine £2).*

(The Lobby Bar)
One Aldwych WC2
1 Aldwych   7300 1000   2–1D
This very stylish design-hotel on the edge of Covent Garden has been a great success. This is perhaps partially accounted for by the fact that its double-height entrance lobby is largely given over to the cocktail bar, which offers an elegant space in which to enjoy a drink at any time of day. / **Food:** bar snacks 5.30pm-10pm, cakes noon-4pm, Sun brunch.

190 Queensgate SW7
190 Queen's Gt   7581 5666   5–1B
With its comfy leather sofas and panelled walls, this large and clubby room (entered off the lobby of a South Kensington hotel) is one of the few bars in town which might reasonably be said to be both 'louche' and 'charming' at once. Not the least of its attractions is the ability to drink into the early hours, though being technically part of a club, entry is sometimes restricted – particularly later on at the weekends. / **Details:** Mon-Thu noon-midnight, Fri & Sat noon-2am, Sun 12.30pm-11.30pm. **Food:** till 1.30am, Sun till midnight.

Opera NW3
68 Heath St   7435 3140   8–1A
Known for a time as China Dream (and, before that, as the Horse & Groom), this impressively refurbished Hampstead pub has been turned, surprisingly successfully, into an elegant and atmospheric oriental bar/restaurant. It's a fun destination whether you're eating or drinking, and there's a DJ on Saturday nights. / **Details:** Mon-Wed noon-3pm & 6pm-10.30pm, Thu-Fri noon-3pm & 6pm-11.30pm, Sat & Sun noon-11.30pm (Sun 10.30pm). **Food:** L&D. **DJ:** Fri-Sat (hip hop). **Live music:** jazz Tue-Thu.

The Opera Tavern WC2
23 Catherine St   7379 9832   4–2D
Directly opposite Covent Garden's Theatre Royal, this ornately-fronted Victorian tavern is useful for a pre-theatre drink (or snack). It's a large and comfortable place (and one that's quite welcoming to families). / **Food:** Tue-Sat L till 3pm, D till 8pm.

Opium W1

1a, Dean St   7287 9608   3–1D

Lavish, boudoir-esque décor makes this Vietnamese basement bar/restaurant, at the top end of Soho, a great spot for a loungey cocktail. Drinks are quite pricey, so this might make a better place for a rendezvous than to spend the whole evening. Alternatively, come late to take advantage of the late opening and clubby entertainments (DJs and cabaret).
/ *Website:* www.opium-bar-restaurant.com *Details:* Mon-Thu 6pm-1.30am, Fri & Sat 6pm-3am, closed Sun. *Food:* 6pm-10pm. *DJ:* Thu-Sat.

The Orange Brewery SW1

37 Pimlico Rd   7730 5984   5–2D

A basement brewery provides the beer for this popular hostelry overlooking Orange Square (as 'Pimlico Green' seems to be called nowadays), and a short walk from Sloane Square. It's been around for ages, certainly pre-dating the current micro-brewery trend. The interior – where the vital statistics of each new brew are posted – is plainly but comfortably furnished, but in good weather people often prefer to drink outside.
/ *Details:* no-smoking area in restaurant. *Food:* till 8.30pm, bar snacks till 9.30pm.

Oriel SW1

50-51 Sloane Sq   7730 2804   5–2D

In spirit – if not in culinary achievement – this prominently-located bar/brasserie on a corner of the square is perhaps London's closest match to its Parisian equivalents. It's busy around the clock and – especially if you can get an outside table – makes a great place to watch the world go by. Alternatively, there's a downstairs wine bar which is a particular haunt of local after-work drinkers. / *Details:* no-smoking area. *Food:* till 10.50pm.

Oscar
Charlotte Street Hotel W1

15 Charlotte St   7907 4000   4–1A

The restaurant and bar open off the lobby of this Fitzrovia design hotel. We've never been great fans of the former, but the latter is a popular, spacious venue and has the added attraction of doors which open on a sunny day to allow drinkers to spill out onto the street. There's a fair wine list and list of cocktails (somewhat wince-makingly named for the likes of 'Posh Spice' and 'Jennifer Lopez'). / *Details:* Sun 6-9pm. *Food:* till 10.30pm.

OSP W6

Fulham Palace Rd   8748 6502   7–2B
*If this large new Greene King pub wasn't on a pretty barren stretch of highway it might not rate a mention. As it is, though, it deserves credit for providing an OK watering hole in the dull area south of Hammersmith Broadway. / **Details:** no-smoking area. **Food:** till 8pm. **DJ:** Fri. **Live music:** Sat.*

Oxo Tower SE1

Barge House St   7803 3888   9–3A
*Location, location and, er, location – those are the attractions of the bar at this famous bar/brasserie/restaurant, on the seventh floor of the landmark complex, which enjoys splendid views over the river, and of the north bank of the Thames. If you want to check the place out, it's a much lower-risk option that visiting the neighbouring, overpriced restaurant or brasserie. / **Website:** www.harveynichols.com **Food:** till 11pm.*

Pacific Oriental EC2

1 Bishopsgate   7621 9988   9–2C
*Prominently located in the heart of the City, this large, glossy modern venue is a slightly unlikely combination of bar, oriental brasserie and microbrewery. It's a popular 'personal account' venue for the workers in the local money factories, but while the oriental scoff is OK, it is arguably drinkers who are best served. / **Website:** www.pacificoriental.co.uk **Details:** closed weekends; no-smoking area. **Food:** till 9.30pm.*

Page's Bar SW1

75 Page St   7834 6791   2–3C
*To all intents and purposes, this is a pretty ordinary sports bar, lost in the backwoods of Westminster (and, if you're into that sort of thing, adjacent to some of the most architecturally interesting council-housing in town). Over the pool table, however, hangs a large model of the Starship Enterprise. This, together with other whimsical decorative touches, has given the place something of reputation as a Trekkies' delight – beware the 'special' nights! / **Website:** www.pagesbar.com **Details:** closed weekends. **Food:** L till 2pm.*

Paradise by Way of Kensal Green W10

19 Kilburn Ln   8969 0098   1–1B

The first and still the best (if not quite still the only) bar in Kensal Green continues to exert a pull on a very hip media crowd from far and wide – particularly nearby Notting Hill. There's nothing obviously cutting-edge about it – it's just a comfy and relaxed place, with a nice garden and some pretty good food. / Website: www.theparadise.co.uk Details: Fri & Sat noon-midnight; no Amex. Food: till 10.50pm. DJ: once/month Sun. Live music: salsa Mon.

Paviours Arms SW1

75 Page St   7834 2150   2–3C

How this very large Fullers pub – which so often appears bereft of custom – remains in business is something of a mystery. There aren't many pubs about, though, where the décor gives every impression of being genuine '30s, so it's certainly a destination for connoisseurs of pub architecture (and ideal for those who like their pints really quiet). / Website: www.fullers.co.uk Details: closed weekends. Food: till 10.30pm.

The Paxton's Head SW1

153 Knightsbridge   7589 6627   5–1D

A palace among pubs, this large and very popular Knightsbridge boozer offers three floors, all of which are of interest in their different ways. The ground floor is traditional, with lots of dark wood and frosted glass, and heaps of charm which even the fruit machine doesn't manage to take away. In the basement, there's a loungier bar, complete with big-screen TV, and upstairs a rather cool restaurant, called Pan-Asian Canteen. / Food: till 10pm. DJ: Fri. Happy hour: Mon all day, otherwise 5.30pm-7.30pm (Mon 2 for 1 cocktails, all week bottle wine £5).

The Peasant EC1

240 St John St   7336 7726   9–1A

This corner pub (the large mosaic of St George slaying the dragon hints at its former name), was one of the first a few years back to be sympathetically-converted into classic Clerkenwell gastropub mode. A fair selection of beers (including Bombardier and Hoegaarden) and tapas-style snacks satisfy the punters – there's also an airy restaurant upstairs (with a terrace). / Website: www.thepeasant.co.uk Details: Sat 6pm-11pm, closed Sun. Food: till 11pm.

The Pelican W11

45 All Saints Rd 7792 3073 6–1B

Part of a trio of organic (Soil Association-approved) London pubs, this recently renovated corner boozer, near the Portobello Road, is an ideal place to test the theory that organic beer leaves no trace of a hangover. Alternatively, you could go and enjoy some cooking that comes with a fine degree of flair.
/ **Website:** www.singhboulton.co.uk **Details:** no-smoking area. **Food:** till 10.45pm.

The Pen SW6

51 Parson's Green Ln 7371 8517 10–1A

This sleek bar opposite Parson's Green tube was – a decade ago – the first in Fulham to chuck out its old pub knick-knacks, and re-invent itself. Its sleek styling has kept moving with the times, though, and the overall look remains well above that of a typical modern pub or gastropub. The food in the restaurant upstairs is very good, and there are also quality snacks in the bar. / **Website:** www.thepenrestaurant.co.uk **Details:** no Amex. **Food:** till 10.30pm.

Pentagon SW4

64 Clapham High St 7498 8822 10–2C

There's little to hint from outside as to the size of this newish hang-out, which opens Tardis-like into two levels at the back. It's full of a friendly twentysomething crowd, and its relaxed atmosphere and funky music (not to mention late opening) make it a better venue than many on the Clapham strip.
/ **Details:** Mon-Thu 4pm-midnight, Fri 4pm-2am, Sat 3pm-2am, Sun 2pm-midnight; no Amex. **Food:** Sun L only.

La Perla WC2

28 Maiden Ln 7240 7400 4–3D

It's not the last cry in sophistication, but for a fun night out that won't break the bank there are far worse places than this Tex/Mex cantina – packed on busy nights with a raucous, largely twentysomething crowd. Margaritas and bottled lagers are the order of the day, and there's some cheap (and not bad) Tex/Mex scoff to help soak 'em up.
/ **Website:** www.cafepacifico-theperla.com **Details:** Sun from 4pm. **Food:** till 10.50pm. **Happy hour:** 4pm-7pm (cocktails £2.95, beer & wine £1.80).

The Perseverance WC1

63 Lamb's Conduit St   7405 8278   2–1D

The generations of London University students who knew this Bloomsbury boozer as 'The Sun' might have some difficulty in recognising it nowadays. It's now a smarter-than-average gastropub (diners even getting tablecloths!) serving some great food. At lunchtimes you can't actually just drink here – the whole place is given over to eating. At night, though, diners get shifted upstairs and the ground floor operates as a regular bar. About as many drinkers go for wine as go for the lagers and bitter on tap. / **Details:** Mon-Sat 12.30pm-11pm, Sun 12.30pm-10.30pm. **Food:** till 9.30pm.

Pharmacy W11

150 Notting Hill Gate   7221 2442   6–2B

The colourful molecular sculpture (once spuriously described as Damien Hirst's DNA) over the entrance, plus a façade like a Continental pharmacy have made this large bar/restaurant a Notting Hill landmark for about five years now. The ground floor bar has been revamped somewhat in recent times, but still looks like a chemist shop on acid, with its surgically white décor and rows of medicine cabinets. / **Website:** www.pharmacylondon.com **Details:** Mon-Sun noon-3pm & 5.30pm-1am (Fri & Sat 2am). **Food:** L till 3pm, D till 10.30pm. **DJ:** Wed-Sun.

The Phene Arms SW3

9 Phene St   7352 3294   5–3C

Dr Phene was the man who had the idea of prettifying streets by planting them with trees, so it's appropriate that this rather hidden-away gem of a Chelsea pub is most famous for its large garden (complete with impressive tree). An interesting clientèle which extends all the way from bright young things via some famous locals to the odd mature regular only adds to its attractions. / **Food:** L only.

Pillars of Hercules W1

7 Greek St   7437 1179   4–2A

Even if it does have a DJ one night a week, this traditional panelled pub (mentioned in 'A Tale of Two Cities') is a welcome alternative to the trendy bars now prevalent in Soho. It's quite small and narrow so can get crowded, but the locals are pretty friendly. / **Food:** L&D. **DJ:** Wed.

Pilot W4

56 Wellesley Rd   8994 0828   7–2A

There aren't many places to drink or eat in the area south of Gunnersbury Tube, and this new gastropub fills both needs. It's the latest in a small chain (which includes the Mason's Arms and Stonemason's) and adopts the same casual and relaxing style. In summer, the outside area out back comes into its own. / **Food:** *L till 3.30pm, D till 10pm.*

The Pineapple NW5

51 Leverton St   7284 4631   8–2C

Local activists recently thwarted the proposed redevelopment of this old Kentish Town boozer by succeeding in getting the building listed. Posterity's the gainer, as it's a charming small place, and the new managers are putting considerable effort into making it a success, not least on the cooking front. / **Website:** *www.thepineapplelondon.com*

Pitcher & Piano

1 Dover St, W1   7495 8704
10 Pollen St, W1   7629 9581
69-71 Dean St, W1   7434 3585
40-42 King William IV St, WC2   7240 6180
42 Kingsway, WC2   7404 8510
214 Fulham Rd, SW10   7352 9234
316-318 King's Rd, SW3   7352 0025
871-873 Fulham Rd, SW6   7736 3910
18-20 Chiswick High Rd, W4   8742 7731
68 Upper St, N1   7704 9974

Pitcher & Piano (continued)
94 Northcote Rd, SW11   7738 9751
8 Balham Hill, SW12   8673 1107
11 Bellevue Rd, SW17   8767 6982
4-5 High St, SW19   8879 7020
11 Bridge St, TW9   8332 2524
200 Bishopsgate, EC2   7929 5914
28-31 Cornhill, EC3   7929 3989
The Arches, 9 Crutched Friars, EC3   7480 6818
67-69 Watling St, EC4   7248 0883
*A few years ago – when it made the move from being a couple
of bars in Fulham to becoming a West End (later national)
chain – these 'yuppie' wine bars were briefly stylish symbols of
the time. Now part and parcel of any high street (along with All
Bar One) they've largely lost their individual character, though
they can still be useful standbys (and are usually packed after
work). / **Website:** www.pitcherandpiano.com **Details:** vary. **Food:** L&D &
bar snacks.*

PJ's SW3
52 Fulham Rd   7581 0025   5–2C
*The 'always buzzing' cliché is more than usually accurate when
it comes to this clubbily panelled bar/diner in Chelsea. Although
the place is notionally American (and baseball)-themed,
it generally seems most popular with the local Brits and Euros.
Food is always available but, except at weekend brunch (which
is very popular), it's probably better to eat elsewhere.
/ **Details:** Mon-Sat noon-midnight, Sun noon-11pm. **Food:** till 10.50pm.*

Plan Bar SW9
418 Brixton Rd   7733 0926   10–2C
*Opened in October 2002, this late-night DJ bar (specialising in
soul and funk, with some house) is Brixton's newest hip 'n'
happening place of the moment. The entrance gives no hint of
the large (300-capacity) main area, fringed with tables, chairs
and booths – the middle is devoted to meeting, greeting,
moving and grooving. / **Website:** www.plan-brixton.co.uk
Details: Sun-Thu noon-2am, Fri & Sat noon-3am. **Food:** till 10pm.
DJ: Thu-Sun. **Happy hour:** Mon-Fri 5pm-7pm (discounts in cocktails & wine).*

Play EC1

58 Old St   7737 7090   9–1D

*From the team behind the Dogstar, Red Star and Living, this two-floored '70s-retro (think swirly brown wallpaper) Clerkenwell DJ/lounge bar attracts a hip crowd of twentysomethings who like to shimmy into the early hours to a mix of disco, funk and house. Main drinks: draft and bottled lager, or wine. / **Website:** www.playbar.co.uk **Details:** Mon-Thu noon-2am, Fri & Sat noon-4am, closed Sun. **Food:** L&D. **DJ:** nightly (house & 70's/80's).*

The Player W1

8-12 Broadwick St   7494 9125   3–2D

*If you didn't know it was there, you'd pass by this inconspicuous door in a sleazy part of Soho and never think to descend the stairs to one of the best-reputed cocktail bars in town. Its plush banquettes make ideal lounging points, typically for execs who fancy themselves as Players in the music biz. It was formerly a members' bar, but now it's open to all – an invitation it would be rude not to take up. / **Website:** www.thplyr.com **Details:** Mon-Thu 5.30pm-midnight, Fri 5.30pm-1am, Sat 7pm-1am. **Food:** till midnight. **DJ:** nightly.*

Pleasure Unit E2

359 Bethnal Green Rd   7729 0167   1–1D

*Formerly a gay bar called the Cock & Comfort, this groovy DJ bar feels quite out of place in gritty Bethnal Green. There's plenty of custom (young, trendy types and students) for the late-night weekend opening, however, so perhaps this place will one day be hailed as the first to drag this part of the East End into the 21st-century. / **Details:** Mon-Thu from 5pm, Fri 5pm-2am, Sat 4pm-2am, Sun from 3pm; no Amex. **Food:** Fri-Sat pm. **DJ:** Mon (open deck), Wed-Sat (reggae & house Wed, indie Thu.*

The Plough WC1

27 Museum St   7636 7964   4–1B

*Just down from The Museum Tavern, this traditional boozer similarly appeals to both locals and tourists alike. Though not as old as it's neighbour, it still has an air of Victoriana and a good range of ales from Adnams to Broadside and Pedigree. One concession to modern times is a TV which regularly shows football nights. However, if you want to escape you can go to the non-smoking bar upstairs. / **Food:** till 7pm (Sun till 4pm).*

Plumbers Arms SW1

14 Lower Belgrave St   7730 4067   2–3B

Students of recent history will not wish to miss out on a visit to this Georgian boozer, off Eaton Square, famously the place where Lady Lucan, in 1974, announced the murder of her children's nanny as well as an attempt on her own life. That's as aristocratic as the place's associations get, however, and it's really a pretty typical local boozer nowadays. / **Details:** *closed weekends.* **Food:** *till 9.30pm.*

Po Na Na

220 Fulham Rd, SW10   7352 5978   5–3B
316 King's Rd, SW3   7352 7127   5–3C
259 Upper St, N1   7359 6191   8–2D

In the space of about ten years, this Bedouin-themed bar brand has gone from being a late night drinking den for Chelsea's gilded youth, to a national chain that's increasingly seen as pretty mass-market. These days its the Hammersmith branch (what used to be the Palais) which is best-known, on account of all the tube posters of scantily clad schoolgirls (well twentysomethings dressed as school girls), advertising the regular "School Disco". / **Website:** *www.ponana.co.uk* **Details:** *vary.* **Food:** *bar snacks only.* **DJ:** *nightly.* **Happy hour:** *Mon-Wed (reduced prices).*

The Poet EC3

20 Creechurch Ln   7623 2020   9–2D

The City down Aldgate way is not the most enticing area for a drink (or a light bite), so this rather cavernous modern gastropub is a destination worth knowing about if you should find yourself in these parts. Unsurprisingly, it's especially crowded at lunchtime. / **Website:** *www.thepoet.co.uk* **Details:** *closed weekends.* **Food:** *L only.*

The Point SW17

16-18 Ritherdon Rd   8767 2660   10–2B

In the no-man's-land between Balham and Tooting, this Gallic wine bar understandably attracts a fair amount of custom, not least on account of the happy-hour deals and friendly staff that create a buzzing atmosphere almost every night. There's decent plonk, and some European beers on draught, plus good bar snacks (or if you're hungry, a restaurant at the back). / **Details:** *Mon-Sat 9.30am-11pm, Sun 9.30am-10.30pm.* **Food:** *till 10.30pm.* **Happy hour:** *6pm-8pm (2 for 1 on cocktails & beer).*

Le Pont de la Tour Bar & Grill SE1

Butlers Whf   7403 8403   9–3D
*Stunning views of the Thames and Tower Bridge alone make it
worth a trip to Sir Terence Conran's riverside 'gastrodome.'
Regular musicians and jazz bands make it a chilled-out place,
especially if you can bag one of the outside seats.
The restaurant is pricey, so if you want to eat, stick to the steak
'n' seafood fare in the bar.* / **Website:** *www.conran.com* **Food:** *till
10.45pm.*

The Pool EC2

104-108 Curtain Rd   7739 9608   9–1D
*With its large picture windows (looking over to rival The Elbow
Room) and high ceilings, this bright pool hall-cum-bar strikes
some people as trendy, but others as rather cavernous and
soulless. There's a basement, where they pump up the volume
in the evenings.* / **Website:** *www.thepool.uk.com* **Details:** *Mon-Tue
noon-11pm, Wed-Thu noon-1am, Fri & Sat noon-2am, Sun noon-midnight;
no Amex.* **Food:** *till 10.30pm, Sun noon-4pm.*

The Porterhouse WC2

21-22 Maiden Ln   7379 7917   4–3D
*Modelled on the original, in Dublin's Temple Bar, this cavernous,
tastefully done, multi-level theme bar offers decent Guinness,
as well as some own-brand Irish tipples. It's big enough to
swallow the inevitable crowds of stag parties and office juniors,
while still leaving nooks and crannies for smaller groups.*
/ **Website:** *www.porterhousebrewco.com* **Food:** *till 9pm.*

Porters WC2

16-17 Henrietta St   7836 6466   4–3D
*This colourful, modern Covent Garden bar couldn't be more
different in style than its older restaurant sibling nearby (which
shares the name, and ploughs a decidedly dated and touristy,
English-theme furrow). Some might find it a touch anonymous,
but it's comfortable (with a big basement), handy, and the fact
that it's usually busy boosts the atmosphere levels.*
/ **Website:** *www.porters.uk.com* **Food:** *till 10.45pm.*

Portobello Gold W11
95 Portobello Rd   7460 4900   6–2B
*Despite its position in the heart of Notting Hill, and despite
having been one of the first pubs in town to be given the bar
treatment, this gentrified boozer has never attracted the more
self-conscious local trendies. Market traders rub shoulders with
tourists in the bar and large dining conservatory, and there's
quite an interesting list of drinks including Belgian beers on
draft. Bill Clinton gave the place its 15 minutes of fame when
he stopped by for a pint in 2000.* / **Website:** *www.portobellogold.com*
Details: *Mon-Sun 10am-11pm.* **Food:** *till 10pm (Sun till 8pm).*
Happy hour: *5pm-7pm (special offers).*

Portobello Star W11
171 Portobello Rd   7229 8016   6–1B
*This small Notting Hill pub – with the front largely open to the
street on sunny days, and a few benches on the pavement –
is a favourite with the local market traders. Opened in 1838,
originally as a "Jug and ale house", it retains an old-fashioned,
down-to-earth atmosphere and serves a full range of tipples,
including Heineken Export, Stella, Flowers Original and
Boddingtons on tap.* / **Details:** *no credit cards.* **Food:** *bar snacks Sun-Fri,
Sat full menu.*

Potemkin EC1
144 Clerkenwell Rd   7278 6661   9–1A
*There's nothing particularly Russian about the décor at this
bright, minimalist bar, on a corner-site just north of Hatton
Garden. The drinks selection, though, could do even Boris
Yeltsin proud – a bewildering selection of vodkas, cocktails,
beers and spirits. In the basement there's a restaurant, but the
bar itself offers a good range of zakuski (snacks), from pickles
and soups to caviar.* / **Website:** *www.potemkin.co.uk* **Details:** *Mon-Fri
noon-midnight, Sat 6pm-11pm, closed Sun.* **Food:** *L till 3pm (closed Sat L), D
till 10.30pm.*

Pride of Spitalfields E1
3 Heneage St   7247 8933   9–1D
*Hidden away just off the south end of Brick Lane, this popular,
traditional boozer (once known as The Romford Arms) makes a
cosy, comfortable meeting place for locals, curry-lovers and
miscellaneous East End visitors. Many punters opt for a lager (a
mainstream selection), but there's also fair selection of real ales
including guest beers.* / **Food:** *L only.*

The Prince N16

59 Kynaston Rd   7923 4766   1–1C

This smarter-than-average gastropub to the south of Stoke Newington Church Street features etched windows and a funky interior design. There's an extensive wine list, and beers on tap include San Miguel, Flowers and Staropramen. Just in case you're shy of asking, the motto "Clowns Fear Pie", over the bar, is – of course – an anagram of the pub's name in its former incarnation. / **Details:** Mon-Fri from 4pm. **Food:** L&D.

The Prince Alfred W9

5a, Formosa St   7286 3287   6–1C

This gorgeous Grade I listed Victorian pub in Maida Vale – one of the few in London still divided by screens into numerous separate drinking areas – was sleekly restored a couple of years ago, and it's now a very superior drinking establishment indeed. The Formosa Dining Rooms, in a stylish extension, offers full restaurant service. / **Food:** bar snacks till 6pm, L till 3pm (Sun L till 4pm), D till 10.30pm,.

The Prince Bonaparte W2

80 Chepstow Rd   7313 9491   6–1B

It's basic, bright, crowded, noisy and smoky, but that seems to be almost why fans like this no-nonsense Bayswater boozer, which appeals to the less poncey end of the Notting Hillbilly set. The food is good (the Sunday roast in particular) and there's a fair array of wine and guest beers to add interest to the selection of ales and lagers. / **Details:** no smoking at bar. **Food:** till 10pm.

The Prince of Teck SW5

161 Earl's Court Rd   7373 3107   5–2A

London's huge Aussie community has pretty much moved on from Earl's Court nowadays, but this loud Finch's corner boozer remains something of a rallying point (and for Kiwis too). If you're looking for a shrine to Antipodean 'culture', it's a good choice for atmosphere to the max, visit during the rugby. / **Details:** no Amex. **DJ:** will be during the week until Thu. **Live music:** Sun from 7pm.

Prince of Wales SW4
38 Clapham Old Town   7622 3530   10–2C
*A traditional-looking Clapham boozer with a difference or two –
namely the neon sign outside and the bric-à-brac hanging from
the ceiling, which encompasses such items as bicycle wheels
and bongos. A fun and friendly place with a reasonable range
of beers.* / **Details:** *Mon-Fri from 5pm, weekends from 1pm; no credit cards.*

The Princess Louise WC1
208 High Holborn   7405 8816   4–1C
*A slightly unfortunate location – stuck out on a limb on a very
busy road – sadly limits the charms of this monumental late-
Victorian Sam Smith's pub in Bloomsbury. That said, it is worth
a visit for the architecture alone, and the place attracts a
reasonable crowd, which tends to be businessy at lunch,
and younger in the evening.* / **Food:** *L till 2.30pm, D till 8.30pm.*

Princess of Wales SE3
1a, Montpelier Rw   8297 5911   1–3D
*Traditional, but not twee, this large Blackheath pub at the edge
of the heath is quite a local favourite. There's a charming patio
garden for summer (and a large conservatory extension for less
clement times) and a small panelled parlour filled with rugby
memorabilia (fascinating fact: the first-ever England XV is
apparently organised here.)* / **Details:** *no-smoking areas.* **Food:** *till 9pm.*

Priory W14
58 Milson Road   7371 3999   7–1B
*Lost in the backstreets of Olympia, this relaxed lounge bar was
converted from a pub a couple of years back. Done out with a
Gothic theme, it makes a fun hang out for a local crowd with
draft lager (Stella, Hoegaarden, Fosters…) the most popular
tipple. It's no a gastro-destination, but the food is OK and
reasonably priced.* / **Website:** *www.priorybars.com* **Food:** *L till 3pm
(weekends 4pm), D till 10pm.*

Priory Arms SW8
83 Lansdowne Way   7622 1884   10–1C
*For those who really like their ales, the ever-changing selection
on offer at this South Lambeth boozer is a potent attraction.
Otherwise, it's just a nice and fairly unremarkable place –
if you're looking for an occasion to check it out, it does a nice
Sunday roast.* / **Food:** *L only.*

Prism EC3

147 Leadenhall St   7256 3888   9–2D

This low-ceilinged bar is hidden away in the bowels of Harvey Nichol's City restaurant outpost – it couldn't be in starker contrast to the cavernous former banking hall restaurant above. Comfortable white leather banquettes add to the character of the chic décor and – at lunchtime – make rousing yourself to head back to the office that bit more difficult.
/ **Website:** www.harveynichols.com **Details:** closed weekends. **Food:** till 10pm.

The Prophet EC2

5-11 Worship St   7588 8835   9–1C

There are some nice funky touches to the styling at this large new bar/restaurant near Finsbury Square, which opened in August 2002. (It's part of a promising new group which includes The Assembly on Seething Lane and The Interval by Leicester Square.) As suggested by the large kitchen on view as you enter, there is quite a serious menu, but it's a fine place just for drinking too. / **Details:** closed weekends. **Food:** till 9pm (8pm Fri). **DJ:** Fri.

The Prospect of Whitby E1

57 Wapping Wall   7481 1095   11–1A

Built in 1520, this famous Wapping hostelry is – as proudly proclaimed over the door – the oldest of London's riverside taverns. Past customers include Henry VIII, Pepys, Dickens, Turner and Cap't Cook. It's well on the tourist trail, but still of interest to locals. Although the décor has seen the addition of a few cutesy flourishes over the years (especially in the upstairs restaurant), the place retains many wonderful period features including flagged floors, a lovely pewter bar and pillars made from ships' masts. All this and a pleasant riverside terrace.
/ **Details:** no-smoking area. **Food:** till 10pm.

Public Life E1

82A, Commercial St   7375 2425   9–2D

Possibly one of the smallest – and most unusual – drinking spots in London, this converted Victorian public lavatory is located in front of Spitalfields' imposing Hawksmoor church. It makes an intimate venue for the regular live gigs – which attract a local, arty crowd – but the slightly cold, hard-edged décor is a constant, and not entirely welcome, reminder of days gone by. / **Website:** www.publiclife.org **Details:** Mon-Sun noon-midnight; no Amex. **Food:** till 9pm.

The Punch & Judy WC2

40 The Mkt   7379 0923   4–3D

Few self-respecting Londoners would admit to being regulars of this expensive tourist-trap pub – located in the eaves of Covent Garden's covered market. Pop in at a quiet time, though, and the view from the terrace of the "Actors' Church" – or, if you prefer, the one featured in 'My Fair Lady' – is impressive.

/ **Website:** www.punchandjudycoventgarden.com **Details:** no-smoking area. **Food:** till 7pm (Sun 6pm), bar snacks till closing.

The Punch Tavern EC4

99 Fleet St   7353 6658   9–2A

This City-fringe pub is rather grander than your average boozer, appropriately enough for the building where the famous magazine of the same name was conceived in 1841. The décor and exhibits commemorate the puppet first recorded in England in 1662 (by Pepys), and the companion with whom he became inseparably twinned in subsequent centuries, Judy.

/ **Details:** closed weekends. **Food:** till 3pm (closed weekends). **Happy hour:** Wed-Fri (2 shots for £5).

Purple
Sanderson Hotel W1

50 Berners St   7300 9500   3–1D

The inner sanctum of Ian Schrager's poseurs' paradise design-hotel just north of Oxford Street. It's a superior choice to the better-known Long Bar, but more difficult to enter – if you're not a resident (or "on the list"), you're really not coming in.

/ **Website:** www.ianschragerhotels.com **Details:** Mon-Sun 5.30pm-3am (Residents only). **Food:** till 3am.

Putney Bridge SW15

Lower Richmond Rd   8780 1811   10–1A

Nominations for architectural awards came thick and fast a few years ago when this striking and unusual landmark was built, just upstream from the namesake river-crossing. Upstairs is an acclaimed restaurant, while the swish ground floor bar is done out with the kind of muted, understated (and expensive) style that's usually reserved for the West End. A range of nibbles is available to accompany the list of cocktails.

/ **Website:** www.putneybridgerestaurant.com **Details:** Mon-Fri noon-midnight, Sat noon-1am, Sun noon-10pm. **Food:** L till 2pm (2.30pm weekends), D till 10pm (10.30pm weekends).

Puzzle

187-189 High St, W3   8752 1925
175-177 Fulham Palace Rd, W6   7381 8682   10–1A
25-27 Westow Hill, SE19   8761 4396   1–3D
47-49 Lavender Hill, SW11   7978 7682   10–2B
90-92 Balham High Rd, SW12   8772 1155   10–2B
332 Garratt Ln, SW18   8874 4209   10–2A
Small but fast-expanding chain of modern pubs popular with twentysomethings and Aussies (often both at once). With their chunky wooden furniture and sofas, the look is pretty off-the-peg, but standards seem quite high. Quiz nights and sports screens are consistent features. / **Details:** *vary; no Amex.* **Food:** *L&D & bar snacks.*

Quaglino's SW1

16 Bury St   7930 6767   3–3D
How glamorous it all seemed when this vast Conran-owned venture opened a decade ago. These days, it doesn't draw the 'A'-list as once it did (or even the 'B'- or 'C'- list). Still the comfortable bar – which to an extent overlooks the diners below – still makes an unusual venue, and is still pretty popular, especially with St James's locals. / **Website:** *www.conran.com* **Details:** *Mon-Sun noon-3pm & 5.30pm-midnight (Fri & Sat 1am), Sun 5.30pm-11pm.* **Food:** *till 11.30pm.*

Queen's Head W6

Brook Grn   7603 3174   7–1B
If it wasn't under the dead hand of big brewery ownership, this wonderful, rambling old tavern on Brook Green could be one of the most atmospheric pubs in London. As it is, it still makes a cosy place in winter, and in summer there is the added attraction of a vast, and very well-maintained beer garden – one of the best in west London. There's a huge menu, from quite good snacks to over-pricey main dishes. / **Details:** *management declined to provide information; no-smoking area.* **Food:** *till 10pm.*

Queen's Head & Artichoke NW1
30-32 Albany St   7916 6206   8–3B
This revamped old tavern near Euston's Little India is popular with locals, and medics from the nearby Royal College of Physicians. It advertises itself as a gastropub these days (serving tapas at lunchtimes and modern British cuisine in the restaurant in the evenings). The wine list is fairly extensive but many opt for a pint of lager or bitter.
/ **Website:** www.theartichoke.net **Food:** L till 3pm, D till 10.15pm, Sun till 10pm.

The Queen's Larder WC1
1 Queen Sq   7837 5627   4–1C
A pretty location, outside tables, a decent range of ales and a good dose of historical interest add charm to a visit to this tiny pub north of Holborn. It's named in honour of Queen Charlotte who, during one of George III's bouts of madness, used the basement here as a store for provisions. / **Details:** no-smoking area. **Food:** till 8pm.

The Queens NW1
49 Regents Park Rd   7586 0408   8–3B
This impressive Young's tavern overlooking Primrose Hill was on the receiving end of a modern makeover a few years ago and has designs (in its upstairs dining room) on gastro-status. A friendly place, it has fewer pretensions than some of the competition hereabouts. / **Website:** www.youngs.co.uk **Details:** no Amex. **Food:** till 9.30pm.

Quod SW1
57 Haymarket   7925 1234   2–1C
As big brash Theatreland venues go, this vast, noisy and artified bar/brasserie – the latest creation of the man who originally started the Browns chain – has a hint more style than most. If you decide to stay, there's a menu which offers pizza and other Italian fare. / **Website:** www.quod.co.uk **Details:** Mon-Sat noon-midnight, closed Sun. **Food:** till 10.45pm. **Happy hour:** 8pm-10pm (half-price cocktails).

The Railway Tavern SW4
18 Clapham High St   7622 4077   10–1C
As the name suggests, this brightly converted Victorian corner pub, with large windows looking out on to the street, is right by the tracks (at Clapham High Street BR). With tables outside, it's a useful place – if, perhaps, not quite as nice as its siblings, the nearby Falcon and Sun. Lager is the most popular drink, and Thai scoff is also available. / **Details:** no Amex. **Food:** L till 3pm, D till 10.30pm.

The Rampage WC2
32 Great Queen St   7242 0622   2–1D
Falling somewhere between a wine bar (Bollinger logo on the awning), a boozer (tiles depicting old battle scenes on the walls) and an All Bar One (chunky blond furniture and young Antipodean staff), this modern bar is a useful Covent Garden standby. Those of a sensitive disposition may wish to avoid the times when rugby (and other international sports events) are on the big screen. / **Website:** www.frontpagepubs.com **Details:** closed Sun. **Food:** L till 3pm, D till 10pm.

Rapscallion SW4
75 Venn St   7787 6555   10–2C
This small (some say cramped) restaurant/bar opposite Clapham Picture House offers a range of wine and cocktails (and imported beers), mainly to a local crowd. It can get very crowded and noisy, but those who like the place really go a bundle on its buzzy atmosphere.
/ **Website:** www.therapscalliononline.com **Details:** Mon-Sat 10.30am-midnight, Sun 10.30am-11.30pm. **Food:** till 11pm.

Red Cube WC2
1 Leicester Pl   7287 0101   4–3B
Combining a bar, a restaurant and a dance floor, this is quite a place. Its location just off Leicester Square may not attract – how can one put it? – the most discerning crowd, but that's not to detract from the fact that the venue is impressive. You'd go here to 'make a night of it', not just drop by.
/ **Website:** www.redcubebarandgrill.com **Details:** Mon-Sat 5pm-3am, closed Sun. **Food:** till 3am. **DJ:** nightly. **Happy hour:** Mon-Fri 5pm-7pm (half-price wine, £10 off champagne, cocktails £3, spirits £1.75).

The Red Lion W1

1 Waverton St   7499 1307   2–2A

This charmingly located traditional boozer – which was converted from a farmhouse in 1742 – draws much of its 'tone' from its bijou Mayfair news location. It's not on an obvious road to anywhere, though, so a truly local crowd – residents and workers – is one of its key attractions.
/ Website: www.scottishnewcastle.co.uk Details: Sat 6pm-11pm, Sun noon-3pm & 6pm-10.30pm. Food: L till 2.30pm, D till 9.30pm.

The Red Lion SW1

23 Crown Passage   7930 4141   2–2B

With its cute location in a narrow St James's alleyway, this ancient boozer (which claims its 350-year-old licence is the second-oldest in the West End) looks every bit the quaint 'Olde English Pub'. Rather than tourists, though, its small and comfortable interior is generally packed with local workers, supping a pint of Adnams or Stella. Evenings can be quite a crush. / Details: closed Sun; no Amex. Food: L&D.

The Red Lion SW1

48 Parliament St   7930 5826   2–2C

Proximity to Parliament is a fundamental part of the atmosphere of this large, late-Victorian pub – it even has a division bell, by which MPs may be summoned to vote. It boasts all the aspects of an English pub a tourist would expect: fine etched glass, hanging baskets and people holding pints bursting out of the doors. The ground floor is mostly standing room only. Upstairs, there's a restaurant. / Website: www.redlionlondon.co.uk Details: Sun noon-7pm; no Amex; no smoking in restaurant. Food: L only.

The Red Lion SW1

2 Duke of York St   7930 2030   3–3D

One of the few half-way acceptable pubs in the heart of the West End, this richly decorated jewel of St James's has long been a popular rendezvous for local pinstripes. The interior is so small that the crowd on the pavement is a pretty much permanent installation. (NB: if you're attending a concert at St James's Piccadilly, a few yards away, this place provides the ideal interval bar which Wren so carelessly failed to provide.) / Details: closed Sun. Food: L till 3pm.

The Redstar SE5

319 Camberwell Rd 7703 7779 1–2C
*This converted boozer – Camberwell's cousin to Brixton's Dog
Star and Living – comes with a fine pedigree. On two floors,
the layout is along similar lines to Living – club tunes in the
ground floor bar, retro disco upstairs (weekends only). During
the week it's much more relaxed – Sundays see it at its
loungiest.* / **Website:** www.redstarbar.co.uk **Details:** Mon-Thu noon-2am,
Fri & Sat noon-4am, closed Sun. **Food:** L&D daily. **DJ:** nightly.

Reliance EC1

336 Old St 7729 6888 9–1D
*There's something of a 'frat' house atmosphere about this loud
and boozy bar south of Hoxton Square. Thanks to its bare and
grungy décor, it would be fair to say that it doesn't head the list
of local 'style' destinations.* / **Details:** Mon-Wed noon-11pm,
Thu noon-midnight, Fri noon-2am, Sat 6pm-2am, closed Sun. **Food:** L till 3pm,
D till 9.30pm. **DJ:** Wed-Sat. **Live music:** Tue fortnightly.

The Retreat N1

144 Upper St 7704 6868 8–3D
*Live music, DJs – hip hop, R&B, disco, soul – and sports TV are
the main attraction to this '70s-style Islington bar. It's also
sometimes open until the early hours, and later arrivals may
face an entrance charge.* / **Website:** www.the-retreat.fm
Details: Tue-Sat 5pm-2am, Sun 2pm-midnight (closed Mon); no Amex.
Food: till midnight. **DJ:** nightly.

Revolution

2 St Anne's Court, Off Dean St, W1 7434 0330 3–1D
95-97 Clapham High St, SW4 7720 6642 10–2C
*This North of England chain of funky vodka bars has only
recently hit the capital, but is already proving a huge hit.
The large, low-lit, Soho branch has been joined by a glazed two-
storey sibling in Clapham, and both are buzzing every evening –
and also popular for weekend brunch – with crowds of twenty-
and thirtysomethings fuelled by pitchers of cocktails, and vodka
shots.* / **Details:** W1 standard pub hours, SW4 11am-midnight. **Food:** till
8pm.

Richard I SE10
52 Royal Hill   8692 2996   1–2D
*The crowd is mostly local, but it's worth sniffing out this lovely friendly Young's pub, about ten minutes walk up Royal Hill from Greenwich Station. The small and cosy interior is still divided into separate bars, and there's an outside terrace where there are BBQs in summer. / **Details:*** management declined to provide information.

The Ring SE1
72 Blackfriars Rd   7928 2589   1–2C
*Archive fight footage on the TV, boxing paraphernalia on the walls and a sparring gym upstairs spell out the theme at this Southwark pub, opposite the new Jubilee Line station. You don't have to be a sarf London heavy to visit, though – the Thai scoff and outside seating help draw quite a mixed crowd. / **Details:*** no Amex. **Food:** L till 3pm, D till 10.30pm.

The Rising Sun EC1
38 Cloth Fair   7726 6671   9–1B
*You'd expect a Sam Smith's pub in the shadow of one of London's oldest places of worship (St Bartholomew-the-Great, founded 1123) to be suitably traditional and old-fashioned, and you wouldn't be disappointed here. The comfortable lounge bar has leather seating and a real fire, while the more sparsely furnished public bar has a dartboard and a rather 'men-only' atmosphere. / **Food:*** L till 2.30pm, D till 8pm.

(Rivoli Bar)
Ritz Hotel W1
150 Piccadilly   7493 8181   2–2B
*It hasn't yet taken enough knocks to have acquired much character, but the Ritz's new cocktail bar (removed from its old location, off the Palm Court) has been expensively decorated in just the sort of understated Deco style that should develop nicely over the next few decades. It's a small place, but well broken up, making this a great spot for a tête-à-tête, ideally over a couple of Martinis. / **Website:*** www.theritzhotel.co.uk **Food:** till 10.50pm.

River Walk
Oxo Tower SE1

Bargehouse St   7928 2864   9–3A
*Less flashily obvious than the bar on the top floor of this South
Bank landmark, the new second-floor cocktail
bar/brasserie/restaurant is in some ways rather more
atmospheric. If you're lucky, you may get one of the tables
overlooking the Thames, swirling a few feet below.* / **Food:** L&D.
Happy hour: 5pm-7pm.

The Rivington Grill EC2

28-30 Rivington St   7729 7053   9–1A
*This new bar/brasserie has already made itself something of an
all-day standby for Shoreditch locals – besuited business folk for
lunch, and a rather cooler crowd at night. They make quite a
thing of the food, but our visit didn't impress on this front – so a
better choice might be to settle in to one of the comfy sofas for
a cocktail or a glass of wine.* / **Details:** Sat 6:30pm-11pm. **Food:** L&D.

Rocket W1

4-6 Lancashire Ct   7629 2889   3–2B
*It may be hidden away in a cobbled mews, off Bond Street,
but don't expect this bar to be anything remotely approaching a
secret. On almost any weekday evening it's packed with post-
office drinkers hell bent on having a good time, and the two
small rooms regularly spill out on to the courtyard (come rain or
shine). The first-floor pizza restaurant offers tasty tucker at
keen prices for this part of town, so booking is always advisable.*
/ **Website:** www.freedombrewery.com **Details:** closed Sun. **Food:** till 11pm
(no D Thu & Fri).

Rockwell
Trafalgar SW1

2 Spring Gdns   7870 2959   2–2C
*Much of the ground floor of this trendy design hotel (a Hilton in
disguise) is given over to the bar, and it works pretty well as a
chilled space to laze around in. They've made Bourbon the
house speciality, and there are over a hundred types on offer.
In summer, you can also drink up on the sixth floor – see Roof
Garden.* / **Food:** 10am-11pm. **DJ:** Wed-Sat 8pm-1am.

The Roof Garden
Trafalgar Hotel SW1

2 Spring Gdns   7870 2959   2–2C

It's not always open to the public, so check ahead, but if you're looking for a classy and interesting place for a summer sundowner it's well worth seeking out this design-hotel roof terrace on Trafalgar Square. Enjoy your champagne or martini as you look out on the extraordinary jumble of roads and rooftops which make up central London.
/ Website: www.trafalgar.hilton.com Details: 6pm-midnight, closed Sun (May-Aug only).

The Rose & Crown SW19

55 High St   8947 4713   10–2A

The coach used to depart for London from this old hostelry on the fringe of the village by Wimbledon Common. These days it's one of Young's pub/hotels, and its large bar – lit by rose-coloured wall lights – has a hospitable, cosily-dated atmosphere. There's also a large cloistered garden out back.
/ Website: www.youngs.co.uk Details: no Amex; no-smoking area. Food: L till 3pm, D till 10pm (bar snacks all day).

Rosie's Bar
Cafe Grand Prix W1

50a Berkeley St   7629 0808   2–2B

Evoking the style of the transatlantic liners of the '30s, this elegant subterranean bar – beneath a swanky restaurant called Rascasse, which has a sibling establishment in Monaco – is something of a hidden gem. It makes a perfect Mayfair hide-away for cocktails, or a bottle of champagne. / Details: closed Sun. Food: D only.

The Round House WC2

1 Garrick St   7836 9838   4–3C

A prominent location on a Covent Garden corner (next to Tesco) has helped make this good-all-round pub extremely popular. It prides itself on its changing selection of real ales – on our visit, Butcombe bitter, Old Peculier and Bombardier were on offer. During the summer, local workers and tourists alike spill out on to the surrounding pavement. / Food: till 10.30pm.

Royal Court Bar
Royal Court Theatre SW1

Sloane Sq   7565 5061   5–2D

If you don't mind your architecture brutal, there's something quite satisfying about the bare concrete of this basement theatre bar, which actually extends a fair distance underneath the road into the square, and attracts many non-theatre-goers. It feels a bit like a grown-up students' union (and the bar grub, though cheap, is close to canteen fare). / **Details:** *closed Sun.* **Food:** *11am-10.30pm.*

Royal George SE8

85 Tanners Hill   8692 2594   1–2D

This attractive, red-painted corner boozer is simply decorated and attracts a mainly local and (with Goldsmith's not far away) student crowd. Not a 'destination', but a handy place to know if you find yourself down Dartford/New Cross way. / **Details:** *no credit cards.* **Food:** *till 8.30pm.*

Royal Inn on the Park E9

111 Lauriston Rd   8985 3321   1–1D

A great venue for summer, when you can spill out into the large beer gardens – or even, as the name would suggest, Victoria Park – this big wedding cake of a pub attracts a varied crowd. Non-standard beers are available on tap (including Ridleys, Old Bob and Litovel). Sunday lunch is a big event here, and if it's too wet and windy to go outside console yourself with the eclectic selection on the jukebox. / **Details:** *no Amex.* **Food:** *till 10.30pm (Sun 10pm).*

The Royal Oak SE1

44 Tabard St   7357 7173   9–3C

Rarely-seen – and very good – ales by Harvey's of Lewes make it worth seeking out this pretty Victorian pub (with impressively carved bar), if you find yourself down Borough way. The clientèle seems to be local, and mainly male. / **Details:** *closed weekends; no Amex.* **Food:** *L till 2.15pm, D till 9.15pm.*

La Rueda SW4

66-68 Clapham High St   7627 2173   10–2C
This large, long-established Clapham tapas bar, lined with bottles, has a big reputation for its buzzing atmosphere (aided by the fact that until recently it was one of the few places in the area where you could party till late). There is dancing until the wee hours, but be warned that they close the doors to newcomers at around 11pm, and sometimes earlier.
/ Details: Mon-Sat noon-11.30pm, Sun noon-10.30pm; no-smoking area. **Food:** *till 11.30pm.*

The Rugby Tavern WC1

19 Great James St   7405 1384   4–1C
*A fairly traditional, somewhat spartan Bloomsbury pub. It's themed (if that's the word) as the name suggests, but its main attraction is a good range of real ales. As you might expect quite a blokey sort of place, attracting a lot of workers from the local hospitals and so on. During the summer there are outside tables. / **Details:** closed weekends. **Food:** L till 2.30pm, D till 9.30pm.*

Saint WC2

8 Great Newport St   7240 1551   4–3B
*This basement 'style bar' (entered down an unpromising-looking staircase near Leicester Square) was an "'A'-list" kind of place when it opened a few years back. Nowadays, getting past the entrance isn't quite as tough as once it was, but the place still serves some decent cocktails and can still pull in a trendy-looking crowd. / **Website:** www.thebreakfastgroup.co.uk **Details:** Tue-Thu 5pm-2am, Fri 5pm-3am, Sat 7.30pm-3am (closed Mon & Sun).* **Food:** *Tue-Thu till 1.45am, Fri & Sat till 2.45am.* **DJ:** *nightly.*

The Salisbury WC2

90 St Martin's Ln   7836 5863   4–3B
*With its mirrors and mahogany, this lovely pub is one of the most attractive Victorian boozers in the West End. By virtue of its location – in the heart of Theatreland, next to the Albery – it's always very busy, but well worth a quick visit nonetheless. / **Food:** till 10.30pm.*

Salisbury Tavern SW6
21 Sherbrooke Rd 7381 4005 10–1A
*A classy makeover a couple of years ago transformed this large,
backstreets Fulham boozer into an unusually stylish gastropub –
more a bar/restaurant. The large dining room at the back is
pretty smart for a pub and they also do snacks in the bar
proper. Drinkers most commonly go for a pint of Bombardier or
Pride – but there's also a fair wine selection (and numerous
draft lagers). / **Food:** L only.*

Salmon & Compasses N1
58 Penton St 7837 3891 8–3D
*Abandon any thoughts that this misnamed establishment might
be a bucolic riverside boozer – this low-lit Islington 'Late Nite
Venue' is more a vodka and glitter-ball sort of place than one
where you settle down for a quiet pint. DJs spin funk and hip
hop as the evening progresses. / **Details:** 5pm-2am (Sun midnight);
no Amex. **DJ:** nightly.*

Salsa WC2
96 Charing Cross Rd 7379 3277 4–2B
*A hangar-like basement dance venue (with beginners and
advanced Salsa and Brazilian dance classes every night) that
attracts a post-office, up-for-it crowd, fuelled by cheap cocktails,
loud Latin music and Tex-Mex bites. It can be a laugh, but it's
not for the faint-hearted. There's an entry charge later on
(generally under a fiver, except on Saturday nights).
/ **Details:** Mon-Sat 5.30pm-2am, Sun 6pm-12.30am. **Food:** till 10.30pm,
bar snacks till 2am. **DJ & Live music:** nightly. **Happy hour:** Mon, Tue, Fri
5.30pm-7.30pm, Wed-Thu 5.30pm-7pm and 11pm-2am (half-price cocktails,
spirits & beer).*

The Salt House NW8
63 Abbey Rd 7328 6626 8–3A
*This former boozer was revamped a few years ago into a
thoroughly civilised neighbourhood bar and restaurant.
Attractions include sensible, well-priced food and nice outside
seating, and it's a local favourite as well as a superior stopping-
off point for those plying The Beatles tourist trail of London.
/ **Website:** www.thesalthouse.co.uk **Food:** till 10pm.*

Salusbury NW6
50-52 Salusbury Rd   7328 3286   I–IB
*With an atmosphere somewhere between a coffee house and a pub, this cosy, cocooning establishment makes an excellent, slightly surprising find in up-and-coming Queen's Park. Though there's a fair selection of wines, drinkers largely go for beers (Bass, Adnams, Caffrey's) or lagers (Carling, Grolsch, Staropramen). The dining room next to the bar serves some very good Italianate food. / **Details:** Mon from 5pm; no Amex. **Food:** till 10.15pm.*

The Salutation Inn W6
154 King St   8748 3668   7–2B
*In a slightly grungy location, opposite Hammersmith Town Hall, the smart façade of this ordinary-looking Fullers pub gives little hint of its hidden asset. Inside it's just another high-streety boozer, but out back, there's a large and very attractive beer garden. / **Details:** no Amex; no-smoking area. **Food:** till 9pm Mon-Fri (weekends 8pm).*

Sanctuary W1
4-5 Greek St   7434 3323   4–2A
*Previously called Form, this three-storey Soho venue was re-launched in late-2002. Upstairs is a spacious and chic piano bar (complete with white baby grand, mirror balls and leather sofas), downstairs in the basement is slightly more intimate with alcoves and there is a small dance floor on the ground floor. For its mainly gay crowd, we'd be surprised if it didn't quickly become a major destination. / **Website:** www.SanctuarySoho.com **Details:** Mon-Fri 5pm-3am, Sun 5pm-midnight. **Food:** from 5pm. **DJ:** nightly. **Live music:** pianist upstairs.*

Sanctuary House SW1
33 Tothill St   7799 4044   2–3C
*Big windows and Art Nouveau-style lamps give this Westminster corner site a welcoming and rather unusual appearance, more like a Viennese coffee shop, than the Fullers Ale & Pie House it actually is. Hard to beat if you're looking for a female-friendly drinking (and eating) environment with a touch more character than, say, your typical All Bar One. / **Website:** www.fullers.co.uk **Details:** no Amex. **Food:** till 8.45pm.*

Sand SW4

156 Clapham Park Rd   7622 3022   10–2C
*This late-licence bar opened a couple of years ago at the top of
Acre Lane. It's cool décor and trendy crowd (and communal
loos) add to its glamour, but some visitors find staff attitudes
rather negative.* / **Website:** www.sandbarrestaurant.co.uk
Details: 5pm-2am (Sun 1am); no Amex. **Food:** till 10.30pm. **DJ:** Thu-Sun.

Santa Fe N1

75 Upper St   7288 2288   8–3D
*There's a restaurant at the rear – where the fare is Tex/Mex-
going-on-southern American in style – but it's the welcoming
and comfortable bar at the front which is the star attraction of
this prominently-sited (slightly-themey looking) spot, by Islington
Green. Drink bottled beers or one of their (reasonably priced)
margaritas and other cocktails.* / **Website:** www.santafe.co.uk
Food: till 10.50pm.

Satay Bar SW9

447-450 Coldharbour Ln   7326 5001   10–2C
*A location just round the corner from the Ritzy cinema makes
this long, thin outfit a useful Brixton meeting place, especially
before or after the flicks. As its name hints, it's primarily a
Thai/oriental eatery, but many people do go just to drink,
and there's a wide range of cocktails and mixers. There's a
happy hour every day till 7pm when you're assured a seat,
but beware – later on its gets very busy.*
/ **Website:** www.sataybar.co.uk **Details:** Mon-Thu noon-midnight, Fri & Sat
noon-2am, Sun noon-11pm. **Food:** L till 3pm, D till 11pm, bar snacks also
available. **Happy hour:** 5pm-7pm (cocktails £3).

(American Bar)
Savoy Hotel WC2

Strand   7836 4343   2–1D
*A mainstay of London's cocktail scene since the late 1890's –
and, in the 1920s, the home of the dry Martini – the American
Bar still has a special place in many hearts, and few places can
equal its complimentary nibbles. The main problem with this
refurbished Art Deco room is that it's just too popular.
The jacket and tie rule has been relaxed in recent years (a
shame, as if they liked the look of you they used to loan you
some spectacularly nasty ties to make good sartorial
shortcomings), but a degree of formality of dress remains
advisable.* / **Details:** closed Sun. **Food:** L only.

The Scarsdale W8

23a, Edwardes Sq   7937 1811   7–1C

Located in a graceful square, just round the corner from the Kensington Odeon, this is the pub with arguably the cutest location in town. It has the added benefit of an extremely pretty, if very small, front garden (and, in summer, competition for seats is cut-throat). With a roaring fire, the place is also quite a winter pub, and hearty English fare is served. / **Food:** till 10pm.

Scott's W1

20 Mount St   7629 5248   3–3A

The new owners of this grand English restaurant – who also own Home House, the trendy club – have decided to reformat it in keeping with its heritage. The basement cocktail bar is now in a much more intimate and comfortable style, which is well at home in this part of Mayfair. The aim, apparently, is to make it something of a members' club, but we suspect you're unlikely to be turned away on quieter nights, or if you're dining. / **Website:** www.homehouse.co.uk, www.scottsrestaurant.co.uk **Details:** Mon-Fri noon-midnight, Sat 5pm-midnight, closed Sun. **Food:** L&D.

Sebright Arms E2

34 Coate St   7729 0937   1–1D

Should you find yourself on the Hackney Road in search of something to do on a Thursday night, you could do a lot worse than to drop in to the 'Docklands Farmers Music Hall' night at this unpretentious post-war boozer. The speciality is old-fashioned music hall style acts – there's always a drag act, and usually cabaret or a comedian too. / **Details:** no credit cards; no-smoking area. **Food:** L till 3pm (Sun L 4pm). **Happy hour:** 4pm-7.30pm (beer £2, bitter £1.80, spirits £2.30).

The Sekforde Arms EC1

34 Sekforde St   7253 3251   9–1A

A quiet side street location on the Clerkenwell/Finsbury border makes this very much a locals' pub. If, however, you're after a friendly boozer with proper grub and fine ales (Young's), it would be well worth seeking out (and is one of the few remaining such options in this now much-trendified area). / **Website:** www.youngs.co.uk **Details:** Sat 11am-6pm, Sun noon-4pm; no Amex. **Food:** L till 3pm, bar snacks till 9.30pm.

Sequel SW4

75 Venn St   7622 4222   10–2C

Right by the Clapham Picture House, this trendy and smoky bar/restaurant – trendily enhanced by the presence of a "silent video wall" – has established itself as a key destination for local twentysomethings with a Dutch pils Lendebloom the tipple of choice. You can dine (reasonably well) at any time, with brunch a speciality. / **Website:** www.thesequelonline.com **Details:** Tue-Thu 5pm-midnight, Fri 5pm-12.30am, Sat 11am-12.30am, Sun 11am-11.30pm (closed Mon). **Food:** Tue-Fri 6pm-11pm, Sat L till 4pm, D till midnight, Sun L till 5.30pm, D 10.30pm.

Settle Inn

17-19 Archway Rd, N19   7272 7872   8–1C
186 Battersea Bridge Rd, SW11   7228 0395   10–1B

Groovy modern pubs – with quite an emphasis on sports and providing quite solid food – which seem to have gone down well with the twentysomethings of Archway and Battersea Bridge Road (there's another in Kensington High Street called Settle Down). Battersea is the original, with a popular beer garden in the summer. / **Website:** www.thesettleinns.co.uk **Details:** Mon-Sat 12pm-11pm, Sun 12pm-10.30pm. **Food:** L till 3pm, D till 10pm, weekends till 9.30pm .

Seven Stars W12

243 Goldhawk Rd   8748 0229   7–1A

A location on a pair of mini-roundabouts seems like an odd spot for this large and now trendy Shepherd's Bush boozer. The quality of the conversion, however, is way above what you'd expect for this unglamorous location, and it's succeeded in attracting quite a cool crowd. It provides a good selection of wines, beers and cocktails, and there's very decent grub served in the large dining area at the back. (Out front they have quite a number of outside benches, but it's very trafficky). / **Details:** Thu-Sat till midnight, Sun 11am-10.30pm; no Amex. **Food:** L till 2.30pm (Mon-Fri), Sat L&D, Sun L till 4.

The Seven Stars WC2
53 Carey St 7242 8521 2–1D
A glorious Elizabethan pub behind the Royal Courts of Justice, serving a good range of ales to a mainly legal crowd. It's very small, with one side devoted to food (delivered by a dumb waiter) so it can get extremely cramped. The walls are decorated with drawings of judges and movie posters of past crime films (which usually seem to have starred Richard Attenborough or Terry Thomas). / **Details:** closed Sun. **Food:** till 6.30pm.

Shakespeare N16
57 Allen Rd 7254 4190 1–1C
Just off Newington Green, a cool local boozer, decked out with big dome drop lights, cream walls, a wooden bar and, oddly, what looks like a figurehead from the prow of a ship, cut in half and affixed to the wall. Drinks include standards bitters, plus a Czech larger, Litovel. / **Details:** Mon-Fri from 5pm.

Shampers W1
4 Kingly St 7437 1692 3–2D
Piccadilly Circus is a great area to drink – as long as you're looking for tourist-hell or a place where clipboard Nazis rule. If, on the other hand, you feel like a bottle of wine – and perhaps a substantial plate of decent grub – this bubbly (and very '70s) wine bar is well worth truffling out. / **Details:** Mon-Sat 9am-11pm, closed Sun (& Sat in Aug). **Food:** till 11pm.

Shaw's Booksellers EC4
31-34 St Andrews Hill 7489 7999 9–3B
A Fullers pub that's been cleverly contrived not to look like a boozer at all, this large backstreet corner site near Blackfriars tube has all the distressed charm of, well, a second-hand bookseller somewhere in the provinces (though, naturally, there's not a single title on view). Quite a range of food is available, too. / **Website:** www.fullers.co.uk **Details:** closed weekends. **Food:** L till 3pm, D till 9pm.

The Sherlock Holmes WC2
10 Northumberland St   7930 2644   2–2D
*What a genius marketing wheeze it was to give this pub –
far removed from Baker Street – the name it has, which seems
to have succeeded in establishing it on just about every tourist
trail in town. For a central London boozer, though –
near Trafalgar Square – it's a pleasant-enough spot, and it does
have some interesting Holmes 'memorabilia'.* / **Details:** no Amex.
Food: till 9.45pm.

Shillibeer's N7
Carpenter's Mews, North Rd   7700 1858   8–2C
*The simple fact that this bar hidden away in the unlovely no-
man's-land between Holloway and Islington has survived for
some years now is testament to the attractions of its
atmospheric premises – originally created as the garage for the
world's first horse-drawn buses. It attracts a young crowd
(and Thursday night is student night). For those not intending to
hit the bottle, copious off-street parking is a rare attraction.*
/ **Details:** Fri & Sat till 2am. **Food:** till 10pm. **DJ:** Fri-Sat.
Happy hour: Thu-Fri pm (selected beers £1.50).

The Ship SW14
10 Thames Bank   8876 1439   1–3A
*It takes a bit of finding by car, but this Victorian pub (behind
the Mortlake brewery) is an easy-to-find break point for those
strolling along the towpath. In most respects it's a fairly typical
boozer, but its tranquil location (and nice outside tables and
dining conservatory) make it a good, slightly away-from-it-all
destination.* / **Food:** till 9.30pm.

The Ship SW18
41 Jews Rw   8870 9667   10–2A
*The charm of its riverside location may be partially offset by the
proximity of one of south west London's busiest roundabouts,
but this Wandsworth Young's boozer remains amazingly
popular. It's a complete zoo on sunny days – when the food
options are pepped up by the addition of a barbecue – but it
also makes quite an atmospheric destination for a winter pint.*
/ **Website:** www.theship.co.uk, www.youngs.co.uk **Food:** till 10.30pm
(10pm Sun).

Ship & Shovell WC2

1-3 Craven Pas   7839 1311   2–2D

*You'd be forgiven if you thought you were seeing double even before entering this Charing Cross pub – it's actually split into two halves, one on either side of the Arches beneath Charing Cross Station (there's a bar in each half, and an underground passageway for the staff). Novelty is not the only reason for a visit however, as there are also excellent Badger beers from Dorset. / **Details:** closed Sun. **Food:** L till 3pm (Sat till 4pm).*

Shish NW2

2-6 Station Pde   8208 9292   1–1A

*The establishment which brought a whole new concept (style) to Willesden Green must have something going for it, and this impressively-designed, high-tech kebab-house has been a great success. Upstairs, the bar is a popular destination in its own right. / **Details:** Mon-Sun 11.30am-12.30pm (Sun 11.30pm); no-smoking area. **Food:** till 11pm. **Happy hour:** 5pm-7pm (buy 1 get 1 half-price).*

Shoeless Joe's

1 Abbey Orchard, SW1   7222 4707   2–3C
33 Dover St, W1   7499 2689   3–3C
2 Old Change Ct, EC4   7248 2720   9–3B

*This celeb-backed mini-chain of brash sports bars heaves with City types most nights, and is popular for major sporting events. The space-age branch by the Millennium Bridge is worth a look if you're in the area. / **Website:** www.shoelessjoes.co.uk **Details:** vary. **Food:** L&D & bar snacks. **DJ:** Fri. **Happy hour:** 5-8pm Mon-Fri (cocktails half price).*

Shoreditch
Electriticy Showrooms N1

39a, Hoxton Sq   7739 6934   9–1D

*Occupying – you guessed – a former shop, this large, bare bar, with basement restaurant, was one of the front-runner establishments that helped make Hoxton hip. Arguably it just feels rather like a student union bar with big windows, but there seems to be quite a market for that sort of thing. / **Website:** www.electricityshowrooms.co.uk **Details:** Tue-Thu & Sun noon-midnight, Fri & Sat noon-1am (closed Mon). **Food:** L till 3.45pm, D till 11pm. **DJ:** Fri-Sat 9pm-1am.*

Simpson's of Cornhill EC3
38 1/2 Cornhill   7626 9985   9–2C
*For a re-creation of Dickensian London, you couldn't better this ancient City chophouse (est. 1757), which (though it's best known as an eating place) also has a characterful if rather cramped ground floor bar. Its small yard is an ideal open-air location for a lunchtime pint. / **Details:** Mon-Fri 11.30am-5pm, closed weekends. **Food:** L till 3pm.*

Simpsons-in-the-Strand WC2
100 Strand   7836 9112   4–3D
*Best known for serving roast beef (and nowadays big breakfasts), this famed institution also boasts a little-known bar – decorated in calming shades of green, with black-and-white signed photographs of 1920s stars on the walls. It's well worth knowing about for a pre-theatre drink. / **Website:** www.savoy-group.co.uk **Food:** till 10.45pm.*

Sir Alfred Hitchcock Hotel E11
147 Whipps Cross Rd   8530 3742   1–1D
*After a stroll in Epping Forest (which this large roadside establishment overlooks), this agreeable, traditional hotel/free house (converted from a row of houses in the '80s) makes an ideal pit stop for a nice pint (there's a good selection of bitters) or a glass of wine on the way home. It's not just a summer pub, though – the combination of open fires and plenty of nooks and crannies makes it ideal for gloomy-day hibernation. / **Details:** no Amex. **Food:** L till 3pm, D till 10.30pm. **Happy hour:** Thu.*

(Gallery)
Sketch W1
9 Conduit St   0870 777 4488   3–2C
*"Oh my God, the loos are incredible", seems to be the most consistent reaction to Mourad Mazouz's (he of Momo) unbelievably expensive (£10 million plus spent on refurbishment) and wackily-designed Mayfair complex of bars and restaurants. Needless to say, it's not a place to go drinking when counting the pennies, and there are also some pretty mean style police to be faced down to gain access (it's a good idea to call ahead, and see if you can get your name on the guest list). / **Details:** 12-6pm non-members only, 6pm-11pm members only unless have a reservation.*

Slug & Lettuce

11 Warwick Way, SW1   7834 3313
19-20 Hanover St, W1   7499 0707
80-82 Wardour St, W1   7437 1400
14 Upper St Martin's Ln, WC2   7379 4880
474 Fulham Rd, SW6   7385 3209
96-98 Uxbridge Rd, W12   8749 1987
47 Hereford Rd, W2   7229 1503
1 Islington Grn, N1   7226 3864
32 Borough High St, SE1   7378 9999
4 St John's Hill, SW11   7924 1422
4-16 Putney High St, SW15   8785 3081
Riverside Hs, Water Ln, TW9   8948 7733
30 South Colonnade, Canary Whf, E14   7519 1612
36-42 Clerkenwell Rd, EC1   7608 1929
100 Fenchurch St, EC3   7488 1890
25 Bucklersbury, EC4   7329 6222
A well-established – and much-copied – chain of (slightly formulaic) bars and converted pubs that are squarely aimed at sociable twenty- to thirtysomethings. Some branches have more appeal than others, but they all serve a good selection of bottled beers and wines. The gastropub-style grub is tolerably well done, and not expensive. / Details: vary. Food: L&D & bar snacks.

Smersh Bar EC2

5 Ravey St   7739 0092   9–1D
"From behind the Iron Curtain, to behind Curtain Road" – especially if you're fond of all things retro, it's hard not to raise a smile at this small cellar, just off Great Eastern Street, which manages not to take itself at all seriously. Music (from an eclectic range of DJs) spices up the atmosphere, and there's quite an interesting selection of eastern European beers and vodkas. (The name, in case your Russian is rusty, comes from "smert' shpionam" or "Death to Spies!".)
/ Website: www.smershbar.com Details: from 5pm; no credit cards.
DJ: nightly (soul, funk, reggae, ska, rock). Live music: various music nights.
Happy hour: 5pm-7pm (beer £1.50).

Smiths of Smithfield EC1

Smithfield Mkt   7251 7950   9–1A

This NYC-style warehouse conversion was a catalyst in the 'trendification' of the Smithfield Market area, and remains a favourite destination. The ground floor café/bar, with its stripped-back industrial décor, is hugely popular all week, from post-work drinks to Sunday brunch. There's also a funky cocktail bar on the first floor (available for private hire). / **Website:** www.smithsofsmithfield.co.uk **Details:** Thu-Sat till 12.30am. **Food:** L&D (closed Sat L). **DJ:** Wed-Sat.

Smithy's Wine Bar WC1

Leeke St   7278 5949   8–3D

Quite the best place if you're looking for a refuge around King's Cross station, this new wine bar occupies impressively converted former industrial premises, less than five minutes' walk away. It's a 'something for everyone' sort of place – wines stretch from basic New Worlds to top clarets, but there's quite a lot of beer and lager too, plus a menu that stretches from snacks to more substantial dishes. / **Details:** closed weekends. **Food:** L till 2.30pm, D till 10pm.

The Snug Bar SE5

65 Camberwell Church St   7277 2601   1–2C

Camberwell is fast becoming a hotspot for funky late-night bars. This ornately-furnished place – part of the Babushka chain, but different – is quiet during the day, serving snacks to the local workers, but at night transforms itself into a hippy-chic bar for the resident art students and straying Brixtonians. DJs play an eclectic mix of tunes every night from '80s to garage to dance. / **Website:** www.styleinthecity.co.uk **Details:** Mon-Thu 4pm-midnight, Fri 4pm-2am, Sat noon-2am, Sun noon-10.30pm. **Food:** till 9pm. **DJ:** Wed-Sat. **Live music:** jazz Sun. **Happy hour:** 5pm-7pm (£3 cocktails, pitchers £8.50).

So.uk SW4

165 Clapham High St   7622 4004   10–2C

No disrespect to Clapham, but it's impressive how this low-lit and seductive bar conveys a degree of sophistication that seems rather at odds with its high street location. If there is such a tribe as the Clapham Beautiful People, this is where you'll find it, lounging on the low sofas, and toying with a Moroccan snack. / **Details:** Mon-Tue 5pm-midnight, Wed-Thu 5pm-1am, Fri & Sat 2pm-2am, Sun noon-midnight. **Food:** from 5pm. **DJ:** Wed-Sun.

The Social

5 Little Portland St, W1   7636 4992   3–1C
33 Linton St, N1   7226 3628   8–3D

This duo of DJ bars (with an offshoot in Nottingham and a record label, Heavenly) were spawned by a long-running club night (The Heavenly Social). The branch at the top of Regent Street is a chilled, welcoming hang-out, where the action take place in the narrow, boothed basement bar. Islington occupies an old tavern, and is more of a gastropub.
/ **Website:** www.thesocial.com **Details:** vary. **Food:** L&D. **DJ:** N1 Fri-Sun, W1 every night.

Soho Spice W1

124-126 Wardour St   7434 0808   3–1D

During the day, it's the upstairs dining room which you tend to notice at this colourful Asian Indian diner in Soho. When the pubs have closed, though, the attractions of a 3 am licence draws plentiful younger crowds to the downstairs bar, which has a minimal cover charge. / **Website:** www.sohospice.co.uk
Details: Mon-Thu noon-midnight, Fri & Sat noon-3am, Sun 12.30pm-10.30pm. **Food:** till midnight. **DJ:** Fri-Sat.
Happy hour: 5pm-7pm (half-price drinks).

Sosho EC2

2A, Tabernacle St   79200701   9–1C

Originally called Soshomatch, this large hang-out manages to remain one of the hippest hang-outs hereabouts SOuth of SHOreditch), in spite of regular incursions from (the more fashionable end of the) City suits market. Vaguely Warhol-esque pictures of cowboys and western landscapes lend a retro 'Marlboro Man' tone to a nicely understated space, with a raised area for dining. Nightly DJs cover bases ranging from Afro boogaloo to future jazz. / **Website:** www.matchbar.com
Details: Mon till 10pm, Tue-Wed till midnight, Thu till 1am, Fri till 2am, Sat 7pm-3am, closed Sun. **Food:** till 10.30pm. **DJ:** Thu-Sat.

Southern K NW6

205 Kilburn High Rd   7624 2066   1–1B

An airy Kilburn bar, which allegedly offers "the coldest beer in town" for Aussies in need of refreshment. It's furnished with lots of tall tables and bar stools, though there are a couple of loungier areas with sofas. The Antipodean theming is mercifully fairly restrained. / **Details:** Mon-Sat 11am-midnight, Sun noon-11pm; no Amex; no smoking at bar. **Food:** L till 4pm, D till 8.30pm. **DJ:** Fri.
Live music: Sun and occasionally Thu.

Southside Bar W1

125 Cleveland St   7637 5352   3–1C

Aussies and Kiwis in search of their favoured brew can find VB, Tui, Crown and Speights (among others) at this expats' hangout in the warren of streets north of Soho. It's an oddly proportioned place, but has been recently refurbished and you're guaranteed a friendly welcome. Downstairs, there's a cheesy disco. / **Website:** *www.southsidebar.com* **Details:** *Mon-Sat 4pm-11pm, closed Sun; no Amex.* **Food:** *6pm-11pm.*

The Spaniards' Inn NW3

Spaniard's Rd   8731 6571   8–1A

Dick Turpin, Keats and Byron are among the historical and literary associations of this celebrated 16th-century coaching inn, right by Hampstead Heath. It is a fine survivor of days gone by, and its plus-points include a characterful and quite spacious interior, a large and attractive garden, and even a carpark. / **Details:** *no-smoking area.* **Food:** *till 9pm.*

Spice Island SE16

163 Rotherhithe St   7394 7108   11–1B

Converted from an old spice warehouse, this large Rotherhithe pub is quite a destination on account of its Thames-side location and large waterside terrace (with plenty of heaters). There's a good range of bitters and lagers, but many of the punters opt to swig the likes of vodka and Red Bull. / **Details:** *no smoking in restaurant.* **Food:** *till 9.30pm.*

Spirit EC1

2-5 Carthusian St, Smithfield   7253 6009   9–1B

Smarter than the blue neon sign and shop-front window would lead you to believe, this chic bar/restaurant, behind Barbican tube, is a useful lunch venue hereabouts. Half-price happy hour cocktails and weekend dancing until 2am ensure it's lively in the evenings too. / **Website:** *www.spiritbar.com* **Details:** *Mon noon-10pm, Thu noon-midnight, Fri noon-2am, Sat 8pm-2am, closed Sun.* **Food:** *L till 4pm, bar snacks till 10pm.* **Happy hour:** *Mon-Thu 5pm-7pm, Fri 8pm-9pm (half-price cocktails).*

The Sporting Page SW10

6 Camera Pl 7349 0455 5–3B

Many pubs have an awning promoting a popular local tipple, and it's no different at this boozer in the heart of smartest Chelsea, where the red shades bear the single word 'Bollinger'. A pint of Young's is an equally acceptable choice, though, and the atmosphere is relaxed. At weekends it provides community support for those who have inexplicably failed to get away to The Country. / **Website:** www.frontpagepubs.com **Food:** L till 3pm, D till 10pm.

The Sports Café SW1

80 Haymarket 7839 8300 2–1C

Probably still the largest of London's sports bars, this cavernous and tacky two-floor fixture – a short step from Trafalgar Square – features waitresses in netball skirts and skimpy T-shirts and 120 TVs pumping out constant action. Much of the action is away from the screens, though, given the place's reputation as a pick-up joint for young professionals – it's open till late, and there's a dance-floor. / **Website:** www.thesportscafe.com **Details:** Mon noon-2am, Tue-Thu noon-2am, Fri noon-3am, Sat 11am-3am, Sun noon-midnight. **Food:** till 2.30am. **DJ:** nightly. **Happy hour:** Mon-Fri 3pm-7pm (beers & bacardi breezers £1.20, cocktails £2.50).

The Spot WC2

29 Maiden Ln 7379 5900 4–3D

The smart crowd is most notable by its absence from this no-frills central dive (a 'modern retro bar', whatever that is). It's worth keeping in mind, though, because it's open late and has a convenient location, just south of Covent Garden. As a result there's often a crush. / **Details:** Mon-Sun noon-1am. **Food:** till 12.30am. **DJ:** Thu-Sat, Sun open mic. **Live music:** Mon live band. **Happy hour:** noon-7pm (all drinks £2.20).

St John EC1

26 St John St 7251 0848 9–1B

Minimalism is taken seriously at this strikingly-converted Smithfield smokehouse – a lofty, glass-roofed, white-walled space. It's best known for its restaurant specialising in traditional British offal dishes (motto: "nose-to-tail eating"), but the bar is an attraction in its own right, and there's a good range of ales and lagers (and wines), plus some gutsy snacks. / **Website:** www.stjohnrestaurant.co.uk **Details:** Sat 6pm-11pm, closed Sun. **Food:** L till 3pm, D till 11pm.

St John's N19

91 Junction Rd   7272 1587   8–1C
One of George Michael's favourite boozers, apparently, this is a welcome oasis of civilisation on the edge of Archway. The high point of the show is the splendid rear dining room (which was once a Victorian music hall, and where good food is now served), but the whole joint is relaxed and civilised. / Details: Mon from 5pm. Food: till 11pm (Sun 10.30pm).

(The American Bar) Stafford Hotel SW1

16 St James's Pl   7493 0111   2–2B
Hidden away in a very cute St James's backwater, this is the sort of classic, cosy cocktail bar of which London is all too short. It is nicely cluttered with mementoes of past customers – the ceiling comes festooned with ties, hats and the occasional cuddly toy. A lot of the punters live up to the place's name, but there are plenty of locals, too. / Food: L till 2.30pm, D till 11.15pm.

Star NW8

38 St John's Wood Terr   7722 1051   8–3A
A traditional pub – complete with real fire and booth seating – on a quiet street, handily located for St John's Wood High Street. A corner case with a display of crystal gives something of a 'front parlour' feel – younger souls may prefer the outside tables, at the front.

The Star Tavern SW1

6 Belgrave Mews West   7235 3019   5–1D
This Fullers pub occupies an elegant Georgian building in a hidden-away Belgravia mews. It claims its place in the history books, as the site for the planning of the Great Train Robbery (but then South Kensington's Anglesea Arms does too). / Website: www.fullers.co.uk Details: Sat 11.30am-3pm & 6.30pm-11pm, Sun noon-3pm & 7pm-10.30pm. Food: till 9pm.

The Station W10
41 Bramley Rd   7229 1111   6–2A
Even by West Kensington's often gritty standards, this large, newly converted pub occupies a decidedly 'urban' location (with large picture windows looking on to the arches of Latimer Road tube). If anything, though, the view adds to the atmosphere, though, and means that the enormous and very nicely decked out garden comes as even more of a surprise. The food's better than at many rival gastro-boozers and comes in vast portions. / **Website:** www.priorybars.com **Details:** Mon-Sat noon-midnight, Sun noon-10.30pm; no Amex. **Food:** till 10pm.

Steam
London Hilton, Paddington W2
1 Eastbourne Tce   7850 0555   6–1C
If you're looking for a smart place for a drink round Paddington there ain't a whole lot of choice, so this long, thin room – with its huge monochrome photos, set off by brightly-coloured chairs – is well worth seeking out. As you'd expect, given the location and setting, it can often attract a rather businessy crowd, though DJs funk the atmosphere up in the evenings. / **Details:** Mon-Wed till 1am, Thu-Sat till 2am, closed Sun. **Food:** L only, bar snacks till 11.45pm. **DJ:** Wed-Sat.

Stone Mason's Arms W6
54 Cambridge Grove   8748 1397   7–2B
For years now, this trendy boozer (from the same owners as the Mason's Arms and The Pilot) has made an improbable find, perched on a trafficky corner of Hammersmith. With its relaxed atmosphere, it attracts a younger crowd. The food is good, but you may find you have to wait for it. / **Food:** till 9.50pm.

The Street W1
58 Crawford St   7724 4991   3–1A
This amiable Marylebone gastropub with a Moroccan twist has a strong local following. It serves some good North African grub and is well worth knowing about in a part of town still not awash with competing attractions. / **Food:** till 9.45pm.

The Studio Lounge
Waterstones W1

203-206 Piccadilly   7851 2433   3–3D

*When we first heard about it, we thought the fifth floor bar at
Waterstone's flagship store (which has interesting rooftop
views) might be a locals' secret – a stylish destination for a
quiet drink above the tourist hell of Piccadilly. Unfortunately,
the secret seems to be pretty well out, but it's a very handy
rendezvous nonetheless.* / **Website:** www.searcys.co.uk **Food:** till 9pm
(Sun 5pm).

Sugar Hut SW6

374 North End Rd   7386 8950   5–3A

*Come with me to the Kasbah! You knock on the door to enter
this lavish, Fulham bar/restaurant, which combines Middle
Eastern and Oriental design to create a sultry atmosphere.
If that wasn't enough to put you and your hot date in a
romantic frame of mind, you lie virtually horizontal in the
cocktail bar on a raised dais and cushions. (The bar and
restaurant food is all oriental, and the cooking not bad, but very
pricey).* / **Website:** www.sugarhutfulham.com **Details:** 6.30pm-midnight.
Food: till midnight. **DJ:** Wed-Sun.

Sun SW4

47 Old Town   7622 4980   10–2C

*This funky pub is a linchpin of the Clapham social scene,
especially in summer when its Old Town location and large
courtyard (equipped with numerous heaters) really come into
their own. Lagers, wine and mixers are the most popular tipples
and there's also a nice upstairs restaurant serving a Thai menu.*
/ **Food:** L till 3pm, D till 10.30pm, all day weekends.

The Sun & 13 Cantons W1

21 Gt Pulteney St   7734 0934   3–2D

*A location in the heart of Soho helps explain the surprisingly hip
following for this unusually stylish, yet traditional Soho boozer
(named, apparently, after the Swiss watchmakers who used to
trade nearby). Draft lager is the most popular tipple,
with Stella, Carling, Staropramen and Hoegaarden all on tap
(and London Pride for bitter lovers). The pace is hottest on
Friday nights, when there's a DJ in the basement bar.*
/ **Website:** www.fullers.co.uk **Details:** Mon-Fri till 11.30pm,
Sat 6pm-11.30pm, closed Sun. **Food:** L till 3pm, bar snacks till midnight.
DJ: Fri night downstairs bar.

The Sun & Doves SE5
61-63 Coldharbour Ln   7733 1525   1–3C
Well worth seeking out, in the deepest reaches of sarf London, this fab, funky Camberwell pub offers a cool interior (bedecked with art), a great garden and good pub grub. Large without being cavernous, it attracts a crowd that's both trendy and friendly. / **Website:** www.sundoves.com **Details:** no-smoking area. **Food:** till 11pm (Sun 10.30pm).

The Sun Inn SW13
7 Church Rd   8876 5256   1–3A
With its rambling interior, this large, listed hostelry opposite Barnes Green has maintained its traditional spirit. The interior is cosy and characterful (and could be more so if they spent some money on the place), but it really comes into its own in summer when you can sit out on the terrace (and many people like to take their drink over the road by the duck pond). / **Details:** no Amex; no-smoking area. **Food:** L&D.

The Surprise SW3
6 Christchurch Ter   7349 1821   5–3D
Tucked away in the backwoods of residential Chelsea, this quiet, friendly and attractive boozer (whose origins go back to 1651) is one of the best in the area for those in search of a relaxed drink. It's location makes it a bit of a "locals' secret" but, even so, it attracts quite a diverse crowd. / **Details:** no Amex; no-smoking area. **Food:** L till 3pm, D till 8pm, weekends L only.

SW9 SW9
11 Dorrell Pl   7738 3116   10–2C
Refurbished a couple of years ago, this bright, modern bar – in an alley off the main drag – is worth knowing about as a retreat from the Brixton mayhem. Cocktails and trendy lagers are popular tipples, and live music (mostly jazz) is a regular attraction. There are some pleasant tables outside, and you can also eat. / **Details:** Mon-Wed & Sun 10am-11pm, Thu 10am-11.30pm, Fri & Sat 10am-1am. **Food:** till close, except Thu till 6pm, Fri-Sat till 10pm. **Happy hour:** Sun-Fri 4.30pm-7pm (£2).

Swag & Tails SW7

10-11 Fairholt St   7584 6926   5–1C

This small and picturesquely located Knightsbridge boozer is an attractive place, well remembering for a (relatively) quiet drink in civilised surroundings. Food is a big part of the operation, with much of the space being given over to the dining room, and the wine list has aspirations well above the norm.
/ **Details:** *Sat 6pm-11pm, Sun noon-4pm.* **Food:** *L till 3pm, D till 10pm.*

The Swan SW9

215 Clapham Rd   7978 9778   10–1C

This Irish pub opposite Stockwell tube may be a bit tired-looking, but it always attracts a crowd. Queues often stretch around the block, thanks to a tried and tested formula of cover bands and a late licence (entrance charged for later arrivals). The Antipodean masses (or those wishing to bag an Ozzie/Kiwi) booze through the night, spilling drinks on one another and wailing familiar melodies. Don't wear your best shoes. / **Website:** *www.theswanstockwell.com* **Details:** *Thu-Fri 6pm-3am, Sat 7pm-3am, Sun 7pm-2am (closed Mon-Wed); no credit cards.* **Food:** *free barbeque food till 2am.* **DJ:** *2 all nights but Thu.* **Live music:** *regular.* **Happy hour:** *Thu-Fri & Sun (2 for 1).*

The Swan W2

66 Bayswater Rd   7262 5204   6–2C

Despite its position on the motorway-like Bayswater Road, this 18th-century hostelry manages to transcend its location and, though it's largely a tourist place, it is not forgotten by the locals. The outside terrace (which is largely gas-lit by night) is the key attraction and, though a little noisy, it remains a good point to round off a stroll through Hyde Park or Kensington Gardens. / **Food:** *till 10pm.*

Sway WC2

61-65 Great Queen St   7404 6114   4–1D

It's perhaps not quite an 'A'-list destination, but this modern Covent Garden bar – with nightclub attached – is a handy and spacious choice for a glass of wine or a cocktail. There's also a restaurant – if you stick to the cheaper items on the menu, it makes a reasonable-value place to fuel up before a night on the town. / **Website:** *www.swaybar.co.uk* **Details:** *Mon-Wed 5pm-1am, Thu-Sat 5pm-3am, closed Sun; no Amex or Switch.* **Food:** *till 11pm.* **DJ:** *Thu-Sat.* **Happy hour:** *5pm-7pm (wine half-price, £10 off champagne, cocktails £2.75).*

(Temple)
Swissôtel the Howard WC2

Temple Pl   7300 1700   2–1D
From the outside the Howard looks every bit a smart but boring business hotel. This is indeed true, but its unusually smart and comfortable cocktail bar has not just a view of – but also access to – one of London's prettiest courtyard gardens. It makes a charming (and unlikely) location for a cocktail on a sunny day. / **Details:** *Mon-Sun 11-1am.*

Sydney Brasserie SW6

199 Munster Rd   7381 8821   10–1A
This relaxed bar/restaurant in deepest Fulham has been a neighbourhood hang-out for over ten years now. It's a simple kind of place where lager and vino – along with some straightforward food – are the orders of the day.
/ **Website:** *www.sydneybrasserie.co.uk* **Food:** *L till 3pm, D till 10.30pm.*
Happy hour: *5pm-7.30pm (2 for 1).*

Tea Rooms
des Artistes SW8

697 Wandsworth Rd   7652 6526   10–1B
Originally a 16th-century barn (and with the beams to prove it), this lofty bar attracts a friendly, Bohemian crowd. Music is a mix of happy house, funk and soul, with DJs on Fri, Sat and Sun (a famous chillout session). A garden and quite good (mainly veggie/fish) fare complete the place's wide-ranging attractions.
/ **Website:** *www.tearoomsdesartistes.com* **Details:** *only open Fri & Sat 5.30pm-1am, Sun 7.30pm-12.30am; no-smoking area.* **Food:** *till 12.30am.*
DJ: *Fri-Sun.*

(Cobra Bar)
Teatro W1

93-100 Shaftesbury Ave   7494 3040   4–3A
Previously members-only, this long, thin and stylish bar (previously the Glenfiddich) is now open to all. Ownership by ex-footballer Lee Chapman and his actress wife Leslie Ash help the place attract a smattering of celebs and media types, though the place has never quite hit the big time in the way it once aspired to. There's a restaurant, too, which is pricey for what it is. / **Website:** *www.teatrosoho.co.uk* **Details:** *Mon-Wed 5.30pm-11.30pm, Thu-Fri 5.30pm-1am, Sat 5.30pm-11pm, closed Sun.* **DJ:** *Sat.*

The Telegraph SW2

228 Brixton Hill   8678 0666   10–2C

Formerly a studenty-type pub which held gigs, this large venue underwent a revamp and refurb in 2002. It now styles itself as a DJ bar with club nights every night, where the locals can dance away until the wee hours on the downstairs dance floor. Early evenings sees it as more of a boozer serving Thai inspired food during the week, but a traditional roast on Sundays.
/ **Website:** *www.thebrixtontelegraph.co.uk* **Details:** *Mon-Thu 5.30pm-2.30am, Fri 5.30pm-4am, Sat 5.30pm-6am, Sun noon-13.30am; no Amex.* **DJ:** *Wed-Fri.* **Happy hour:** *5pm-8pm (2 for 1).*

The 10 Room W1

10 Air St   7734 9990   3–3D

The reputation of this would-be trendy lounge bar as a hang-out for beautiful people rather precedes it nowadays. Given the location, near Piccadilly Circus, it was always at risk of becoming a bit of a 'bridge and tunnel' favourite, so quieter nights are to be preferred. / **Website:** *www.10-room.co.uk* **Details:** *Mon-Fri 5.30pm-3am, Sat 8pm-3am, closed Sun.* **Food:** *till 1am.* **DJ:** *Mon-Sat.*

Tenth Bar
Royal Garden Hotel W8

2-24 Kensington High St   7361 1810   5–1A

One of the lesser known bars-with-a-view (over Kensington Gardens), this elevated room is worth seeking out, not least because – unusually for a place with a fine panorama – the adjoining restaurant is of a perfectly reasonable standard. Alternatively, you might like to visit the Park Terrace on the second floor – it may lack the special appeal of the room above, but it's a comfortable place where the view lives up to the name. / **Website:** *www.royalgardenhotel.co.uk* **Details:** *Mon-Fri noon-2.30pm & 5.30pm-11pm, Sat 5.30pm-11pm, closed Sun.* **Food:** *L & D.* **Happy hour:** *Wed 5.30pm-8.30pm (half-price on selected champagnes).*

Terrace Bar
Chesterfield Mayfair W1

35 Charles St   7491 2622   3–3B

Hidden away in this discreet and surprisingly charming Mayfair hotel – a short step from Shepherd Market – is a traditional bar with lots of unpretentious but comfortable charm. On Thursday evenings, jazz is a feature.
/ **Website:** *www.redcarnationhotels.com* **Food:** *11am-11pm.* **Happy hour:** *6pm-7pm (draught lager £2).*

Texas Lone Star SW7
154 Gloucester Rd   7370 5625   5–2B
South Kensington may be thought of as a chichi area nowadays, but you wouldn't know it from this unreformed American theme-joint, near Gloucester Road tube. It has a very well worn-in, Tex/Mex roadhouse ambience and its prime virtue is being cheap, especially for the area. / **Details:** *Mon-Sat noon-11.30pm, Sun noon-10.30pm.* **Food:** *L&D.*

The Thatched House W6
115 Dalling Rd   8748 6174   7–1A
This welcoming Young's pub was somewhat trendified a few years ago, but it remains a boozer at heart and offers a slightly less 'yuppie' experience than many of the other Hammersmith gastropubs. That said, the pub grub here is a cut-above, and the place's other attractions include a nice outside terrace. / **Website:** www.youngs.co.uk **Details:** *Mon-Sat 11am-3pm & 5.30pm-11pm; no Amex.* **Food:** *L till 2.30pm, D till 10pm.*

Three Kings of Clerkenwell EC1
7 Clerkenwell Close   7253 0483   9–1A
Funky 3-D signage advertises the presence of this free house, nearly three centuries old – a characterful place, offering a good range of ales and lagers, plus an unusually good range of spirits. It's popular with local office workers, who quite often spill out into the little lane on warm evenings. / **Details:** *Sat 7pm-11pm, closed Sun; no credit cards; no-smoking area.* **Food:** *L till 3pm.*

Tiger Tiger SW1
29 Haymarket   7930 1885   2–1C
If you're on the pull, or up for a Big Night Out in the West End (or both), make a beeline for this three-floored meat-market, whose dine-to-disco attractions include a variety of themed cocktail bars. Wonderful or appalling – depending entirely on your state of mind. Expect to queue for entry. / **Website:** www.tigertiger.co.uk **Details:** *Mon-Sat noon-3am, Sun noon-midnight.* **Food:** *till midnight, bar snacks till 2.30am.* **DJ:** *nightly (commercial).* **Happy hour:** *5pm-7pm (half-price drinks).*

The Tim Bobbin SW4
1-3 Lilleshall Rd   7738 8953   10–1B
*This used to be a fairly traditional, reassuringly worn-in
Clapham pub but, after a late-2001 transformation, it now
proclaims itself a gastropub. It seems to have been a pretty
successful transformation, and there's a good range of beers,
lagers and wines on offer, as well as some quite good (if not
particularly cheap) food. / **Website:** www.thetimbobbin.co.uk
Details: no Amex. **Food:** L till 2.45pm, D till 10pm.*

Toast NW3
50 Hampstead High St   7431 2244   8–1A
*For a West End experience in the heart of Hampstead – rather
implausibly, above the tube station, in fact – this Manhattanite
cocktail bar and restaurant is the place to go. It's won the
hearts and minds of a good number of affluent local trendies, a
fact fully reflected in the prices (especially of the rather ordinary
food). / **Details:** Mon-Fri 6pm-midnight, Sat & Sun 11am-midnight;
no-smoking area. **Food:** D 6pm-midnight, weekends 11am-midnight.
DJ: Mon-Fri from 10pm.*

Tollesbury Barge E14
Millwall Inner Dock, Marsh Wall   7363 1183   11–1C
*Once a working Thames barge (and the only vessel of its kind
to have successfully returned from the Dunkirk evacuation of
1940), this foliage-covered veteran is now moored in genteel
semi-retirement in the Docklands (close to South Quay DLR).
There's usually a cask ale on, and a varying range of wines and
snacks, making it a useful alternative to the Identikit chain bars
around Canary Wharf. / **Details:** no credit cards. **Food:** till 9pm.*

The Toucan W1
19 Carlisle St   7437 4123   4–2A
*A charmingly scruffy Irish boozer, off Soho Square, whose
unaffected friendliness more than makes up for its lack of
space. Guinness – obviously – is a speciality, accompanied with
an impressive range (the largest in London, they say) of Irish
whiskeys. Warm weather and Friday nights see the crowd
spilling out onto the street. / **Website:** www.thetoucan.co.uk
Details: closed Sun; no Amex. **Food:** till 10pm.*

The Town of Ramsgate E1
62 Wapping High St   7488 2685   11–1A
Although it's packed with history – the crew of the Bounty took their last drink here before setting sail – and very atmospheric, this Wapping boozer is less touristy than its more famous neighbour, The Prospect of Whitby. So expect to be joined by locals and journos from the nearby Murdoch empire when you're supping your bitter or lager, and admiring the river views from the tiny garden. / **Details:** no Amex. **Food:** Tue-Sat L till 3pm, Sun L till 4pm.

Townhouse SW3
31 Beauchamp Pl   7589 5080   5–1C
On the site formerly known as Min's Bar, a new cocktail emporium firmly aimed at the cooler end of the Knightsbridge lounge lizard market. They've certainly spent plenty on the modernistic décor, and an impressive range of libations is available. / **Details:** Mon 4pm-midnight, Tue-Sat noon-midnight, Sun noon-11.30pm.

Trader Vics W1
22 Park Ln   7493 8000   2–2A
Elvis Presley was still in the charts when this Polynesian bar opened in the basement of the new Hilton hotel in 1963. Forty years on, the bar – part of a chain which also has branches in the likes of Atlanta, Marbella and Dubai – may similarly be credited with 'classic' status, and if kitsch is your thing it's still hard to beat. A long and pricey list of cocktails is available, accompanied by fairly substantial eats. / **Details:** Mon-Thu 5pm-1am, Fri & Sat 5pm-3am, Sun 5pm-10.30pm. **Food:** till 12.30am.

The Trafalgar Tavern SE10
6 Park Row   8858 2437   1–2D
This famous Regency public house nestles beside Wren's Royal Naval College at Greenwich. Downstairs, its elegantly proportioned rooms have huge bow windows looking right over the river. Upstairs, apart from banqueting rooms which would put many hotels to shame, the intriguing Hawke & Howe bar (not always open) is worth seeking out. Famous names associated with the place include Dickens, and the atmosphere is absolutely in keeping. / **Website:** www.trafalgartavern.co.uk **Details:** no Amex. **Food:** till 9.15pm.

Trinity Arms SW9

45 Trinity Gdns   7274 4544   10–2C

Sitting at one of the outside tables in this leafy and tranquil square, it's hard to remember that Brixton High Street is a mere 90 seconds stroll away. The décor similarly couldn't be further apart from most of the gritty urban style bars that dominate the area. So relax, and get yourself a pint of Young's bitter. / **Website:** www.youngs.co.uk **Details:** no credit cards. **Food:** till 3pm (closed weekends).

Troubadour SW5

265 Old Brompton Rd   7370 1434   5–3A

It may lack the eccentricity of its former ownership (not altogether a bad thing), but the overall attractions of this wonderfully Boho Earl's Court coffee shop have been much enhanced by the new proprietors. Now – apart from being much bigger – the place really is a 'café' in the Continental style, busy at almost all hours. In the evenings, this leads to an ambience which – paradoxically – is rather like your classic English wine bar. The basement club has been re-opened and now offers a programme of jazz, comedy and poetry. / **Website:** www.troubadour.co.uk **Details:** Mon-Sun 9am-midnight; no Amex. **Food:** till 11pm.

25 Canonbury Lane N1

25 Canonbury Ln   7226 0955   8–2D

A tucked-away location (in a side street off the top of Upper Street) adds to the appeal of this attractive local cocktail bar. A converted pub whose style impressively combines the modern and the traditional. / **Details:** Mon-Fri from 5pm; no Amex. **Food:** till 10pm (L only Sat & Sun).

Twentyfour EC2

Level 24, Tower 42, 25 Old Broad St.   7877 2424   9–2C

To oldies it's still the NatWest Tower, but – whatever you call it – Tower 42 still has some of the best views in the City. Actually there's a better vantage point at the top (see Vertigo), but in this neutrally-decorated bar/restaurant there's more comfort, and you can still see for miles. Prices are as elevated as you would expect. / **Website:** www.twenty-four.co.uk **Details:** Mon-Fri 11.45am-10pm (must book in advance), closed weekends. **Food:** till 9pm.

2 Brewers SW4

114 Clapham High St   7498 4971   10–2C
This tacky but busy bar/club in the middle of Clapham really hots up at the weekends, attracting mainly a gay crowd. There's entertainment nightly – including not a few drag acts (they claim Lily Savage started here) and weekly karaoke. On Sundays, the crowd is more chilled, recovering from the rigours of Saturday night. / **Details:** *Mon-Thu 4pm-2am, Fri & Sat 4pm-3am, Sun 2pm-12.30am.* **DJ:** *nightly.* **Happy hour:** *Mon-Sat 4pm-9pm, Sun 2pm-8pm (Carling £1.50, vodka/gin £1.50).*

The Two Chairmen SW1

39 Dartmouth St   7222 8694   2–2C
A short walk from St James's Park tube, this cosy 18th-century establishment is the epitome of a quiet and civilised London pub, and primarily a civil servants' haunt. The upstairs restaurant, with its deep leather chairs and fine, club-like décor, is particularly atmospheric. / **Details:** *closed weekends.* **Food:** *till 9.30pm.*

Two Floors W1

3 Kingly St   7439 1007   3–2D
When it opened about eight year ago, this spacious west Soho hang-out was frighteningly trendy for a time, as one of the new wave of loungey bars hitting town. Even if the world around has changed, this place hasn't much, and it remains a mellow place to chill out. / **Details:** *closed Sun; no Amex.* **Food:** *till 4.30pm.*

291 E2

291 Hackney Rd   7613 5676   1–1D
This impressive Cambridge Heath gallery/art bar (opened in 1998) occupies a deconsecrated neo-Gothic church. In the nave, there's a range of events from live performances to exhibitions. Having had your cultural fill you can adjourn to the swanky bar next door for a reviving cocktail or half of lager (though you don't escape the art completely, as there's a cinema-sized display screen synchronised with the music). / **Website:** *www.291gallery.com* **Details:** *Tue-Thu 6pm-11.30pm, Fri & Sat 6pm-2am, closed Sun & Mon.* **DJ:** *nightly.* **Live music:** *bands Fri-Sat.*

Urban Bar (LHT) E1
176 Whitechapel Rd   7247 8978   1–1D
The initials stand for London Hospital Tavern, the former name
for this old boozer that's been given a 'wacky' makeover. If a
tiger-striped exterior doesn't appeal, then you probably won't go
for the 'pets' – lizards and anacondas (in glass cases). However,
if you're after a buzzing (quite studenty) atmosphere, fuelled by
good-value beers and regular live music, this may well be the
place for you. / **Details:** Sun-Wed noon-midnight, Thu-Sat noon-1am;
no Amex. **Food:** Sun-Wed till 11.30pm, Thu-Sat till 12.30am. **DJ:** Sat.
Live music: jazz night Tue, classic rock musician Sun and Wed.

Vats WC1
51 Lamb's Conduit St   7242 8963   2–1D
A favourite of the local business and legal crowd, this cosy and
woody Bloomsbury wine bar is done out in a very atmospheric
early-'70s style. Owned and run for over 30 years by a husband
and wife team, it has a traditional wine list strongest in clarets,
and provides a menu of quite substantial (and quite expensive)
food. In summer there are a few pavement tables.
/ **Details:** closed weekends. **Food:** L till 2.30pm, D till 9.30pm.

Vertigo
Tower 42 EC2
Old Broad St   7877 7842   9–2C
For an unbeatable panorama of the City, where better (until
they finish the 'Erotic Gherkin', anyhow) than glugging
champagne and nibbling seafood in the bar on the top floor of
the building formerly known as the NatWest Tower? As 30
varieties of bubbly hint, though, this is not a place to
economise. Nor can you just walk in – reservations must be
made in advance and you'll also need to take a photo ID.
/ **Website:** www.vertigo42.co.uk **Details:** Mon-Fri noon-3pm & 5pm-11pm,
closed weekends. **Food:** till 10.20pm.

Vesbar W12
15-19 Goldhawk Rd   8762 0215   7–1B
Estate agents may claim that the area around Shepherd's Bush
Green is up-and-coming, but it's still not over-provided with nice
places to eat, drink and hang out. There's nothing fancy about
this modern bar/pub (a short walk from the fancier Bush Bar &
Grill), but it does what it does well and without attitude.
/ **Website:** www.fullers.co.uk **Food:** 11am-10pm.

The Vibe Bar E1
91-95 Brick Ln   7377 2899   9–2D

Almost solely responsible for turning Brick Lane into a place to be seen, rather than just somewhere for a late-night curry, this large venue (with a courtyard garden that quickly fills up in summer) still draws a young, funky, lager-fuelled crowd. Mismatched décor – with uneven wooden flooring, Gothic iron chairs and a large mural on one wall – adds to the rather self-consciously cutting-edge feel. / **Website:** www.vibe-bar.co.uk
Details: Fri & Sat till 1am. **Food:** L till 3pm, D from 6pm. **DJ:** nightly.
Live music: bands (see website for details) Sun and Tue .

Vic Naylors EC1
40 St John St   7608 2181   9–1B

Since the late-'80s, this brick-lined bar/restaurant has been a popular and convivial rendezvous for Smithfield workers – more a food place during the day, more a popular wind-down-with-a-drink place after work. There are those who discern a needn't-try-too hard attitude in recent times, but the place is still always busy. / **Details:** Tue-Sat 5pm-1am (closed Mon & Sun).
Food: till 12.50am. **DJ:** nightly.

Victoria SW14
10 West Temple   8876 4238   10–2A

To say this revamped gastropub in a leafy backstreet is Sheen's most stylish place is not the double-edged compliment it might seem. You just didn't get places like this distinctively decorated, rambling pub in the 'burbs a few years ago. The restaurant operation dominates (and there's a huge rear dining conservatory), but there is also a small bar for drinkers. Most regulars opt for wine, but there's also, for example, Brakspears, Hoegaarden or Guinness on draft.
/ **Website:** www.thevictoria.net **Details:** Mon-Sun 8.30am-10pm. **Food:** L till 2.30pm (weekends till 3pm), D till 10pm.

Village Soho W1
81 Wardour St   7434 2124   3–2D

Entrances on both Wardour and Brewer Streets give this large Soho spot something of a split personality – it's a gay bar that seems to attract lots of mixed couples (perhaps thanks to the cheap late-night drinking possibilities). DJs every night, extended happy hours and entertainments at weekends create a jolly party atmosphere. / **Details:** Mon-Sat 11am-1am, Sun noon-midnight.
Food: L&D. **DJ:** Mon-Sat from 8pm. **Happy hour:** till 8pm & all Mon pm (jug cocktail £7, spirits £2, beer jug £5).

(Club Bar)
Waldorf Meridien Hotel WC2

Aldwych   7836 2400   2–1D

*This well-known hotel, on the fringe of Covent Garden, has just one bar – the Club Bar – open to the public (the Footlights Bar now having closed). Done out in clubby, traditional style, it would make a convenient spot for a pre-theatre drink – or is suitably low-lit for illicit romance. / **Details:** Mon-Sun 11am-3am.* **Food:** *till 2.45am.*

Walkabout Inn

11 Henrietta St, WC2   7379 5555   4–3D
Charing Cross Rd, WC2   7255 8620   4–2B
Temple Pl, WC2   7240 7865   2–1D
58 Shepherds Bush Green, W12   8740 4339   7–1B
56 Upper St, N1   7602 6433   8–3D
Hill Hs, Shoe Ln, EC4   7353 7360   9–2A

*Don't wear your best clothes and don't put anything on the floor – it may stick – at these infamous Aussie-themed bars, where ex-pats congregate to drink cheap beer and shout over loud music. Especially popular when the rugby's on and great place's to watch most big sporting events, the chain is expanding fast, with new branches at Temple (formerly Shoeless Joe's) and at the former Limelight nightclub. / **Website:** www.walkaboutinns.com **Details:** vary. **Food:** L&D. **DJ:** N1, WC2 nightly, W12 Thu-Sat, EC4 Thu & Fri (popular). **Happy hour:** Mon & Tue (2 for the price of 1 on selected drinks).*

Walker's of Whitehall SW1

13 Craig Court   7925 0090   2–2C

*Tucked down a small alley off Whitehall, this traditional pub is one of the better places near Trafalgar Square. It mainly serves the local civil servant/office crowds, but is useful for anyone looking for a reasonably tranquil West End rendezvous. / **Details:** closed weekends; no-smoking area.* **Food:** *till 9pm.*

Walmer Castle W11

58 Ledbury Rd   7229 4620   6–1B

*In another postcode this would just be a nice traditional boozer, but a location at the heart of trendy Notting Hill has made this one a fave rave with a trendy twenty- and thirtysomething crowd. Its popularity is most evident in summer when there's a pavement-clogging crush outside its front door. Good cheap Thai scoff (served in the intimate upstairs dining room) adds to its appeal. / **Food:** till 10pm.*

The Warrington Hotel W9

93 Warrington Cr   7286 2929   6–1C

*For students of Victoriana, this vast, magnificently fitted-out Maida Vale pub is a must – they just don't build 'em like this anymore. It's actually best known outside the immediate area for its first-floor restaurant (Ben's Thai), which has quite a reputation as a fun budget destination. The pleasant outside terrace for drinking in summer is a further attraction. / **Details:** no Amex; no-smoking area. **Food:** L till 2.30pm, D till 10.30pm.*

Warwick Castle W9

6 Warwick Pl   7432 1331   6–1C

*A short step from the canal in Little Venice, this sedate but very pleasantly decorated Victorian pub (where much of the décor looks original) is a quiet and civilised spot for a drink. In summer, when the windows are open, the seats at the rear, overlooking Clifton Nurseries, are particularly nice. / **Details:** Mon-Thu noon-2.30pm & 5pm-11pm, Fri & Sat noon-11pm; no-smoking area until 5pm. **Food:** L only.*

Washington NW3

50 England's Ln   7722 8842   8–2A

*A slick redevelopment of this large Belsize Park boozer has left many of its original features (such as the impressive carved bar) intact, but has also introduced some very clearly contemporary touches. Fortunately, the fusion has worked well, creating a loungey and comfortable place to drink, with food available all day. / **Details:** no Amex; no smoking at bar. **Food:** till 10pm.*

The Water Rat SW10
1-3 Milman's St   7351 4732   5–3B
This cosy pub near World's End is worth remembering as one of the nicer watering holes on this bit of the King's Road. Low-lit and done out with dark wood floors and tables, and some tasteful photos of nudes on the walls, its crowd includes a fair proportion of younger Chelsea pinstripes. / **Food:** L&D.

Waterloo Bar & Kitchen SE1
131 Waterloo Rd   7928 5086   1–2C
Handy for Waterloo, or a pre-Old Vic drink, this cosy bar/restaurant offers a more genteel alternative to the nearby Fire Station (and attracts a more sophisticated, older crowd). The better-than-average range of drinks is a bonus – there's a decently-priced wine list (and for beer drinkers Nastro Azzurro on tap) – and the food is good. / **Details:** Sat 5.30pm-11pm, closed Sun. **Food:** L till 2.45pm, D till 10.30pm.

The Waterloo Fire Station SE1
150 Waterloo Rd   7401 3267   1–2C
When it was converted almost a decade ago, this huge Waterloo hang out set a new standard for good food and drink in an interesting warehouse-type setting. These days, it's not the gastronomic destination it was and service can be off-hand, but it's still a lively watering hole, troughing spot and rendezvous for huge numbers of commuters, students and assorted others. / **Food:** till 10.45pm.

The Waterway W9
54 Formosa St   7266 3557   6–1C
A few years ago, no-one could have dreamt that the grotty, tatty old 'Paddington Stop' (which had a nice Little Venice location going for it but nothing else) would one day be revamped into one of the more glamorous-looking bars in town. Opened in the summer of 2002, this cool-looking joint combines a sleek interior with a beautiful outside terrace. Many drink wine (especially as there's a substantial food operation), but there's also Stella, Heineken, Hoegaarden and London Pride on tap. / **Website:** www.thewaterway.co.uk **Details:** no Amex. **Food:** L till 3.15pm, D till 10.15pm.

Waxy O'Connor's W1

14-16 Rupert St   7287 0255   4–3A
*Queues down the street testify to the unfailing popularity of this
vast Irish pub, on the fringe of Chinatown. Despite being a
theme-joint, it's very atmospheric – a rambling warren of bars
and chambers with impressive, whimsical décor (complete with
a full-grown tree in the main bar). There's plenty of Murphy's,
Caffrey's and Guinness, to be sure, but also wine and lagers
(Fosters, Carlsberg, Stella) and some OK food.*
/ **Website:** www.waxyoconnors.co.uk **Food:** till 10.30pm.

Waxy's Little Sister W1

20 Wardour St   7287 8987   4–3A
*As compact as its sister is sprawling, this corner bar affiliated
with the behemoth over the road is a little-known Soho secret.
The 'lounge' upstairs is little more than a balcony with sofas,
but makes a great romantic rendezvous.*
/ **Website:** www.waxyoconnors.co.uk **Food:** L&D.

The Well EC1

180 St John St   7251 9363   9–1A
*This is a 'classic' gastropub in every respect: converted pub
premises, unfussy décor, picture windows, exposed brickwork,
good-quality grub and a strong local following. But there's more
– this Clerkenwell stalwart also boasts a sumptuous cocktail
lounge in the basement (Aquarium Bar, open Wed-Sat only),
with leather panelling and fish tanks in the walls.*
/ **Website:** www.downthewell.com **Food:** till 10.15pm. **DJ:** Fri.

The Wellington WC2

351 Strand   7557 9881   2–1D
*This narrow, traditional boozer on the corner of Aldwych
benefits from its proximity to the Lyceum Theatre. It caters to
the family-orientated show likely to run there for the next few
years (The Lion King) by welcoming children in its upstairs bar.*
/ **Details:** no smoking at bar. **Food:** till 9.45pm (Sun 7.45pm).

Wenlock Arms N1

26 Wenlock Rd   7608 3406   9–1C

It may not have the most 'obvious' location, ten minutes' from Old Street tube, but this really nice old boozer (1835) is worth seeking out. It's garlanded with CAMRA awards, but it's not just a place for beer-anoraks – if you're contemplating a trip, check out the (much above-average) website for a fuller description that we can give here. / **Website:** www.wenlock-arms.co.uk **Details:** no credit cards. **Food:** till 9pm.

West 12 W12

74 Askew Rd   8746 7799   7–1A

Despite all the hype about the trendification of Shepherd's Bush, there are still not that many places in the heart of the postcode which offer much in the way of stylish hang-outs. This narrow cocktail bar is a brave exception, and with its darkly glam' décor attempts to bring a little metropolitan chic to a grungy streetscape. Cocktails are the main thing, and simple food is also available. / **Website:** www.west12bar.com **Details:** Mon-Sat 4pm-midnight, Sun 4pm-10.30pm; no Amex. **Food:** till 10pm. **Happy hour:** Mon-Fri 5pm-7pm (half-price cocktails).

West Central WC2

29-30 Lisle St   7479 7980   4–3A

Blacked out windows set the scene at this converted pub on a Chinatown corner – these days a busy three-floor gay bar and club. Inside the look has been called Victorian pub meets brothel – lots of red, plain furniture and fairy lights. Upstairs is more relaxed – downstairs the club is more full-on. / **Details:** Mon-Thu from 2pm, Fri & Sat 2pm-3am, Sun from 2pm; no Amex. **DJ:** Mon, Wed-Sat from 8pm.

The Westbourne Tavern W2

101 Westbourne Park Villas   7221 1332   6–1B

A great outside terrace (fight for a space), helps maintain this trendy Bayswater boozer as one of the top posing spots for Portobello trendies, especially in summer. It also does some very decent grub, but – even assuming they haven't run out of what you wanted – it's unlikely to come with great speed. / **Details:** Mon from 5pm. **Food:** L till 3pm, D till 10pm.

Wheatsheaf SE1
6 Stoney St   7407 7242   9–3C
*The regeneration of Borough Market has lead to this old boozer
being taken under the benign wing of Young & Co. It now
attracts a fairly wide-ranging crowd, and is, of course, especially
busy on market days (and the pub fare makes much use of
market produce). The tiny patio is worth seeking out on a
sunny day.* / **Website:** www.youngs.co.uk **Details:** Sat noon-8pm, closed
Sun. **Food:** L only.

White Cross Hotel TW9
Water Ln   8940 6844   1–3A
*This large Young's tavern is prominently situated by the river,
near Richmond Bridge and is a fine example of a traditional
pub. In summer the good-sized garden – complete with its own
bar – comes into its own, but the warren of cosy rooms inside
makes the place a good winter choice (especially when the real
fires are burning). There's a large variety of wines by the glass
and a good selection of pub grub (and the nice family room
upstairs makes it an OK option with kids in tow).* / **Details:** no
Amex; no-smoking area. **Food:** till 3.30pm.

White Hart SW13
White Hart Ln   8876 5177   1–3A
*Though the interior of this impressive, turn-of-the-century
Young's pub is perfectly pleasant – and though it has a good
reputation for the quality of its beers and wines – it's for its
terrace and Thames-side location (five minutes walk upstream
of Barnes Bridge) that it's most worth knowing about.*
/ **Details:** no Amex. **Food:** Tue-Sun L.

The White Horse SW6
1-3 Parson's Gn   7736 2115   10–1A
*It's fashionable to knock this classic Fulham boozer as the
'Sloaney Pony', but few traditional pubs have moved with the
times so effectively. The selection of real ales and over 50
bottled beers is impressive, and there's an excellent selection of
wines (with over 20 by the glass). Add to all that an increasingly
professional food operation, nice outside terrace by the Green,
and comfortable interior (with huge leather Chesterfields) and
it's not really so hard to put up with one Hackett polo shirt too
many.* / **Website:** www.whitehorsesw6.com **Details:** no smoking in
restaurant. **Food:** till 10pm.

The White House SW4

65 Clapham Park Rd 7498 3388 10–2C

Just round the corner from 'Sand', this hip and happening bar/club/restaurant attracts a similarly style-conscious Claphamite crowd (and some accusations of operating a ridiculous door policy). It's doing something right, though, as it's often very very busy – especially into the early hours.
/ **Website:** *www.thewhitehouselondon.co.uk* **Details:** *Mon-Sat 5.30pm-2am, Sun 5.30pm-midnight.* **Food:** *till 10pm.* **DJ:** *Thu-Sun (R&B).*
Happy hour: *Mon-Fri 5.30pm-7.30pm (2 for 1 cocktails, all food half-price).*

William IV NW10

786 Harrow Rd 8969 5944 1–1B

Despite – or perhaps because of – a busy location which doesn't seem propitious, this large Kensal Green gastropub has maintained high culinary standards for a number of years. If you're just looking for a pint, it's worth a visit at any time, but especially in summer when the large courtyard-garden comes in to its own. / **Website:** *www.william-iv.co.uk* **Details:** *Mon-Wed noon-11pm, Thu-Sat noon-midnight, Sun noon-10.30pm.* **Food:** *L till 3pm (weekends 4pm), D till 10.30pm.* **DJ:** *Fri-Sat.*

Williamson's Tavern EC4

1 Groveland Ct 7248 6280 9–2B

You enter through a fine pair of wrought iron gates (a 17th-century gift from William and Mary) to this traditional city pub, which occupies what was once the residence of the Mayor of London. Big brewery ownership hasn't done much to boost the atmosphere, but some of its Georgian charm lingers, and helps raise the place above the City norm. There's a fair range of bitters, including the odd guest ale. / **Details:** *no-smoking area.* **Food:** *L till 2.45pm, D till 9pm.*

Willie Gunn SW18

422 Garrett Ln 8946 7773 10–2A

This welcoming and stylish bar (leading on to a large dining room) would be a useful addition to any area. In Earlsfield, though, it's absolutely amazing and enjoys cult status amongst the locals as a cheerful hang-out for a glass of wine, quick beer, or full meal. / **Food:** *till 11pm.*

Windmill W1

6-8 Mill St   7491 8050   3–2C
Perhaps not the grooviest pub in town, but if you're looking for a decent Young's boozer that's handy as a respite from Regent Street shopping, this is just the place. The food – in a traditional English style you don't find much of round Savile Row – is pretty good too. / **Website:** www.youngs.co.uk **Details:** Sat noon-5pm, closed Sun. **Food:** L till 2.30pm, D till 9.30pm.

The Windmill Tavern SE1

86 The Cut   7787 9487   1–2C
In the unlovely environs of Waterloo, it's worth knowing about this stripped-down boozer near the Old Vic (which, if you can take the traffic, has a few outside tables in summer). Many punters drink lager, but there's a fair selection of bitters (Spitfire, Directors, J Smith) and some cheap and tasty Thai nosh. / **Details:** closed Sun; no Amex. **Food:** L till 3pm, D till 10.30pm. **Happy hour:** from 6pm (pitchers of beer £8-£9).

The Windmill on the Common SW4

Clapham Common Southside   8673 4578   10–2B
About as countrified as you'll find in south London, this large (going-on-cavernous) and ancient Young's pub on Clapham Common is a popular destination. There is a restaurant and hotel attached, and a huge car park to boot. / **Website:** www.youngs.co.uk **Details:** no Amex; no-smoking area. **Food:** L till 3pm, D till 10pm, Sat all day, Sun L.

Windows on the World Park Lane Hilton W1

22 Park Ln   7208 4021   2–2A
Mayfair's glitzy Hilton hotel may have 'naff' written all over it, but for a 'destination' cocktail it's hard to beat this 28th-floor eyrie. The views are quite not as fabulous as from the adjoining French restaurant, but the tab – though still elevated – is considerably less ruinous. / **Details:** Mon-Thu noon-1.30am, Fri noon-2.30am, Sat 5.30pm-2am, Sun noon-10pm; no smoking at breakfast. **Food:** till 10.30pm.

The Windsor Castle W8

114 Campden HI Rd   7243 9551   6–2B

*For many people, this splendid Georgian tavern (named after its
view, before other buildings got in the way) is the classic London
inn, and it attracts traditionalists of all ages. In summer there's
a great walled garden out back, while the nooks and crannies
of the ancient interior recall Dickensian times. All this,
plus simple good pub grub and a good range of ales, bottled
beers and wines.* / **Website:** *www.windsor-castle-pub.co.uk*
Details: *no-smoking area at lunch.* **Food:** *till 10pm.*

Windsor Castle W1

29 Crawford Pl   7723 4371   3–1A

*Royal and Establishment memorabilia cram into every nook and
cranny of this quirky pub (in the anonymous streets surrounding
Marylebone's Seymour Leisure Centre), whose front door is
guarded by a life-sized sentry. Given this patriotic devotion, it is
somewhat surprising to find that the food on offer is Thai,
though the brews on offer tend to be more of the traditional
English and Irish variety.* / **Food:** *L till 3pm, D till 10pm (Sat D only),
Sun all day till 9pm.*

Wine Library EC3

43 Trinity Sq   7481 0415   9–3D

*These basic but civilised cellars provide a convivial way of killing
off an afternoon in the City. They're owned by a wine merchant,
and you can buy any of the bottles available – from a
considerable range – at retail plus £3.50 corkage. Lunch here –
a basic but enjoyable cheese and pâté buffet – is very popular,
so it's best to book.* / **Details:** *Mon-Fri 11.30am-8pm (must book in
advance), closed weekends.* **Food:** *L till 3pm.*

Wine Wharf SE1

Stoney St   7940 8335   9–3B

*The bar of the wine museum Vinopolis, atmospherically
situated beneath vast railway arches, offers the varied list you'd
hope for – but there's no need to be overwhelmed by the
choice, as the staff are knowledgeable, friendly and happy to
help. A must for oenophiles, and – at quieter times – not a bad
choice for a romantic assignation.* / **Website:** *www.winewharf.co.uk*
Details: *closed Sun.* **Food:** *till 9.30pm.*

WKD NW1

18 Kentish Town Rd   77267 1869   8–3B

Squatting in the space created by the outwardly sloping walls of Camden Town's weirdly designed branch of Sainsbury's, this two-level lounge/club bar (motto: "keeping it fresh and funky") has an offbeat vibe, with bands and DJs central to the ambience. A younger crowd drink bottled lagers and cocktails, and there's also some (light) scoff. / **Website:** www.wkdclub.co.uk
Details: Mon-Thu 4pm-midnight, Fri & Sat 4pm-3am, Sun 1pm-midnight.
Food: till 10pm (weekends 2am). **DJ:** nightly (soul, funk, hip hop, jazz, house).
Live music: bands Mon. **Happy hour:** 5pm-8pm (all bottles £2, jugs of cocktails £8, spirit/mix £2).

Yard W1

57 Rupert St   7437 2652   4–3A

This amiable gay bar has a most unusual galleried setting (converted from former stables), around a small open yard, intriguingly hidden away right in the centre of Soho. In summer, it's one of the few venues locally with its own outside space, so be prepared for a crush. / **Website:** www.yardbar.co.uk
Details: Mon-Fri from 4pm, weekends from 2pm. **DJ:** Fri-Sat (house).

Ye Olde White Bear NW3

New End   7435 3758   8–1A

Even the lamp-post outside is on a tilt at this ancient inn, in a pretty part of Hampstead, There's an open fire, too, making this one of the more attractive destinations in what is arguably London's premier historic village. It's an ideal place for a reviver after a walk on the Heath, offering a reasonable range of real ales. / **Details:** no Amex. **Food:** till 9pm, Sun L till 5pm, D till 6pm-9pm.

Yo! Below

52-53 Poland St, W1   7287 0443   3–2D
95 Farringdon Rd, EC1   7841 0785   9–1A

The Clerkenwell and Soho branches of the conveyor-belt sushi chain Yo! Sushi have been much enhanced by the addition of bars. Relax at the long bench tables, or on one of the slouchy leather beds, and enjoy free massages or tarot readings while you watch Manga cartoons, or listen to the all-singing staff on the karaoke machine – they don't need to be serving drinks, as each table has its own beer dispenser! Japanese snacks are available – or pop in to the restaurant for some sushi.
/ **Details:** vary. **Food:** L&D & bar snacks. **DJ:** Thu-Sat (house/Club).
Happy hour: Mon-Sat 5-7pm (2 for the price of 1 on beer and house wine).

Zander SW1

Buckingham Gate 7378 3838 2–3B

*Claiming the longest bar in Europe, this cavernous, modern
Victoria venue (under the same roof as one of two outlets of
the smart Bank brasserie group) has managed to make quite a
name for itself in an area without many competing attractions.
In some ways, not being in the most happening of
neighbourhoods works to the place's advantage – staff lack
attitude, and they work hard here on their cocktails.*
/ **Website:** www.bankrestaurants.com **Details:** Mon-Tue 11.30am-11.30pm,
Wed-Fri 11am-1am, Sat 5.30pm-1am. **Food:** till 11.15pm. **DJ:** Wed-Sat.

Zebrano W1

14-16 Ganton St 7287 5267 3–2C

*An upmarket offering from London's Freedom Brewery Co.
(see also Freedom Bar, Rocket) this "champagne & cocktail
lounge", just off Carnaby Street, is a café during the day. After
5pm, the focus shifts to alcohol, which is far better suited to the
deep-red interior. Sadly, the company's excellent homebrews
are not widely promoted here – instead plump for wine, or buy
a whole bottle of your chosen spirit (from £70, with free
mixers) and huddle in a booth with a few friends. Your bottle
can be kept for your next visit.* / **Website:** www.freedombrewery.com
Details: closed Sun. **Food:** till 10pm. **DJ:** every other Fri.

Zero Degrees SE3

29-31 Montpelier Vale 8852 5619 1–3D

*Microbreweries have yet to catch on in London as they have in
the US, but if they do, let's hope they're much like this buzzy
venture in sleepy old Blackheath. The quality of the brewing is
high, but the striking modern setting makes the place of
interest to much more than CAMRA types. The place is very
popular with a younger crowd at weekends, and the restaurant
does a good line in wood-fired pizzas at any time.*
/ **Website:** www.zerodegrees-microbrewery.co.uk **Details:** Mon-Sat
noon-midnight, Sun noon-11.30pm. **Food:** till 11.30pm. **DJ:** Fri.
Live music: band Mon. **Happy hour:** Mon-Fri 4pm-7pm (all pints £1.50 &
half pints 75p).

Zeta W1

35 Hertford St   7208 4067   2–2A

By far the coolest of the bars at the Mayfair Hilton, this large but oddly proportioned room benefits from not feeling part of the hotel at all – having its own discreet side-street entrance helps. The door policy isn't particularly restrictive either. Inside, lounge on a suede pouffe while you enjoy your fresh fruit juice cocktail (the house speciality). / **Website:** www.zeta-bar.com
Details: Mon-Tue 4pm-1am, Wed-Sat 4pm-3am. **Food:** till midnight. **DJ:** Sat. **Live music:** bands Mon.

Zig-Zag W11

12 All Saints Rd   7243 2008   6–1C

It was All Saints, then it was Anonimato, then it was Nosh Brothers, then it was Saints – for some reason these premises seem to be in a perpetual state of change. The location – on a road which was famed for drug-dealing in the '80s – still inspires a certain frisson and helps explain the house motto ("Party on the front line"). An early visit to this latest red-decorated incarnation found it buzzing with a young-twenties crowd. / **Details:** Mon-Sat 6pm-midnight, closed Sun; no Amex.
Food: 6pm-11pm. **DJ:** occasionally.

Zuma SW7

5 Raphael St   7584 1010   5–1D

If inches generated in gossip columns are a true measure of how hip somewhere is, then this sleek Knightsbridge bar/restaurant is THE place of the moment. The Japanese food is an arm-and-a-leg job, but you can hang out over a sake or a cocktail and some nibbles at the bar (whose rock and glass design is the epitome of Flintstone-chic). / **Food:** L till 2.30pm, D till 11.15pm.

Indexes

Big screen TV

Central

a.k.a. *(WC1)*
Bacchanalia *(WC2)*
Bar Soho *(W1)*
Blue Posts *(W1)*
Blues *(W1)*
The Calthorpe Arms *(WC1)*
Cardinal *(SW1)*
Circus *(W1)*
Claridges Bar *(W1)*
Corner Store *(WC2)*
The Crown & Two
   Chairmen *(W1)*
De Hems *(W1)*
Edgar Wallace *(WC2)*
The Freemason's Arms *(WC2)*
Freud's *(WC2)*
Friendly Society *(W1)*
Globe *(WC2)*
The Grouse & Claret *(SW1)*
Hope *(W1)*
Jamie's: *Charlotte St W1*
Jugged Hare *(SW1)*
Kettners *(W1)*
The Maple Leaf *(WC2)*
The Marylebone Bar &
   Kitchen *(W1)*
Motcomb's *(SW1)*
Nell Gwynne *(WC2)*
Nordic *(W1)*
The Old Crown *(WC1)*
Ye Old White Horse *(WC2)*
Page's Bar *(SW1)*
Paviours Arms *(SW1)*
The Paxton's Head *(SW1)*
The Plough *(WC1)*
Plumbers Arms *(SW1)*
The Porterhouse *(WC2)*
Porters *(WC2)*
The Punch & Judy *(WC2)*
Quod *(SW1)*
The Rampage *(WC2)*
Rosie's Bar *(W1)*
The Round House *(WC2)*
The Rugby Tavern *(WC1)*
Scott's *(W1)*
Shampers *(W1)*
Shoeless Joe's: *all branches*
Soho Spice *(W1)*
The Sports Café *(SW1)*
The Spot *(WC2)*
The Street *(W1)*
The Toucan *(W1)*
Village Soho *(W1)*
Walker's Of Whitehall *(SW1)*
Waxy O'Connor's *(W1)*
The Wellington *(WC2)*
West Central *(WC2)*
Windmill *(W1)*
Zeta *(W1)*

West

Aragon House *(SW6)*
The Art Bar *(SW3)*
The Australian *(SW3)*
Bar Room Bar: *all west branches*
Big Easy *(SW3)*
The Blue Anchor *(W6)*
Blue Elephant *(SW6)*
Brinkley's *(SW10)*
The Bushranger *(W12)*
The Chelsea Ram *(SW10)*
Ciao *(SW6)*
The Collection *(SW3)*
The Crown *(SW3)*
The Crown & Sceptre *(W12)*
The Duke of
   Wellington *(W11)*
The Durell *(SW6)*
Elephant & Castle *(W8)*
The Enterprise *(SW3)*
Finch's *(SW10)*
Frog & Forget-me-Not: *all
   branches*
Front Page *(SW3)*
The Fulham Tup *(SW10)*
Goat In Boots *(SW10)*
Golborne House *(W10)*
The Hillgate Arms *(W8)*
Ifield *(SW10)*
The Imperial Arms *(SW6)*

Comedy

The Marquess of
  Granby *(WC2)*
Nell Gwynne *(WC2)*

West
Troubadour *(SW5)*

North
Bar Risa *(NW1)*
The Camden Head *(N1)*
Enterprise *(NW3)*
The Magdela Tavern *(NW3)*
Narrow Boat *(N1)*

South
Alexandra *(SW4)*
Bread & Roses *(SW4)*
Circle: *SW9*
The Common Rooms *(SW11)*
The Cricketers *(TW9)*
Half Moon *(SW15)*
Hobgoblin: *SW2*
100 Pub *(SW4)*

East
Ember *(EC1)*
Old Red Lion *(EC1)*
Pleasure Unit *(E2)*
Reliance *(EC1)*

Film

Central
a.k.a. *(WC1)*

West
Cranks: *W2*
Electric Brasserie *(W11)*

North
WKD *(NW1)*

South
Film Café *(SE1)*
Living *(SW9)*
The Redstar *(SE5)*

The Ring *(SE1)*

East
Great Eastern Dining
  Room *(EC2)*
Old Red Lion *(EC1)*
Play *(EC1)*
The Pool *(EC2)*
Reliance *(EC1)*
291 *(E2)*

Gay/Lesbian

Central
Bar Code *(W1)*
The Box *(WC2)*
The Edge *(W1)*
Freedom *(W1)*
Friendly Society *(W1)*
G-A-Y Bar *(W1)*
Kudos *(WC2)*
Sanctuary *(W1)*
Village Soho *(W1)*
West Central *(WC2)*
Yard *(W1)*

West
The Coleherne *(SW5)*

North
The Black Cap *(NW1)*
Oak Bar *(N16)*

South
2 Brewers *(SW4)*

Good food

Central
Bentley's *(W1)*
Blues *(W1)*
Bohème Kitchen & Bar *(W1)*
Boisdale *(SW1)*
Boulevard *(WC2)*
Cecconi's *(W1)*

Happy hour

Central

The White House *(SW4)*
The Windmill Tavern *(SE1)*
Zero Degrees *(SE3)*

East

Al's *(EC1)*
Bar Baran *(E8)*
Bar Kick *(E1)*
Bar Room Bar: *all branches*
Bleeding Heart *(EC1)*
Café Kick *(EC1)*
Cargo *(EC2)*
Cock Tavern *(EC1)*
Cocomo *(EC1)*
The Crown *(E3)*
El Paso Club *(EC1)*
Fluid *(EC1)*
Fuego *(EC3)*
The Gate *(EC1)*
Grand Central *(EC2)*
Half Moon *(E1)*
Jamie's: *Ludgate Hill EC4*
Medicine Bar: *EC2*
Play *(EC1)*
The Punch Tavern *(EC4)*
Sebright Arms *(E2)*
Shoeless Joe's: *all branches*
Smersh Bar *(EC2)*
Spirit *(EC1)*
291 *(E2)*

Karaoke

Central
The Maple Leaf *(WC2)*

North
Oak Bar *(N16)*
Southern K *(NW6)*

South
2 Brewers *(SW4)*

East
Ferry House *(E14)*

Late licence

Central
a.k.a. *(WC1)*
Akbar *(W1)*
Amber *(W1)*
L'Apogee *(WC2)*
Atlantic Bar & Grill *(W1)*
Babble *(W1)*
Bar Code *(W1)*
Bar Madrid *(W1)*
Bar Rumba *(W1)*
Bar Soho *(W1)*
Bar Sol Ona *(W1)*
The Berkeley, Blue Bar *(SW1)*
Blues *(W1)*
Boardwalk *(W1)*
Bohème Kitchen & Bar *(W1)*
Café Bohème *(W1)*
China White *(W1)*
Chintamani *(SW1)*
Circus *(W1)*
Claridges Bar *(W1)*
Denim *(WC2)*
Dover St Wine Bar *(W1)*
The Edge *(W1)*
Elysium *(W1)*
Freedom *(W1)*
Garlic & Shots *(W1)*
Hakkasan *(W1)*
Havana: *all branches*
ICAfé *(SW1)*
Jerusalem *(W1)*
Ku De Ta *(W1)*
The Lanesborough *(W1)*
The Langley *(WC2)*
The Long Bar *(W1)*
The Loop *(W1)*
The Bam-Bou *(W1)*
Mandarin Bar *(SW1)*
The Market Place *(W1)*
Mash *(W1)*
Met Bar *(W1)*
Mezzo *(W1)*
Momo *(W1)*
Nadines *(W1)*

Literary events (including Poetry)

Live music

Southside Bar *(WI)*
Trader Vics *(WI)*
Windows on the World *(WI)*
Zeta *(WI)*

West
Abbaye: *all branches*
All Bar One: *W4*
Big Easy *(SW3)*
Cactus Blue *(SW3)*
The Durell *(SW6)*
Eclipse: *SW3, WII*
Havana: *all branches*
King's Head *(SW6)*
The Notting Hill Arts
  Club *(WII)*
Po Na Na: *SW10*
Puzzle: *W6*
Sugar Hut *(SW6)*
Texas Lone Star *(SW7)*
Troubadour *(SW5)*

North
Auld Shillelagh *(N16)*
Bar Lorca *(N16)*
Bar Risa *(NWI)*
Bartok *(NWI)*
The Bull & Gate *(NW5)*
Enterprise *(NW3)*
Ha! Ha!: *N10*
Hope & Anchor *(NI)*
King's Head *(NI)*
Living Room: *all branches*
Oh! Bar *(NWI)*
Opera *(NW3)*
Southern K *(NW6)*
Wenlock Arms *(NI)*

South
Archduke Wine Bar *(SEI)*
Bar Room Bar: *SE5, SWII*
The Bedford *(SW12)*
Brixtonian *(SW9)*
Bull's Head *(SW13)*
The Common Rooms *(SWII)*
Cranks: *SEI*
Eclipse: *SW19*

Frog & Forget-me-Not: *SW17*
Half Moon *(SW15)*
Numidie *(SE19)*
Puzzle: *SWII*

East
Abbaye: *all branches*
Boisdale of Bishopsgate *(EC2)*
Cargo *(EC2)*
Catch *(E2)*
Foundry *(EC2)*
Fuego *(EC3)*
Jamie's: *The Pavilion, Finsbury Circus
  Gdns EC3*
Living Room: *all branches*
New Inn *(EC2)*
Public Life *(EI)*
Spirit *(ECI)*
291 *(E2)*
Urban Bar (LHT) *(EI)*
The Vibe Bar *(EI)*

Lounge/
Cocktail bar
**(and/or spirits a
speciality)**

Central
Akbar *(WI)*
Alphabet *(WI)*
Amber *(WI)*
Atlantic Bar & Grill *(WI)*
The Avenue *(SWI)*
Bank *(WC2)*
The Berkeley, Blue Bar *(SWI)*
Black Bull *(SW10)*
Bohème Kitchen & Bar *(WI)*
Brown's Hotel *(WI)*
Carlton Tower *(SWI)*
Cecconi's *(WI)*
Che *(SWI)*
China White *(WI)*
Chintamani *(SWI)*
Circus *(WI)*
Claridges Bar *(WI)*

The Pelican *(W11)*
The Pen *(SW6)*
The Phene Arms *(SW3)*
Pilot *(W4)*
Queen's Head *(W6)*
The Salutation Inn *(W6)*
The Scarsdale *(W8)*
Seven Stars *(W12)*
The Sporting Page *(SW10)*
The Station *(W10)*
The Swan *(W2)*
The Thatched House *(W6)*
Troubadour *(SW5)*
Walmer Castle *(W11)*
The Warrington Hotel *(W9)*
Warwick Castle *(W9)*
The Water Rat *(SW10)*
The Waterway *(W9)*
The Westbourne Tavern *(W2)*
The White Horse *(SW6)*
William IV *(NW10)*
The Windsor Castle *(W8)*

North

Albert *(NW1)*
Auld Shillelagh *(N16)*
Babushka: *N1*
Backpacker *(N1)*
Bar Risa *(NW1)*
Bar Room Bar: *all north branches*
Bartok *(NW1)*
The Black Cap *(NW1)*
Camden Brewing Co *(NW1)*
The Camden Head *(N1)*
Cane *(NW6)*
Canonbury Tavern *(N1)*
Castle Free House *(N1)*
Cava *(N16)*
Centuria *(N1)*
The Chapel *(NW1)*
Chapel *(N1)*
The Clifton Hotel *(NW8)*
Crocker's Folly *(NW8)*
Dartmouth Arms *(NW5)*
Drapers Arms *(N1)*
The Duke of Cambridge *(N1)*

The Engineer *(NW1)*
Enterprise *(NW3)*
The Flask *(N6)*
The Flask *(NW3)*
Fox Reformed *(N16)*
Harringay Arms *(N8)*
Henry J Beans: *all branches*
The Holly Bush *(NW3)*
Hoxton Square Bar &
  K'n *(N1)*
Lansdowne *(NW1)*
Living Room: *N1*
The Lock Tavern *(NW1)*
The Lord Palmerston *(NW5)*
The Lord Stanley *(NW1)*
Mac Bar *(NW1)*
The Magdela Tavern *(NW3)*
Medicine Bar: *all branches*
Narrow Boat *(N1)*
No 77 Wine Bar *(NW6)*
The Old Bull & Bush *(NW3)*
Ye Olde White Bear *(NW3)*
The Prince *(N16)*
Queen's Head &
  Artichoke *(NW1)*
The Salt House *(NW8)*
Shakespeare *(N16)*
Shillibeer's *(N7)*
Shish *(NW2)*
The Spaniards' Inn *(NW3)*
St John's *(N19)*
Star *(NW8)*
Washington *(NW3)*

South

The Anchor *(SE1)*
Anchor Tap *(SE1)*
Angel *(SE16)*
Archduke Wine Bar *(SE1)*
The Artesian Well *(SW8)*
Babel *(SW11)*
Babushka: *SW2*
The Balham Tup *(SW12)*
Bar Du Musée *(SE10)*
Bar Estrela *(SW8)*
Bar Room Bar: *all south branches*

Pool/Snooker

Central

West

North

Real fire

Central
The Albert *(SW1)*
The Audley *(W1)*
Black Bull *(SW10)*
Brown's Hotel *(W1)*
The Cittie of Yorke *(WC1)*
The Clachan *(W1)*
The Cock Tavern *(W1)*
Connaught Bar *(W1)*
CVO Firevault *(W1)*
De Hems *(W1)*
The Dog & Duck *(W1)*
Dover Castle *(W1)*
Globe *(WC2)*
Goring Hotel *(SW1)*
The Grenadier *(SW1)*
The King's Arms *(WC1)*
The Lanesborough *(W1)*
Mybar *(WC1)*
The Nag's Head *(SW1)*
Newman Arms *(W1)*
The Opera Tavern *(WC2)*
The Salisbury *(WC2)*
The Seven Stars *(WC2)*
The Stafford Hotel *(SW1)*
Vats *(WC1)*
Waxy's Little Sister *(W1)*

West
The Anglesea Arms *(W6)*
The Antelope *(SW1)*
The Art Bar *(SW3)*
The Atlas *(SW6)*
Beach Blanket Babylon *(W11)*
The Bell & Crown *(W4)*
The Bull's Head *(W4)*
The Bushranger *(W12)*
Capital Hotel *(SW3)*
Churchill Arms *(W8)*
The City Barge *(W4)*
Cow *(W2)*
Dove *(W6)*
Eight Bells *(SW6)*
The Fox & Pheasant *(SW10)*

Golborne House *(W10)*
Grand Union *(W9)*
Harwood Arms *(SW6)*
The Havelock Tavern *(W14)*
The Hillgate Arms *(W8)*
King's Head *(SW6)*
The Old Ship *(W6)*
190 Queensgate *(SW7)*
The Phene Arms *(SW3)*
Portobello Gold *(W11)*
Puzzle: *W6*
Seven Stars *(W12)*
The Surprise *(SW3)*
Swag & Tails *(SW7)*
The Warrington Hotel *(W9)*
Warwick Castle *(W9)*
The Waterway *(W9)*
West 12 *(W12)*

North
Albert *(NW1)*
Auld Shillelagh *(N16)*
Babushka: *N1*
Bar Room Bar: *N22*
Blakes *(NW1)*
Camden Brewing Co *(NW1)*
Chapel *(NW1)*
Drapers Arms *(N1)*
The Flask *(N6)*
The Flask *(NW3)*
The Holly Bush *(NW3)*
King's Head *(N1)*
The Lock Tavern *(NW1)*
The Marquess Tavern *(N1)*
Narrow Boat *(N1)*
Oak Bar *(N16)*
The Old Bull & Bush *(NW3)*
Ye Olde White Bear *(NW3)*
Queen's Head &
    Artichoke *(NW1)*
Social: *N1*
The Spaniards' Inn *(NW3)*
St John's *(N19)*
Star *(NW8)*
Wenlock Arms *(N1)*

East

Bar Kick *(E1)*
The Bull *(EC1)*
Café Kick *(EC1)*
The Dickens Inn *(E1)*
Sebright Arms *(E2)*

Traditional pub (and/or beer a speciality)

Central

The Albert *(SW1)*
Argyll Arms *(W1)*
The Audley *(W1)*
The Barley Mow *(W1)*
Blue Posts *(W1)*
Bricklayers Arms *(W1)*
The Calthorpe Arms *(WC1)*
The Chandos *(WC2)*
The Cittie of Yorke *(WC1)*
The Clachan *(W1)*
The Clarence *(SW1)*
The Coach & Horses *(W1)*
The Coal Hole *(WC2)*
The Cock Tavern *(W1)*
Cross Keys *(WC2)*
The Crown & Two Chairmen *(W1)*
De Hems *(W1)*
Dover Castle *(W1)*
Edgar Wallace *(WC2)*
The Fox & Hounds *(SW1)*
Freedom Brewing Company *(WC2)*
The Freemason's Arms *(WC2)*
French House *(W1)*
Globe *(WC2)*
Ye Grapes *(W1)*
The Grenadier *(SW1)*
The Grouse & Claret *(SW1)*
The Guinea *(W1)*
Hope *(W1)*
Horse & Groom *(SW1)*
Jugged Hare *(SW1)*

The King's Arms *(WC1)*
The Lamb *(WC1)*
The Lamb & Flag *(WC2)*
Lowlander *(WC2)*
The Lyceum Tavern *(WC2)*
The Marquess of Granby *(WC2)*
Mash *(W1)*
The Morpeth Arms *(SW1)*
The Museum Tavern *(WC1)*
The Nag's Head *(SW1)*
Nell Gwynne *(WC2)*
Newman Arms *(W1)*
Nordic *(W1)*
O'Conor Don *(W1)*
The Old Coffee House *(W1)*
Ye Old White Horse *(WC2)*
The Opera Tavern *(WC2)*
The Orange Brewery *(SW1)*
Paviours Arms *(SW1)*
The Paxton's Head *(SW1)*
Pillars of Hercules *(W1)*
The Plough *(WC1)*
Plumbers Arms *(SW1)*
The Princess Louise *(WC1)*
The Queen's Larder *(WC1)*
The Red Lion *(SW1)*
The Red Lion *(W1)*
The Red Lion *(SW1)*
The Red Lion *(SW1)*
The Round House *(WC2)*
The Rugby Tavern *(WC1)*
The Salisbury *(WC2)*
The Seven Stars *(WC2)*
The Sherlock Holmes *(WC2)*
Ship & Shovell *(WC2)*
The Star Tavern *(SW1)*
The Sun & 13 Cantons *(W1)*
The Toucan *(W1)*
The Two Chairmen *(SW1)*
Walker's Of Whitehall *(SW1)*
The Wellington *(WC2)*
Windmill *(W1)*
Windsor Castle *(W1)*

Sir Alfred Hitchcock
   Hotel (E11)
Smersh Bar (EC2)
Saint John (EC1)
Three Kings of
   Clerkenwell (EC1)
The Town of Ramsgate (E1)
Williamson's Tavern (EC4)

Wine bar
(and/or wine a
speciality)

Central
Bacchanalia (WC2)
Bar des Amis du Vin (WC2)
Boisdale (SW1)
Carpe Diem (W1)
Cork & Bottle (WC2)
Davy's: The Arches, off Villiers St WC2,
   The Mkt WC2
Dover St Wine Bar (W1)
French House (W1)
Gordon's Wine Bar (WC2)
Hodgson's Wine Bar (WC2)
Kettners (W1)
Motcomb's (SW1)
Noble Rot (W1)
Oriel (SW1)
The Rampage (WC2)
Shampers (W1)
Smithy's Wine Bar (WC1)
Vats (WC1)

West
Albertine (W12)
Brinkley's (SW10)
Ciao (SW6)
Hollands (W11)
Iguacu (SW6)
Julie's Bar (W11)
Lomo (SW10)
Metro (SW6)
Olé (SW6)
PJ's (SW3)

Troubadour (SW5)

North
Le Bar du Café
   Delancey (NW1)
Davy's: NW1
Fox Reformed (N16)
No 77 Wine Bar (NW6)
Odette's Wine Bar (NW1)

South
Archduke Wine Bar (SE1)
Bar Du Musée (SE10)
Boland's Wine Bar (SE24)
Le Bouchon Bordelais (SW11)
Buchan's (SW11)
Davy's: SE10
Franklin's (SE22)
Hartfield's Wine Bar (SW19)
Hop Cellars (SE1)
Mistress P's (SW4)
Numidie (SE19)
The Point (SW17)
Waterloo Bar & Kitchen (SE1)
Willie Gunn (SW18)
Wine Wharf (SE1)

East
The Bar Under The Clock
   (EC4)
Bleeding Heart (EC1)
Boisdale of Bishopsgate (EC2)
Booty's (E14)
The Bow Wine Vaults (EC4)
Cellar Gascon (EC1)
City Limits (E1)
The City Page (EC4)
Davy's: E14, Holborn Viaduct EC1,
   Exchange Sq EC2, EC4
El Vino's: Fleet St EC4, New Bridge St
   EC4
La Grande Marque (EC4)
Jamaica Wine House (EC3)
Lay & Wheeler (EC3)
Leadenhall Wine Bar (EC3)
Ye Olde Wine Shades (EC4)
Wine Library (EC3)

MAPS

MAP I – LONDON OVERVIEW

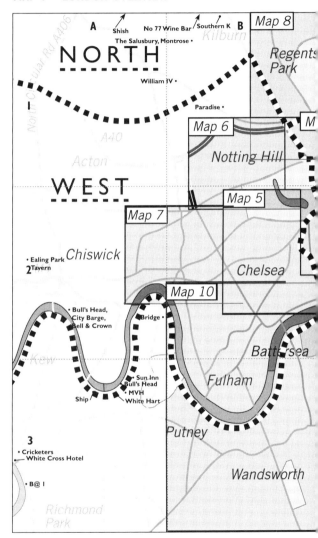

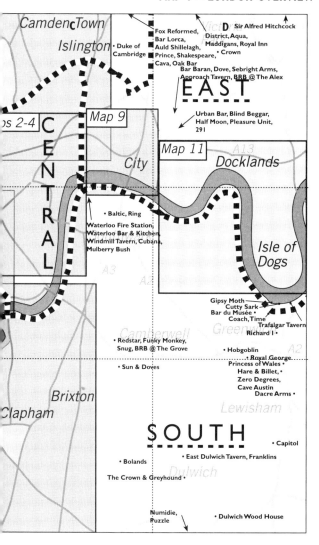

MAP I – LONDON OVERVIEW

Camden Town

Islington

Duke of Cambridge

os 2-4

CENTRAL

Map 9

City

Fox Reformed,
Bar Lorca,
Auld Shillelagh,
Prince, Shakespeare,
Cava, Oak Bar

D Sir Alfred Hitchcock
District, Aqua,
Maddigans, Royal Inn
Crown

Bar Baran, Dove, Sebright Arms,
Approach Tavern, BRB @ The Alex

EAST

Urban Bar, Blind Beggar,
Half Moon, Pleasure Unit,
291

Map 11

Docklands

Baltic, Ring
Waterloo Fire Station,
Waterloo Bar & Kitchen,
Windmill Tavern, Cubana,
Mulberry Bush

Isle of
Dogs

Gipsy Moth
Cutty Sark
Bar du Musée
Coach, Time
Richard I

Trafalgar Tavern

Greenwich

Redstar, Funky Monkey,
Snug, BRB @ The Grove

Hobgoblin
Royal George
Princess of Wales
Hare & Billet,
Zero Degrees,
Cave Austin
Dacre Arms

Sun & Doves

Brixton

Clapham

Lewisham

SOUTH

Capitol

East Dulwich Tavern, Franklins

Bolands

The Crown & Greyhound

Dulwich

Numidie,
Puzzle

Dulwich Wood House

MAP 2 – WEST END OVERVIEW

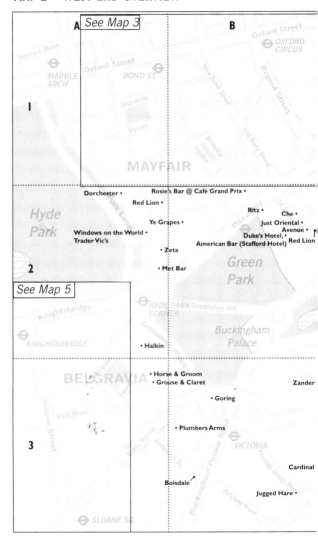

MAP 2 – WEST END OVERVIEW

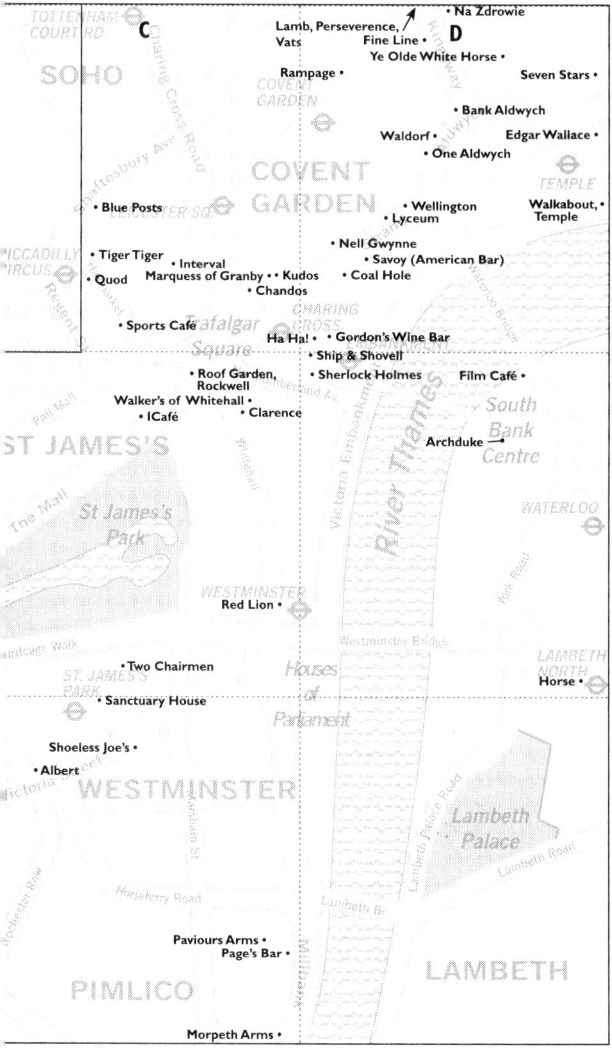
C
D
TOTTENHAM COURT RD.
SOHO
Charing Cross Road
Shaftesbury Ave
Lamb, Perseverence,
Vats
Fine Line
Na Zdrowie
Ye Olde White Horse
Rampage
COVENT GARDEN
Seven Stars
Bank Aldwych
Waldorf
Edgar Wallace
One Aldwych
COVENT GARDEN
TEMPLE
Blue Posts
LEICESTER SQ.
Wellington
Lyceum
Walkabout, Temple
Nell Gwynne
PICCADILLY CIRCUS
Tiger Tiger
Interval
Savoy (American Bar)
Quod
Marquess of Granby
Kudos
Coal Hole
Chandos
Waterloo Bridge
CHARING CROSS
Sports Café
Trafalgar Square
Ha Ha!
Gordon's Wine Bar
EMBANKMENT
Ship & Shovell
Roof Garden, Rockwell
Sherlock Holmes
Film Café
Walker's of Whitehall
Pall Mall
South Bank Centre
ICafé
Clarence
Archduke
ST JAMES'S
Whitehall
Victoria Embankment
River Thames
The Mall
St James's Park
WATERLOO
York Road
WESTMINSTER
Red Lion
Westminster Bridge
Birdcage Walk
Two Chairmen
Houses of Parliament
LAMBETH NORTH
ST. JAMES'S PARK
Horse
Sanctuary House
Shoeless Joe's
Albert
Victoria Street
WESTMINSTER
Lambeth Palace Road
Lambeth Palace
Lambeth Road
Horseferry Road
Lambeth Br
Paviours Arms
Page's Bar
Millbank
LAMBETH
PIMLICO
Morpeth Arms

MAP 3 – MAYFAIR, ST JAMES'S & WEST SOHO

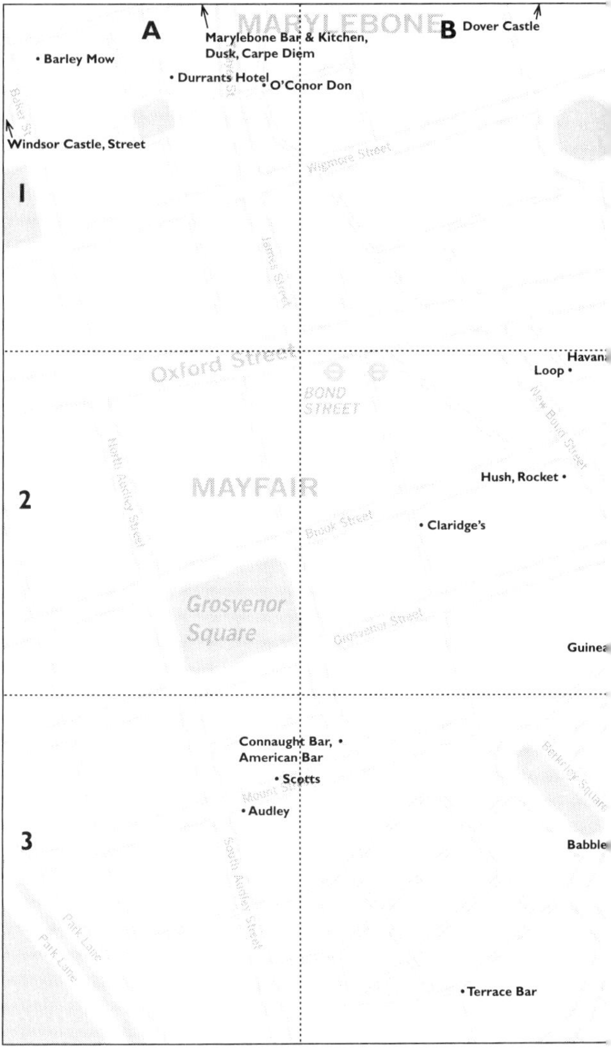

A

MARYLEBONE

B Dover Castle

Marylebone Bar & Kitchen,
Dusk, Carpe Diem

• Barley Mow

• Durrants Hotel

O'Conor Don

Windsor Castle, Street

Baker St

Wigmore Street

1

James Street

Oxford Street

BOND
STREET

Havana

Loop •

New Bond Street

Hush, Rocket •

MAYFAIR

Bour Street

• Claridge's

2

North Audley Street

*Grosvenor
Square*

Grosvenor Street

Guinea

Connaught Bar, •
American Bar

Mount Street

Berkeley Square

• Scotts

• Audley

3

South Audley Street

Babble

Park Lane

• Terrace Bar

MAP 3 – MAYFAIR, ST JAMES'S & WEST SOHO

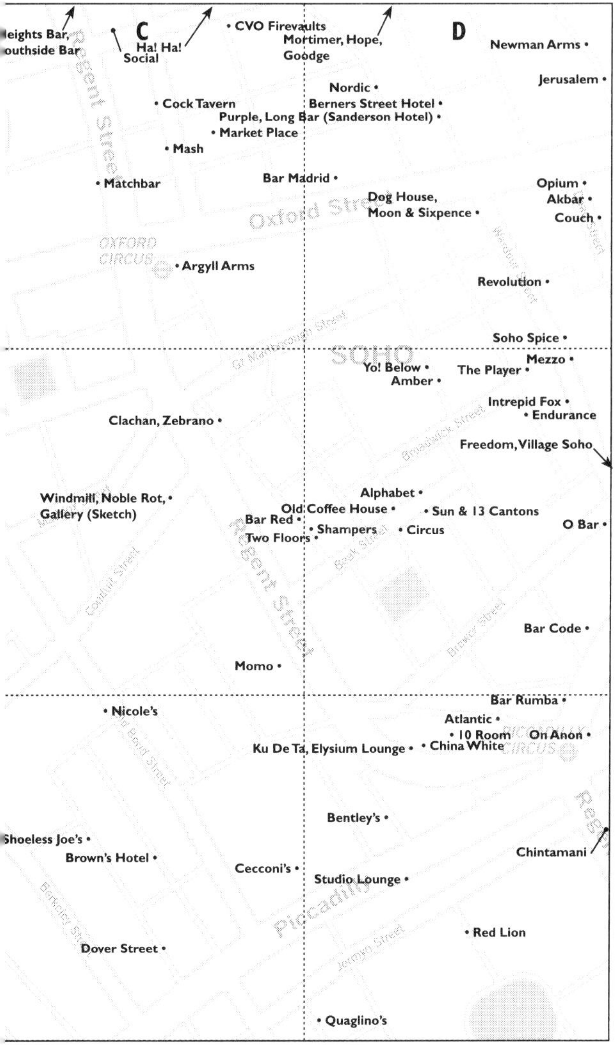

C
D
eights Bar,
outhside Bar
Ha! Ha!
Social
CVO Firevaults
Mortimer, Hope,
Goodge
Newman Arms
Jerusalem
Nordic
Cock Tavern
Berners Street Hotel
Purple, Long Bar (Sanderson Hotel)
Market Place
Mash
Regent Street
Matchbar
Bar Madrid
Opium
Akbar
Dog House,
Moon & Sixpence
Couch
Oxford Street
OXFORD CIRCUS
Argyll Arms
Wardour Street
Revolution
Gt Marlborough Street
Soho Spice
SOHO
Mezzo
Yo! Below
The Player
Amber
Intrepid Fox
Endurance
Clachan, Zebrano
Broadwick Street
Freedom, Village Soho
Alphabet
Windmill, Noble Rot,
Gallery (Sketch)
Old Coffee House
Sun & 13 Cantons
Bar Red
O Bar
Shampers
Circus
Two Floors
Conduit Street
Beak Street
Regent Street
Brewer Street
Bar Code
Momo
Bar Rumba
Nicole's
Atlantic
10 Room
On Anon
Ku De Ta, Elysium Lounge
China White
PICCADILLY CIRCUS
Bentley's
Shoeless Joe's
Chintamani
Brown's Hotel
Cecconi's
Studio Lounge
Piccadilly
Jermyn Street
Red Lion
Dover Street
Quaglino's

MAP 4 – EAST SOHO, CHINATOWN & COVENT GARDEN

MAP 4 – EAST SOHO, CHINATOWN & COVENT GARDEN

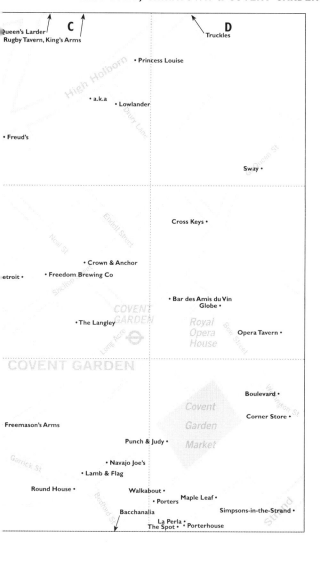

Queen's Larder
Rugby Tavern, King's Arms

C

D
Truckles

• Princess Louise

High Holborn

• a.k.a   • Lowlander

Drury Lane

• Freud's

Sway •

Endell Street

Cross Keys •

Neal St

• Crown & Anchor

etroit •   • Freedom Brewing Co

Shelton St

• Bar des Amis du Vin
Globe •

COVENT
GARDEN

Royal
Opera
House

Bow St

Queen St

• The Langley

Long Acre

Opera Tavern •

COVENT GARDEN

Boulevard •

Wellington St

Covent

Corner Store •

Freemason's Arms

Garden

Market

Punch & Judy •

Garrick St

• Navajo Joe's
• Lamb & Flag

Bedford St

Round House •

Walkabout •
• Porters   Maple Leaf •

Simpsons-in-the-Strand •

The Strand

Bacchanalia

La Perla •
The Spot • • Porterhouse

MAP 5 – KNIGHTSBRIDGE, CHELSEA & SOUTH KENSINGTON

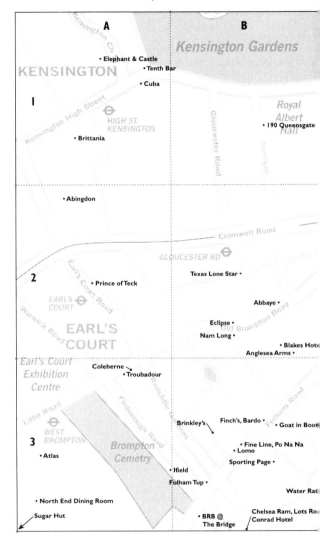

A

B

Kensington Gardens

KENSINGTON

• Elephant & Castle
• Tenth Bar
• Cuba

Royal
Albert
Hall
• 190 Queensgate

I

Kensington High Street

HIGH ST.
KENSINGTON

• Brittania

Gloucester Road

• Abingdon

Cromwell Road

GLOUCESTER RD

2

Earls Court Road

• Prince of Teck

EARLS
COURT

Texas Lone Star •

Abbaye •

Old Brompton Road

Warwick Road

EARL'S
COURT

Eclipse •
Nam Long •

• Blakes Hotel
Anglesea Arms •

Earl's Court
Exhibition
Centre

Coleherne
• Troubadour

Redcliffe Gardens

Lillie Road

WEST
BROMPTON

Finborough Road

Brinkley's

Finch's, Bardo •

Fulham Road

• Goat in Boots

3

• Atlas

Brompton
Cemetery

• Fine Line, Po Na Na
• Lomo
Sporting Page •

• North End Dining Room

Sugar Hut

• Ifield
Fulham Tup •

Water Rat

• BRB @
The Bridge

Chelsea Ram, Lots Ro
Conrad Hotel

MAP 5 – KNIGHTSBRIDGE, CHELSEA & SOUTH KENSINGTON

MAP 6 – NOTTING HILL & BAYSWATER

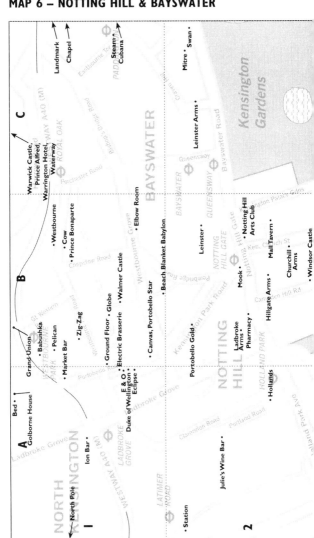

MAP 7 – HAMMERSMITH & CHISWICK

MAP 8 – HAMPSTEAD, CAMDEN TOWN & ISLINGTON

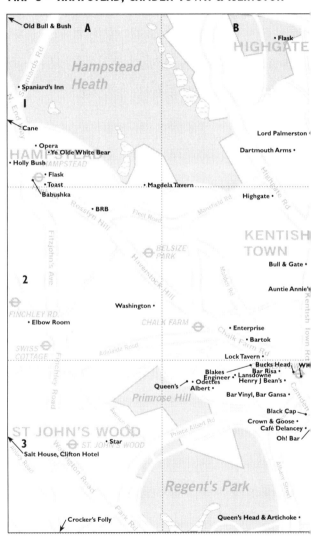

A

B

• Old Bull & Bush

• Flask

HIGHGATE

Hampstead Heath

N. End Rd

Spaniards Rd

• Spaniard's Inn

1

← Cane

Lord Palmerston •

• Opera
• Ye Olde White Bear

Dartmouth Arms •

HAMPSTEAD

HAMPSTEAD

• Holly Bush

• Flask

• Toast

• Magdela Tavern

Highgate •

Babushka

Highgate Rd

Rosslyn Hill

Fleet Road

Mansfield Rd

• BRB

BELSIZE PARK

KENTISH TOWN

Bull & Gate •

Fitzjohn's Ave

2

Haverstock Hill

Maldon Rd

Auntie Annie's •

Kentish Town Rd

Washington •

CHALK FARM

FINCHLEY RD.

• Elbow Room

• Enterprise

SWISS COTTAGE

Chalk Farm Rd

• Bartok

Adelaide Road

Lock Tavern •

Finchley Road

• Bucks Head — **W**

Blakes
Engineer •
Odettes
Albert •

Bar Risa •
• Lansdowne
Henry J Bean's •

Camden

Queen's •

Bar Vinyl, Bar Gansa •

Primrose Hill

Black Cap —

Crown & Goose •
Café Delancey •
Oh! Bar

ST JOHN'S WOOD

Prince Albert Rd

• Star

ST JOHN'S WOOD

Albany Street

3

← Salt House, Clifton Hotel

Grove End Rd

Abbey Road

Park Rd

Regent's Park

Queen's Head & Artichoke •

↙ Crocker's Folly

MAP 8 – HAMPSTEAD, CAMDEN TOWN & ISLINGTON

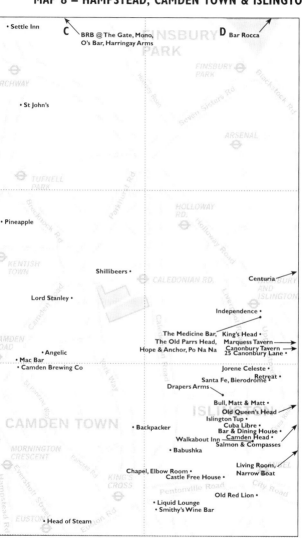

• Settle Inn

C BRB @ The Gate, Mono,
O's Bar, Harringay Arms

FINSBURY
PARK

D Bar Rocca

FINSBURY
PARK

ARCHWAY

• St John's

ARSENAL

TUFNELL
PARK

HOLLOWAY
RD.

• Pineapple

KENTISH
TOWN

Shillibeers •

CALEDONIAN RD.

Centuria •

AND
ISLINGTON

Lord Stanley •

Independence •

CAMDEN
ROAD

The Medicine Bar, King's Head •
The Old Parrs Head, Marquess Tavern
Hope & Anchor, Po Na Na   Canonbury Tavern •
                            25 Canonbury Lane •

• Angelic
• Mac Bar
• Camden Brewing Co

Jorene Celeste •
                    Retreat •
Santa Fe, Bierodrome •
Drapers Arms •

Bull, Matt & Matt •
  Old Queen's Head •
Islington Tup •
  Cuba Libre •
Bar & Dining House •
Walkabout Inn   Camden Head •
          Salmon & Compasses •

CAMDEN TOWN

• Backpacker

MORNINGTON
CRESCENT

• Babushka

EUSTON

Living Room,
Narrow Boat

Chapel, Elbow Room •
        Castle Free House •

KING'S
CROSS

Old Red Lion •

Pentonville Road

• Liquid Lounge
  • Smithy's Wine Bar

• Head of Steam

MAP 9 – THE CITY

A

B

• Al's, Café Kick
• Bull
Filthy McNasty's
• Peasant
Old Street

• Well

• Eagle
Sekforde Arms •
Crown Tavern, Rivington Grill Bar
• Calthorpe Arms
3 Kings of Clerkenwell •
Cicada •
• 19:20
Betsey Trotwood •
• Dovetail
• Yo! Below
• Potemkin
• Match
• Dust
Clerkenwell Road
Jerusalem Tavern •
• The Bear
• Clerkenwell House
• Fox & Anchor
Hope & Sir Loin
Spirit
Beech St
FARRINGDON
BARBICAN
Fluid •
• Charterhouse
• Ember
• Gate
• Vic Naylor's
• St John
• Olde Red Cow
Lifthouse •
• Rising Sun
Barbican
Smiths of Smithfiled •
• Cock Tavern
Abbaye •
Smithfield Market
EC1
Bed •
• Cellar Gascon
• Hand & Shears
• Bleeding Heart
Living Room
• El Vino's
• Cittie of York
• Olde Mitre Tavern
Bishops Finger
London
Holborn
• Nylon

2
Newgate St
Gresham St
• Knights Templar
Corney & Barrow •
Walkabout •
• Hodgsons
Olde Cheshire Cheese
ST. PAUL'S ⊖
Cheapside
• Old Bank of England
Ludgate Hill
Fine Line •
• El Vino's
Punch Tavern
Grand Marque
Old Bull Tavern
Williamson's Tavern •
• Cockpit
Cannon Street
MANSION
Evangelist •
Shoeless Joe's •
HOUSE
El Vinos •
• Shaw's Booksellers
Corney & Barrow •
Blackfriar •
Queen Victoria St
⊖ BLACKFRIARS
Upper Thames St

3
Victoria Embankment
River Thames
Blackfriars Br
Southwark Br
Founders Arms
Oxo, River Walk •
• Doggetts Coat & Badge
Laughing Gravy
Anchor •
Wine Wharf •

MAP 9 – THE CITY

C

Grand Central,
Medicine Bar,
Bar Kick

Smersh Bar •

• Cantaloupe

D

Bricklayer's Arms

• Pool
New Inn

Great Eastern Dining Room,
Home •

Foundry, Cocomo, Play, Cargo
Fox • Rivington Grill, Catch, City Page

• Elbow Room

Bridge & Tunnel

Shoreditch Electricity Showrooms,
El Paso Club, Reliance, Bedroom Bar, Dragon Bar,
Bluu, Hoxton Sq Bar, Charlie Wrights

Venlock Arms,
ifteen

FINSBURY

HAC
(Bunhill
Fields)

• Soshomatch

Prophet •

• Lime

• Liquid Lab

The Light •

Chiswell St

Pride of Spitalfields

• Corney & Barrow

Broadgate
MOORGATE

• Corney & Barrow

Vibe Bar, Public Life

• City Limits

LIVERPOOL ST

Boisdale
of Bishopsgate

Finsbury
Circus

Hamilton Hall •

George, Fishmarket, G E Club

EC2

• Corney & Barrow

• Old Dr Butler's Head

• Corney & Barrow

Twentyfour, Vertigo •

ALDGATE

Bow Wine Vaults

Hoop & Grapes •

Bonds •

• Prism

• Poet

• Pacific Oriental

• Corney & Barrow

Leadenhall St

Corney & Barrow •

Cornhill

• Coq D'Argent

• Lay & Wheeler

• Corney & Barrow

Jamaica Wine House

• Leadenhall

• Bar Under The Clock

• Simpson's Tavern

• Crosse Keys

• Lamb Tavern

Fine Line •

1 Lombard Street

Ide Wine Shades, El Vino's,
Bar
ourse

MONUMENT

FENCHURCH ST

• Bell

• Crutched Friar

Upper Thames St

CANNON ST

Eastcheap

• Corney & Barrow, Fine Line,

Wine Library, •

Fuego

Assembly

ER HILL

EC3

Tower St

Lower Thames St

Tower of
London

Old Thameside Inn

Hop Cellars,

Borough Bar, Fina Estampa,

Market Porter,

George Inn, Mint on Montague,

Dickens Inn, Mint

Wheatsheaf Cynthia's

Royal Oak, Goose & Firkin,

Anchor Tap, Bridge House,

Horniman @ Hays

Pont de la Tour

Thames

London Br

MAP 10 – SOUTH LONDON (& FULHAM)

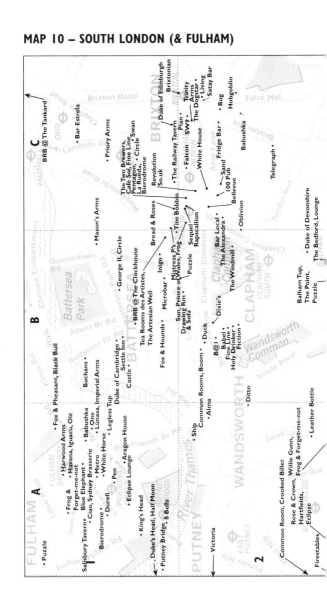

MAP 11 – EAST END & DOCKLANDS

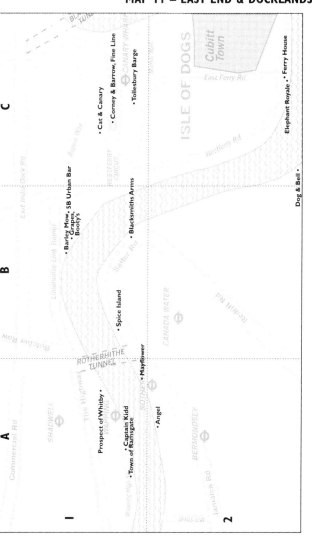